THE BODY AS CAPITAL

The Body as Capital

Masculinities in Contemporary Latin American Fiction

VINODH VENKATESH

THE UNIVERSITY OF
ARIZONA PRESS

TUCSON

The University of Arizona Press
www.uapress.arizona.edu

© 2015 The Arizona Board of Regents
Printed in the United States of America
20 19 18 17 16 15   6 5 4 3 2 1

ISBN-13: 978-0-8165-0069-7 (paper)

Cover designed by David Drummond

Publication of this book is made possible in part by a subvention from the Department
of Foreign Languages and Literatures, the College of Liberal Arts and Human Sciences,
and the Provost's Office at Virginia Tech.

Library of Congress Cataloging-in-Publication Data
Venkatesh, Vinodh, author.
The body as capital : masculinities in contemporary Latin American fiction / Vinodh
Venkatesh.
    pages cm
Includes bibliographical references and index.
ISBN 978-0-8165-0069-7 (pbk. : alk. paper)
    1. Masculinity in literature.   2. Latin American literature—History and criticism.
3. Human body in literature.   4. Sex role in literature.   I. Title.
PQ7081.V429 2015
860.9'353—dc23
                                                    2015005389

♾ This paper meets the requirements of ANSI/NISO Z39.48-1992 (Permanence of Paper).

For Narayini and Venkatesh

Contents

Acknowledgments

Seminars and conversations at the University of North Carolina at Chapel Hill with Oswaldo Estrada, Alicia Rivero, José Manuel Polo de Bernabé, and Pablo Gil Casado set the trajectory and tone of my research on masculinities in contemporary Latin American fiction. I am extremely thankful to have counted on the close reading and thoughtful critique of Juan Carlos González Espitia, Irene Gómez Castellano, María DeGuzmán, and Alfredo Sosa-Velasco during the early drafts of this project. Their feedback was invaluable in moving this project from doctoral work to the book at hand. In the manuscript's final stages, the comments and suggestions by Humberto López Cruz and David William Foster proved to be invaluable. I also want to thank my editor, Kristen Buckles, for believing in this project—she and Scott De Herrera at the University of Arizona Press, as well as Melanie Mallon, have truly been wonderful people to work with. Finally, Oswaldo was and continues to be a pillar behind my research. To him I am grateful for countless e-mails and moments of much-needed revelry, always punctuated by song (his, not mine, as I am tone deaf).

I am appreciative of the Department of Romance Languages and Literatures for its financial support during my (second) tenure at Chapel Hill and for fostering an intellectual climate of collegiality, exchange, and spirited conversation. The department graciously supported this project through the Dana B. Drake and Isabella Payne Cooper Dissertation Research Fellowship. I am further indebted to the Graduate School at UNC for the Thomas F. Ferdinand Summer Research Fellowship. I am also thankful for the mentoring and support of Gillian Lord, Shifra Armon, and Luis

Alvarez-Castro at the University of Florida. My somewhat accidental arrival in this field would not have happened without their guidance. A big thank you as well to my colleagues in the Department of Foreign Languages and Literatures at Virginia Tech.

Nothing in this life would be possible without the laughter and joy shared with those we hold closest. To my *familia chapelhilliana*, thank you for everything throughout these years. I am grateful to Ray Miller and Austin Worley for their friendship and conversations; in fact, it is in these that I first began to critically think about masculinities. In Melilla: Joaquín, Mari Carmen, Chica, Alberto, Kiny, Roma, Luis, Mari Ángeles, and Julia. In Kuala Lumpur: my parents, Narayini and Venkatesh, who saw me through my crazy plans of studying literature. To both of you, for always nurturing me and being the best parents anyone could ask for, thank you for your wisdom, support, and motivation. To my siblings, Vishnu and Sabitha, thank you for being a constant source of amusement and encouragement. Last but not least, I want to thank my better half, my partner in crime, and the person who never forgets to remind me that *la vida sale* (*sale*): Mari Carmen.

Fragments of part 1 have appeared in *Chasqui* and *Explicación de Textos Literarios*. Early versions of the essays on Jaime Bayly and Gioconda Belli have appeared in *Revista Canadiense de Estudios Hispánicos* and *Hispanic Research Journal*, respectively. I am grateful to the editors and publishers of these venues for granting me permission to reprint this work.

THE BODY AS CAPITAL

Introduction
The Body as Capital

In works on issues of gender in Latin American fiction, criticism has tended to largely focus and build up from feminist, and more recently, queer perspectives, where marked genders are examined for their potential to usurp and challenge normative orders that tend to repress many for the benefit of a few. Going against this tide, several recent interventions have flipped the analytic coin by focusing instead on the masculine condition and how it regiments the gendered social structures of patriarchy. In this minoritarian trajectory, several critics have reoriented gender studies to analyze how discourses and representations of masculinity have affected broader cultural processes.[1] Within this line of thought, however, criticism has tended to treat masculinity, the unmarked gender position, as a monolithic construct that is rarely afforded the relativist pluralism given to feminine and queer subjectivities. Therein lies a first point of departure, for I argue that we must conceive of the masculine not as a solidified, unchanging, and eternal subject position, but as a fluid, sociohistorically specific, and interrelational identity that is plural in nature yet often seen as singular in practice.

The second point of departure in these pages is predicated on the impact of recent economic and political policies on the representation and discursive construct of gender positions in Latin America. Although periods of first contact, colonization, and movements of independence have produced tropic and aesthetic conceptions of masculine gendered bodies, an examination of recent shifts is warranted, especially if we are to consider the neoliberal age as what Gareth Williams calls an underlying shift in the telos of the region, where the local moves toward the global and the

3

heterogenous make way for the imperial homogenous.[2] What, then, is the role of the masculine in how gendered bodies are deployed in a new stage, a transnational theater where vestigial semantics and historical symbols slowly give way to a homogenizing grammar of gender and identity?

In the following pages, I argue that the writing of masculinities in contemporary Latin American fiction is reflective of and reactive to the social and economic processes of neoliberalism. Working through what I contend to be a neoliberal aesthetic, that is, a distinctly market-based system of representation and an economically conscious poetics, I focus on the male body as a dialogic site of enunciation, arguing that the writing of masculinities is a project that centers socioeconomic and political concerns and paradigms on specific sites of the male anatomy. In novels published after 1990 by canonical, well-known, and newer writers from Mexico, Central America, the Caribbean, Peru, and Chile, the male body is a capital commodity that is metaphorically bartered, segmented, marketed, and sold in works coinciding with the neoliberal experiment; its movements and circulations code for textual anxieties and considerations of the changing politico-economic landscape. The male body as capital is a variant of Gayle Rubin's notion of the feminine as a commodity, and a development of Raewyn Connell's theorization of "the body inescapable" (*Masculinities* 52), that the body as metaphor provides a discursive point of entry into how gender is constructed and conceived. The body as capital thus operates on micro and macro levels; that is, it is singularly commoditized in the writing of specific bodies yet also rendered as a whole in what I argue to be a market of masculinities.

Such a framework of a "market" and "commodities" is propitious to a study of how masculinities are written in the neoliberal age. Aside from being a set of economic and political strategies with defined steps of action, neoliberalism is a comprehensive paradigm that cannot be ignored as a dialoguing agent in late capitalist cultural configurations. It is positioned at the crossroads of cultural production, ontological to the representation of social realities and their circulation and, perhaps more important, a vital step toward the dissemination of a market of homogenizing popular cultural artifacts. Neoliberalism is, furthermore, involved in any collective processes of identity politics as it subscripts borders, effectively severing the ties that previously bound both representations of the body and self to the symbolic collective or/of nation and non-identitarian notions of sexuality.[3] In essence, neoliberalism can be located in the background—as a shading of a tabula rasa—in the equation of contemporary gender formations. Its organizational presence underlines current theorems in masculinity studies, where shifts to transnational gender positions are being theorized as an overarching matrix to sustained local inquiries. Within this equation is the proposal that the neoliberal episteme has caused a crisis of sorts in traditional gender structures, where singular masculinity, or what Raewyn Connell calls hegemonic masculinity, has historically held an apical position.[4] Through economic liberalization and the untethering of labor and production markets, masculinity as hegemon has entered a crisis stage, because renegotiated labor and familial orders have triggered a widespread cultural renegotiation of how masculinity operates and is represented as an organizational position in relation to other gender expressions. This holds especially true in Latin America, where governments have, since the late 1970s, enacted to varying degrees social and familial policies that are side effects of the replacement of import substitution industrialization.[5]

By crisis, I am referring to a change in the order or roles, as women are increasingly permitted and encouraged to work and lead lives that were once accorded only to men. Economic autonomy, sexual liberation, and the right to an education are some of the changes that have affected gender politics in Latin America. In examining the contemporary constructions of masculinities, Mabel Burin underscores that relatively recent socioeconomic shifts have led to "la pérdida de un área significativa de poder del género masculino, y las nuevas configuraciones en las relaciones de poder entre géneros" (Burin and Meler 124). Such socioeconomic shifts and their resultant gender reconfigurations are salient results of the broader macro openings of local markets to foreign economies and economic policies, as free trade agreements and foreign direct investment increase labor demands and supply and thus shift familial economic roles. These measures, as can be expected, democratize societies to the extent that conventional structures and relations are no longer compatible with an open-framed notion of the market and, as a result, of the social. Writing on the change of gender roles, Irene Meler furthers the idea that these factors "configuran, en este período de acumulación capitalista, un contexto adverso en lo que se refiere al bienestar de los varones" ("La construcción" 122). The crisis in masculinity, as such, triggers a critical interest in the strategies of change and coping that men undertake as a result. Meler (121) and Burin ("Precariedad" 87) develop this notion of crisis in Latin American societies to argue that forces of globalization and neoliberal tendencies have led to changes in personal, intimate constructions of masculinity, which in turn affect the formulations of the masculine in cultural production. A second line of inquiry, then, which is perhaps more appropriate for cultural criticism, is how and in what configurations masculinity has been

renegotiated, because the traditional system of (national) hegemony is ob-
solete in a postnational age.

We can find within this investigation into the traditional representation
of masculinity an emphasis in creating a hegemonic position based on certain desired and idealized characteristics (which are both physical and psychical). Looking, for example, at the caudillo, or dictator, novels produced
in Latin America since the nineteenth century, we see a preponderance of
textual constructions of gender that stress the role of male virility, stylized
corporal aesthetics, and an epistemological focus on logic and science as
parts that construct a masculine whole.[6] There is a direct linkage made
between the male body and the nation, an idea that George Mosse uses to
create a theoretical framework around the stereotype and countertype in
the production of masculinities. He argues that any bona fide stereotype
of the male ideal must be accompanied by a series of undesirable countertypes to politically justify the idealized masculine. This framework is ex-
ceedingly apt at reading male gender structures in cultural texts but is
somewhat inaccurate and unwieldy when it comes to examining these
same structures when the nation-state is blurred by transnational markets.
The neoliberal system engages in what is effectively a break from the cus-
tomary symbolic and semantic processes of creating and deifying the
masculine, because the tenets of a closed gendered order are incapable of
adapting to a polyvalenced and global system of bodies and its parts.

The masculine is therefore no longer hinged on only the physical penis
and virility or economic prosperity but is, instead, tangential to globalized
and commercial influences; the philosophy and principles of free market
economics, I argue, are integral to the formation (and subsequent examination) of gendered bodies in contemporary Latin American cultural production.[7] Masculinity enters in a direct relationship with the pervading
politico-economic model and is constituted around a capitalization of the
body. I say "capitalization" in two senses: first, the body is metaphor for real
and virtual capital, as a tradable and productive resource; second, there is
a semantic capitalization, that is, the body becomes the BODY, as an em-
phatic site of enunciation and of discursive potential for negotiating constructs of subjectivity. On the one hand, we evidence that writing the body
is undertaken primarily through corporal analogisms of free market ideologies, where stress is placed more on the marketability of the body (and
its accompanying symbolic sites, such as the penis, testes, and anus) and
not necessarily on its potential as political symbolic capital.[8] On the other
hand, and in a process that is not mutually exclusive to the first, masculinities become a circulating commodity that is quantified, bartered, and

moved across transnational lines and can no longer be considered a closed national position of gender supremacy or organization. The examination of contemporary Latin American masculinity, therefore, emphasizes it to be a plural position and pluridirectional process that is paradoxically local and global yet not necessarily exemplary in discussions of a transnational gender order. With this in mind, we can consider neoliberalism as more than a simple backdrop to recent cultural production and instead as an aesthetic and politico-organic point of reference.

Fundamental in this reading and analysis of masculinity is a working definition. I will use the Masculine to identify the idealized and multifaceted position of what Connell terms hegemonic masculinity. It is akin, in a structural sense, to Connell's apical position but functions on other semantic and symbolic levels, beyond, yet at times in tandem with, variable structural hierarchies of gender. Through dialogue with the Masculine, femininities, masculinities, and queerities come into being, taking the Masculine as a sociohistorically specific normative position. The Masculine, as Ben Sifuentes-Jáuregui argues, "designs itself from the outside of culture and society, and doubles an idea of itself as the very interior of that culture and society" (*Transvestism* 108). Those characteristics deemed powerful, desirable (both to the projected and real heterosexual and to the repressed homosocial imagination vis-à-vis desire), and viable as the pillars of the social matrix—as organizational tenets—are enshrined as the Masculine, intrinsically linked to the male body by patriarchal systems. The Masculine is consecrated and assimilated through aesthetic, discursive, behavioral, and even sartorial cues and practices and is enabled and reiterated/reproduced by all gendered bodies within a given culture and society. The reverse process, I want to make clear, is what creates the other non-Masculine gender expressions, for whatever does not lie within or loosely follow this specific epistemology of power is relegated to alternative and subservient roles and positions. This includes the creation of masculinities, those male (though at times female) approximations to the Masculine that in some shape or form fall short of embodying the socially and culturally enabled construct. Aside from being performative, iterative, and sociocultural in constitution, gender is a tableau vivant defined and brushed over by the previously (and simultaneously) enabled strokes of the Masculine.

Within this framework of masculinities, the body is engaged in a dialectic process of identification where gender is not attributed to or defined simply by performance. As Connell, Sifuentes-Jáuregui, and José Quiroga have restated, gender is a verdant association between the physical body and those social traits outlined earlier that sustain the image of the Masculine (as it is nothing more than a projected ideal, a méconnaissance that, depending on level of adherence to or disassociation from, establishes a gender expression), and we cannot completely do away with the anatomy of the subject when talking about masculinity. The body is, as Guillermo Núñez Noriega thoroughly argues, "burdened and crisscrossed by multiple demands and preconceptions that entail ideas about desire, erotic practices, and the ultimate expected configuration of one or another gender identity" (77). It is indeed "inescapable" and becomes a point of critical focus, for it opens a discussion on how gender systems come into play.

Masculinity is pertinent to any discussion of contemporary gender formations and gains special importance in the Latin American context, where it has often been minted for its symbolic potential in the cultural productions in the postindependence era. Doris Sommer's well-known and archetypal *Foundational Fictions* is a case in point, where the Masculine (and its associated female lover) facilitates the semantic construction of the nation. In the neoliberal age, however, this connection still remains tangible, though the link between the male body/character and the nation has been fragmented, just as neoliberalism has done away with the autonomy of national economies. The crux of studying the Masculine at this point, then, is the need to understand how neoliberalism has reconfigured the Masculine, or perhaps more accurately, how the neoliberal episteme has redesigned it from the "outside" and within its "interior." Connell, for example, has theorized transnational business masculinity as a successor or most recent iteration of hegemonic masculinity, to better reflect the late capitalist mode ("Masculinities and Globalization" 9). This model, while valuable, is not always met as necessarily true or descriptive, especially in the Latin American context, where competing local masculinities, which may be regional in deployment, have long been established prior to any real positioning of a hegemonic variant. They may resist transnational positions, just as these societies resist the seeming inevitability of cultural homogenization. We will see this later in the analysis of Jaime Bayly's *El cojo y el loco*, where historical hegemonies are pitted against the transnational business position to develop a discursive challenge to cultural homogenization. What is being planted, then, is an analytics that focuses on the Masculine and its relationship to plural masculinities, femininities, and queerities at the sociohistorical moment of neoliberalism, because what is being posited is a reimagining of both how gender is constructed and how it is interplayed with representations of broader entities, such as the nation, or in this case, its lack.[9]

It is at this juncture that we can open the previous affirmations to an analysis of Latin American cultural production that addresses the shift in gender structures as the Masculine is renegotiated. While at first glance a broad multidisciplinary perspective may seem most appropriate, I suggest that a structured interrogation of recent literary production provides a useful litmus for studying contemporary Latin American masculinities. We can stress, in this instance, the importance of the literary as a historical artifact, because current narratives can be dialogued with past works—a privilege not afforded to newer media. This is fundamental, if we take as axiomatic the importance of the region's literature in shaping national and individual identity from the colonial period to the present (or the role of the literary/textual in identity formation). Questions asked here include an interrogation of how current texts written in, and through the marketing and distribution of, neoliberal mechanisms dialogue with older works and genres. The literary's historicity is not its only advantage, for we can also glean from the written text several intertextual referents to other artifacts of popular culture, such as the moving image and lyrical music, where the semantics of gender construction and the negotiation of the Masculine can take place in what is sometimes called the "low" arts. Recent Latin American fiction is valuable here as a source of study, because post-boom and McOndo writers have made it a point to reference, develop, and serially link to other manifestations of popular culture. Important, in this regard, is the diegetic reception of the popular cultural artifact (whether it be musical or cinematic) within the narrative, as a symbolic representation of how subjects may react to the planted gendered imagery/imaginary. I am, however, by no means stating that the literary is the only viable source material for an examination of contemporary Latin American masculinities, for similar studies can and should be undertaken across disciplines such as the visual arts, mass media, and even ethnography (akin to the latter section of Connell's *Masculinities*).

The advantages that I prescribe to the literary inform the subsequent chapters in this study, as I link contemporary Latin American textual artifacts to critical approaches that draw freely from cultural studies. The point regarding the relativity of current literature to past iterations is addressed and developed over the course of part 1, where I examine recent new historical novels produced in different regions of Latin America. The organization of this part stresses the need for geographic sensitivity when approaching such a vast cultural and spatial amalgamation, as I include texts from Central America, Mexico, the Andean region, the Southern Cone, and the Caribbean in the subsequent sections. Important in this survey is the fact that the neoliberal age is not universal to Latin America, for different countries and regions have had very different relationships with its tenets. What is notable, however, is that neoliberalism as a politico-social episteme is far-reaching, going beyond true neoliberal experiments in how it affects the everyday lives of people.[10] The underlying theorem behind this textual analytics is that local, subnational actors and bodies can successfully domesticate or scale down macro processes to a tangible system of representation, manifested through the aesthetics of the text or, more importantly, in the semantics of the body. Part 1, divided into four chapters, examines four new historical novels in juxtaposition to the traditional hegemonic dictator novel to identify how contemporary fiction rewrites the apical position of the Masculine. These novels provide a diachronic mint of gender constructions, because their "newness" stems, in some ways, from recent takes on gender in relation to history. I am interested here in unearthing how cultural production can highlight how the current politico-economic episteme influences a traditional genre of gender construction. I examine how authors such as Cristina Rivera Garza, Pedro Lemebel, Mario Vargas Llosa, and Sergio Ramírez chose to write and undermine the dictatorial body to construct, instead, different yet converging masculinities. These novels, I argue, successfully deconstruct the nationalistic hegemonic position (in this case, represented by the literary caudillo) and posit alternate textual sites of male identification. There is an acute authorial focus on how the male body is written, as specific anatomical positions become the loci that capture broader sociocultural processes of change. The penis and its potential for masculine virility no longer codify the Masculine, as what takes their place is an economic understanding of the body, reflective perhaps of the destabilization of national politics in the interest of transnational economics. In this section, my analysis focuses on the writing of the penis, the testes, and the anus as textual markers of the neoliberal episteme. I argue that the anus is not only a site of queering challengers to the Masculine, but also in its inversion a point of politico-economic critique, as the subsequent staining of the dictator who loses control of his sphincter muscles expels him from any position of reproductive viability. There is, as I will develop in later chapters, an underlying critique of neoliberalism, as the anus emphasizes the scatological possibilities when talking about free market policies and their social aftermath.

The analysis of these new historical fictions sets the stage for the second benefit I assign to the literary as source material, for it is through Lemebel's *Tengo miedo torero* that we transition toward an examination of popular music as a referent in studying contemporary takes on masculinities. The novels in part 2 are useful in examining how other means of cultural production (in this case, literature) assimilate and react to popular musical compositions (though a case can easily be made for studying the usage of popular songs in recent cinema from the region). Intrinsic to this chapter is a methodology that takes into account the intricacies of the lyrical text as an inter- and intratextual referent to the diegesis. I analyze how traditional genres like the bolero are employed as popular codings of how gendered bodies are constructed, and how they are placed or deployed in relation to each other, which invariably accentuates their positionality in relation to the Masculine. An alternative would be to analyze the incursions of the cinematic into the literary, because the latter provides a contextual matrix for understanding the reception and assimilation of visual gendered bodies. Such a study falls outside the scope of these pages but would be welcome in identifying how neoliberalism affects masculinity in the cinema, which is arguably a more postnational medium than literature or popular music. That being said, the novels examined in this chapter directly involve neoliberalism as a dialoguing influence in the constitution of transnational gender expressions. This argument is brought to a climax through the analysis of Franz Galich's use of the popular music of the Mexican rock band Maná to create fluid, nonnational masculinities that defy traditional norms that dictate male identity.

This critical reading, in turn, sets up the questions to be tackled in the final section, where I examine how contemporary Latin American fiction reacts to Connell's theorized position of transnational business masculinity. The readings here may inform scholars in other geocultural fields, because the neoliberal episteme tends to find synonymous relationships between a Global North and South. We may ask, then, how local gender positions react to transnational bodies that erect new relations of hegemony over traditional power systems. I examine works by Hernán Rodríguez Matte, Jaime Bayly, and Enrique Serna to elucidate how masculinities are reconstituted during and as a result of the crisis in gender brought about by neoliberalism. Intrinsic to this investigation is an understanding that Latin American masculinities are malleable by, yet challenging of, transnational processes and discursive subjectivities. In this line of argumentation, I furthermore question some of the recent theorizations regarding global gender positions coming from the field of masculinity studies, suggesting instead that local considerations cannot be ignored in favor of homogenizing notions of Masculine uniformity. This line of inquiry segues into the conclusion, which proposes several masculine tropes that can be theorized as common archetypes repeated in recent literary production. I look at cyborg masculinity in Santiago Roncagliolo's *Tan cerca de la vida* as an example of how technology problematizes the body as a symbolic and semantic referent in conceiving gender and argue that the cyborg allows for a way out of transnational hegemony. In this section, I also look at Gioconda Belli's *La mujer habitada* as an example of what I term revolutionary masculinity, a trope that is often repeated in narratives that recount the failure of the Left vis-à-vis the onset of the neoliberal age.

As a final note, the texts and authors examined in *The Body as Capital* are reflective of what Aníbal González calls writing after the nation (83), because these fictions escape the traditional boundaries of a national corpus. Many of the authors here, in fact, do not claim any one nationality, moving seamlessly across borders like the very commodified gendered bodies that inhabit their fictions. At times holding multiple passports, living in foreign capitals, and publishing through the powerhouses of transnational presses, or in multiple venues such as newspapers, academic journals, editorials, anthologies, and on social media sites such as Facebook and Twitter, the writers collected together here are intimately linked to the neoliberal paradigm as they partake in a transnational free trade, the marketing and distribution of both their cultural products and themselves as editorial capital. They are, in most cases, equally adept at writing about Tokyo and Barcelona and no longer necessarily locate their fictions in the traditional spaces and ideologies of Latin American fiction. We can further note that this grouping of authors does not follow traditional definitions of what constitutes a literary generation or movement, but they are instead held together by their participation in a global literary market that is triangulated around the writer, the publisher, and the (mostly North American) academy, as subject positions generating global fictions that are reactive to equally global processes. They are effectively grouped under a system of distribution that prizes, prints, and markets specific texts that are valued for their potential to enter a global interchange of readers and ideas. Their selection, however, is fruitful for the cultural critic, because they provide a wide-angle lens for examining (and in a very real sense, simplifying) the intricacies of Latin American masculinities (within the idea, of course, of "Latin American" fiction as a placeholder). Their texts, we must note, serve as reactive agents to the neoliberal episteme and thereby fabricate polydimensional matrices of textual masculinities that permit an analysis of how masculinity can be renegotiated in a global(ized) stage. I am hesitant to name such a corpus but would tentatively call them Generation Alfaguara, though one could equally substitute the name of any other large publisher.

As a conclusion to this introduction, I want to invite the reader to view masculinity outside the constrictions of unmarkedness and to examine and mint it for its ability to explain and challenge systems of oppression. In that sense, and in addition to proposing an original methodology to viewing gender in contemporary Latin American fiction, that is, through an adoption of Raewyn Connell's system of masculinity, the following pages dialogue in some instances with previous gender-based criticism on well-known works by posturing a masculine-centric analysis. Seen less as a challenge to previous interventions, these readings move toward a more holistic approximation of discursive gender that may feed into other angles of criticism.

PART ONE

New Historical Masculinities

In a print culture focused on the past, where writers both rising and established have repeatedly followed the strategy of fictionalizing the history of the continent, authors (and critics) have become key instruments in societies' rewriting of societies. This remembering by means of fiction has continued to examine the figure of the dictator in Latin America as an organizational position in political and sexual spheres, as these caudillos sit up as discursive targets, which we can understand to be characterized by an omnipotent and hypervirile masculinity. The importance of history and the examining of the past have contemporary implications in Latin America before, during, and after the 1990s. As María Cristina Pons reckons, the rewriting of the past from the margins and peripheral positions "le da a la novela histórica latinoamericana contemporánea una dimensión reflexiva y un carácter político, y no meramente filosófico" (268). These reflections on the self in relation to the nation, history, and gender lie at the center of the following pages.

The search for identity is paired with what Gareth Williams calls a shift in "the underlying telos of the nation" (23), which "is not a single process of evolution but an accumulation of distinct and uneven processes of transition toward so-called globalization," which has been brought about by "neoliberal restructuring of the nation-state together with the emergence of the transnational marketplace as a new and dominant force throughout Latin America" (23). As a foundational work to Williams's thesis, Néstor García Canclini observes that part of this process revolves around a dissolution of the great narratives that "used to order and hierarchize the periods

of the patrimony and the flora of cultured and popular works in which societies and classes recognized each other and consecrated their values"
(243–44). This search is not a process within the nation but is, by necessity
and consequence of economic and political developments, a transnational
questioning. This need for identity comes into play just as capital markets
enjoy a free-floating and deterritorialized era of inversion, where "the goal
of production no longer lies in any specific market, any specific set of con-
sumers or social and individual needs, but rather in its transformation into
that element which by definition has no content or territory" (Jameson, *Cultural Turn* 153). This shift has necessarily led to both a deterritorialization
and a dematerialization of economic systems. These processes are products
of what economists and politicians call neoliberalism, though the term is
neither an official designation of policy nor a rulebook for states to follow.
It is characterized by three broad components: the privatization of state-
owned enterprises, the implementation of austerity programs to curb public spending, and the opening of trade barriers, normally through treaties
and accords that often lack a true juridical backbone. As I explicate in the
introduction, research regarding gender and sexuality has followed a similar course, with what can be observed as a deterritorialization of theorists
and theories onto the Latin American episteme. While this has taken place
on both economic and critical fields, literary production, in turn, has experienced a relative boom in caudillo novels.[1]

These new narratives are not so much concerned with exploring polyphonic voices of the dictator (which was in vogue in earlier pieces) as they
are geared toward a presentation of a singular alternative to the official history championed by regimes. This alternative history, I argue, is substanti-
ated by and fashioned through a retooling of the male body and an exploration of the shift in the underlying telos of masculinity that has been
brought about by neoliberal policies.[2] Taking into account Sergio Ramírez's
Margarita, está linda la mar (1998), Cristina Rivera Garza's *Nadie me verá
llorar* (1999), Mario Vargas Llosa's *La fiesta del chivo* (2000), and Pedro
Lemebel's *Tengo miedo torero* (2001), in these pages I focus on the process
of writing masculinities and the dictator, the construction of texts that are
brought alive by characters inscribed on the surface in black ink yet are
created and come to life in a more than three-dimensional space. This
space, beyond the imaginary and beyond the literary, is polytemporal, polyphonic, and polyveracious. Some critics have chosen to call this space the
new historical novel as it decenters traditional constructs of the past in
favor of a new configuration of historical events.[3]

The choice of novels provides a variety of authors that do and do not
subscribe to the phallic voice of patriarchal systems: Ramírez writes from

a position of authority within the Sandinista government; Rivera Garza writes with a female, though gender-ambiguous, pen; Vargas Llosa takes the pen at its most phallic, in textual and political terms, though his own defeat and exile from Peru can be read in his version of the caudillo; and last, Lemebel queers the text by dressing, transgendering, and metaliterizing the pen, providing a glimpse into a countervoice of the hegemonic that Vargas Llosa explores in his retelling of the death of the Chivo. These multiple positions in the writing of history vis-à-vis identity are auto-reflexive of their own tools, as they plant the problematic of the legitimacy of alternative versions of history against the traditional dominant masculinity of the South American dictator figure. These authors, importantly, circumscribe the figure of the dictator not through polyphonic confusions or ambiguities, but instead by putting their own mark on the trope by displacing the figure along lines of gender composition and sexual expression that come into dialogue with a socio-structuralist theorization of hierarchical and plural masculinities.[4] In the seminal *Masculinities* (1995), Raewyn Connell argues that masculinities exist in a matrix of power dominated by a hegemonic variant that permits and perpetuates the subjugation of the feminine subject and gender position by an effective social, political, and economic strategy (77). These authors, I contend, engage in a displacement of the dictator that is scripted by and in reaction to the economic and social changes brought about by end-of-the-century politics in Latin America. As José Olavarría notes, "los procesos macrosociales y económicos, así como la disponibilidad de recursos que hacen de nexo entre esas políticas macros y la vida cotidiana" ("La investigación" 328) have come to form a crisis in masculinity that these novels are reactive to in their literary reimaginings of the dictator, which, in turn, implicate all compositions of the individual in the face of the ever-changing nation-state.

CHAPTER ONE

Commoditizing the Male Body in Margarita, está linda la mar

The possibilities of both spatial and temporal displacements within the new historical novel are perfectly evidenced in Sergio Ramírez's *Margarita, está linda la mar*. By means of a dual inquiry into the past, Ramírez puts under the microscope the political dictator Anastasio Somoza García and the poet and father of *modernismo*, Rubén Darío, in an intricate wordplay that stresses the connection between aesthetics and politics in the construct of the nation-state. In terms of structure, the novel juxtaposes the return of Darío to Nicaragua in 1907, after his stay in Europe, with the plot to assassinate Somoza García in 1956; Ramírez recounts in candid detail both the alcoholism of the poet and the antics of the conspirators as they attempt to organize a foolproof plan to liberate the country.

In a study on contemporary novels of the dictator, Gabriela Polit Dueñas notes that the novel marks a new phase in the caudillo genre, as "el carisma, la personalidad y la capacidad personal de encarnar un poder absoluto—elementos que obsesionaron a los escritores en décadas anteriores—dejan de ser la preocupación del autor," and that "tampoco hay una idealización de la militancia de izquierda" (130). (The latter point serves as a sort of preemption of postwar Central American fiction that is ethico-aesthetically disenchanted with the political process.) Polit Dueñas rightly notes that the assassination of Somoza is carried out by individuals and is captured as a political happening instead of as a product of a common political ideal, as the text marks a new phase that shows "un profundo desencanto con el poder y el quehacer de la política" (130). While this can be read in the context of apolitical ennui from the Left after the fall of the

Communist bloc and the failure of popular revolutions, such as the Sandinistas, the novel can further be conceived along the place of the authorial and corporal subject within the imagination of the historical past; in the latter case, we may ask what is the role of the body in fictive rehashes of the past? *Margarita, está linda la mar* can be read as a reflection of the personal on the political, as Ramírez draws parallels between two masculinities that represent the modern Nicaraguan state—the authoritarian politician and the eloquent man of letters. This dualism in the imagining of the nation is systematically approached in the novel through the temporal displacements between the assassination of Somoza by the poet Rigoberto López Pérez and the return of Darío to the continent after a stay in Europe.

In her attempt to trace Ramírez's published work in tandem with his political life, Polit Dueñas hesitates in performing a close reading of the text and how it writes gender and sexuality, and what ramifications these have on the national imaginary. Though she employs a psychoanalytic reading to construct a connective thread between Darío, López Pérez, and Ramírez, her analysis does not account for the constructions of masculinities within the text. This is not to say that the national imaginary is left aside completely, for she argues that the figure of the poet competes with the dictator to assert a phallic masculinity that identifies the former as a founding father of the nation (150). The physical brain of the former, furthermore, is juxtaposed with the penis as representative of power, best evidenced in the final pages of the novel as Quirón buries a jar containing Rigoberto's castrated testicles next to the interred jar containing Darío's stolen brain.

A psychoanalytic reading of the novel emphasizes the physical and psychical phallus as being the locus mundi of the body politic of the male subject. This critical practice is not strange to Latin American letters, where the penis traditionally textualizes the subject's social position and psychological makeup. Ramírez's text, however, upon closer inspection seems to displace the physical phallus from the penis to the testicles, asserting these reproductive factories as the source of masculinity and power. Hegemony is not defined by being able to urinate standing up, as is the desire of La Caimana, or by being able to sustain an erection, as we note Darío's impotence, but is instead characterized only by possessing the reproductive testes of the male. The novel consecrates the centrality of the testes as physical loci of power when one of the conspirators asserts, "éste es un país de cunucos. Se engorda más fácil cuando no se tiene testículos" (218). The eunuch, as we know, lacks testicles but not necessarily a penis, thereby emphasizing the importance of these productive sexual organs in the construct of the masculine subject. I underline the (economic) productivity of the testicles because unlike the penis, which serves a coital and urological purpose, the testicles are solely responsible for creating, storing, and disseminating the subject either through the prosthesis of the offspring or through the aesthetics of a copious ejaculation that, in turn, defines virility. The anatomy of the male thus suggests a deviation from José Piedra's notion of the pen(is) in the writing of fiction and historicity, for it is not necessarily the organic phallus that circumscribes masculinity and power, but a paradigm of economic productivity that leads to a writing of the past with the aim of understanding contemporary Latin American society.[1]

By emphasizing the corporeality of the male subject in *Margarita, está linda la mar*, Ramírez highlights the construct of masculinity within the novel as a crossroads in understanding the present through a mythification of the past in his native Nicaragua. As José Ángel Vargas has studied, Ramírez mythifies and then demythifies important historical figures in order to construct "un ícono de la realidad de un país que aparece por una parte pletórico de gloria, y por otra, castigado terriblemente por el poder político" (33). The leftist revolutionary figure of Sandino is described as having "los huevos . . . enormes y sonrosados, como la postura del ave fénix" (*Margarita* 218). The failure of the Left in contemporary Nicaraguan politics is addressed in the description of the male's testicles, albeit in a positive light, as the novel suggests that they will rise again like the mythical bird. Their productivity is stressed in opposition to the relative impotency of the penis, for the novel is rife with characters who have failing organs and belong to the homosocial. To further emphasize the connection between the testes and subjectivity, Somoza on his deathbed orders his troops to castrate Rigoberto: he stresses the cutting of the "huevos" and not the penis. The testes, thus, are codified as corporal signifiers of the male subject within a broader imaginary of the writing of the nation.

As Somoza's men round up the plethora of suspects, Rigoberto's testicles in a bottle are described as resembling a fetus. This last observation suggests that the nation is birthed from the testicles of the poet, and not necessarily from the site of ejaculation, that is, his penis. The testes as a site of origination of biological and ideological seed establish a genealogy among sons and fathers, and only by eliminating them can the son avenge the father. Trujillo's sons in *La fiesta del Chivo* best represent this trope, but it is also extant in Ramírez's narrative. When one of the conspirators, Cordelio, returns to León, a priest asks him if he is going to hang by the testicles the colonel who killed his father. The testes represent the connection between the father and the son, between aesthetic and political genealogies, for the son is merely a prosthesis produced in the scrotal sac. By focusing on the testes, the text hints at an economic understanding of the nation that is not necessarily connected to the equivalency of the penis to the Lacanian phallus that Polit Dueñas suggests is pervasive in the novel (143–50), but instead suggests a model of progeny that is metaphorical of systems of (re)production.

From an etymological standpoint, the testicles originate from the Latin *witness*. They witness virility, masculinity, reproduction, and even, as in *Margarita, está linda la mar*, the subjectification and desubjectification of individuals. From an anatomical standpoint, the testes house the development of germ cells into reproductive gametes: only by means of the testicles can the male individual reproduce. The onus placed on (re)production as a systemic and epistemological practice establishes a writing of subjectivity onto the testicles, and not necessarily through the psychics of the phallus. Masculinity is, therefore, not solely formed by a psychoanalytic construct; it is also (corporally) manufactured in tandem with the economic idea of anatomical productivity. We may see this corporal shift as reactive to the economic changes in Nicaragua after the handover of the government from Ramírez's party to the rightwing Unión Nacional Opositora. The new government headed by Violeta Chamorro institutes socioeconomic policies that attempt to align the country with neoliberal tendencies in Latin America. Unlike Vargas Llosa's Peru, which undergoes a Fujishock in the early nineties, Sandinista Nicaragua refused to incorporate the economic policies disseminated from the Global North. Written during a shift away from leftist economic ideals, and Ramírez's own divorce from national politics, which he would enshrine in *Adiós muchachos: Una memoria de la revolución Sandinista* (1999), *Margarita, está linda la mar* seems to be conscious of the economic pinnings of nationhood as borders are permeated. Ramírez's emphasis on the testes as a source of masculinity, as a source of virility for both the leftist poets and the rightist caudillos, reflects the importance of a bodily coding of economics in imagining the nation. In imagining the years of Sandinista control, for example, the castrations of Sandino, Rigoberto, and three other conspirators reconciles the lack of economic growth in Nicaragua during the revolution and its inability to undergo an urban boom. This is reflected in the descriptions of the capital, Managua, in contemporary Nicaraguan fiction: it is not the urbanized, cosmopolitan expression of McOndo, as are other cities such as Santiago and Lima, but is instead deathly and lost, emphasizing Seymour Menton's notion of a poetics of disillusionment and Beatriz Cortez's aesthetics of cynicism in contemporary Central American fiction, which I explicate in the study of Franz Galich's novels.

Just as the testicles are paramount to the connection between masculinity and the national, the printing press is similarly connected to the community's imagining of the nation (Anderson 6). This comes as no surprise, as Ramírez continues publishing fiction during his tenure as vice president and during his charge of the National Council of Education from 1979 to 1984. The press in *Margarita, está linda la mar* is the institution under Somoza that Ramírez undermines by writing gender and sexuality onto its body. I say "undermines" because he does not adhere to Connell's ideas of the hegemonic and how it establishes itself through discourses of science, objectivism, and the official reporting of history. While the text highlights the importance of science as a discourse of modernity and progress in the building of the nation, its interpretation of the topic is centered on Godofredo, the cuckolded husband of Darío's lover, who functions as the demythified man of science. Nicaragua does not enjoy a precise and overbearing figure such as Somoza in the latter half of the twentieth century and must instead contend with "el inventor paralítico que se había caído del caballo el día de San Juan Bautista" (96). Science is further castrated from the discussion of the national through the figure of Dr. Baltasar Cisne, a Darío fanatic and supporter of Somoza's regime. On the way to León, the doctor shares a beer with some of the conspirators, who know him from La Caimana's brothel. A fictive Jorge Negrete addresses Cisne by asking him to recount how "le pidió a *La Caimana* que le consiguiera la mejor de las muñecas" (108). Cisne ignores the comment, only to have Negrete follow with "cuénteles por qué ninguna quería con usted, y cuénteles lo que al fin le dijo aquella morenota rolliza, la *Flor de un día*: '¡Ay, no, yo con usted no, doctor! No voy a saber si me está cogiendo, o lo estoy pariendo'" (108). The man of science in Ramírez's early twentieth-century Nicaragua is, through interpersonal relationships with other masculinities, without a doubt not the mobilizing, domineering voice associated with Connell's hegemonic masculinity in the structuralizing of society; instead, he's a weakened object of ridicule, emasculated by competing masculinities within the gendered theater.

Margarita, está linda la mar does, however, include a reference to Connell's last strategy of control. The official reporting of history is carried out by the printing press, which in the novel serves as a meeting point for the conspirators. The building is guarded by an "empleada, calzada con zapatos de varón" (144). This is the first step in Ramírez's undermining of hegemonic power, as the quasi-transvestite sweeper is hesitant to allow the preacher Cordelio, one of the conspirators, to enter, because printed on a tattered sign on the door is a warning: "AQUÍ SOMOS CATÓLICOS Y

NO ADMITIMOS PROPAGANDA PROTESTANTE" (146). Ramírez is careful to connect the press to established hierarchies of the hegemony, such as religion, yet at the same time sidesteps gender norms to subvert the power of the press under Somoza.

This strategy of connecting the press to authority and then sublating this very authority by means of gender constructs and writings is best evidenced in the figure of Rafael Parrales and his journal *El Cronista*. The journal is housed in a city block with a funeral parlor and a professional school of commerce, both of which represent legislative bodies of the state, with the former legalizing death and the latter education. The funerary alludes to the military and traditional branches of virile masculinity, with its emphasis on the shield. Within the journal, the printing press is operated by human labor. Ramírez asserts the connection between *El Cronista* and the government when he notes that Kid Dinamita, a disgraced boxer who is condemned to jail after stabbing his wife, physically powers the press; he is loaned to Rafa by the authorities during the working week, allowed to leave his cell "como reo de confianza, para que haga girar la pesada rueda de la prensa manual" (216). Dinamita subscribes to the virile and violent masculinity that precedes the agenda of science and knowledge, which dominates movements toward modernity in the early twentieth century. He represents a violent and hypersexualized masculinity that Polit Dueñas connects to the dictator figure. More importantly, though, he reflects the commoditization of the body—the emphasis on it as bartered capital—as his virility and strength are no longer symbols of the nation or the hegemon but are instead only cogs in the industrial complex of the state and the Masculine.

Returning to the construction of hegemonic masculinity during Somoza's regime in reference to the printing press, note that the owner of the journal merits attention as he conforms to the thesis of connecting to and then subverting the institution. The novel provides a genealogy of ownership of *El Cronista* ending with Rafael Parrales, who buys the journal with a loan from his godmother, doña Casimira, who is the mother-in-law of Somoza. Parrales is further linked to the regime when one of the conspirators suggests that using the journal as a hideout for Cordelio would be "como si lo llevaras directo a manos del coronel Melisandro Maravilla" (288). The apotheosis of this association occurs at the banquet, moments before Rigoberto assaults Somoza, when Parrales sits at the dictator's table and tells him that Rigoberto would be an ideal candidate to work in the national press (read: propaganda machine) in Managua. Rafa's penetration into the hegemonic is formalized when he flirtatiously invites Somoza's wife to dance (339). This action evokes the notion that women are traded among hegemonic subjects as capital; in other words, Parrales's invitation inserts him into the dominating group.

In this act of courtship, we are reminded that though owning the press and belonging to the intimate table of the dictator, Parrales is homosexual. There is some confusion in the novel regarding his sexuality, as he is described both as a *cochón* (302), who in Nicaraguan homosexual circles is solely penetrated, and as a penetrator. As the conspirators approach *El Cronista*, Rafael is described as a "loco peligrosísimo" (208), who sensually fixates on Norberto. When the other conspirators mock Norberto for this attention, he staunchly denies any connection with Parrales. Only when one of the conspirators affirms that "tuyo es tu culo. En eso, yo no me meto" (209) does Norberto laugh, suggesting that he has been penetrated by the journalist. Herein lies the subversion of the press, for Parrales is not only a queered figure but also sexually ambiguous within practice. He is not the willing penetratee that Roger Lancaster conceptualizes in his sociological study of homosexuality in Nicaragua but is instead a new archetype that does not conform to traditional tenets of sexual expression, introduced in the national imaginary perhaps as a side effect of the shift to open borders. Parrales ritualizes a practice of seduction, evoking Reinaldo Arenas's joys in hunting flesh in the liminal space of the seaside in *Antes que anochezca* (1992), as he is the "pescador" who catches a "pez" (205).[2] His bait is "un billete de mil córdobas con el perfil en óvalo de Somoza" (205). The inclusion of this caveat has a dual significance in the text. On the one hand, sexuality and masculinity can be bought and sold, as it is alluded that the otherwise heterosexual Norberto fell trap to the "pescador." Such a seduction highlights the importance of the body and its productive parts in constructing the Masculine subject, for masculinity is for all intents and purposes a commodity that subscribes to the laws and pressures of the market: it can be bought, sold, negotiated, and ultimately put into a hierarchical system. Even seemingly heterosexual men can be priced and convinced to open their orifices (the ultimate sign of emasculation). Heterosexuality, it seems, is fluid and undefined, particularly in a neoliberal episteme, where cash is king and the buyer has the last word.

The inclusion of Somoza's profile in the scheme, that is, on the bank note, hints at the dictator's economic policy, which was shrouded by under-the-table dealings, oligarchic structures, and hierarchies built around nepotism and cronyism. This system impoverished the populace and increased the divide between rich and poor in Nicaragua. By following the metaphorical banknote printed with the caudillo's portrait, the novel affirms that the nation as the unassuming and anonymous "pez" assumed the role of the sodomee, giving in to bodily and economic pressures to open up. The nation under such a historical regime effectively becomes a cochón, which, as one of Somoza's sergeants asserts, is an "invertido" (302). Similarly, the nation under any regime that holds capital to be king (such as the neoliberal state in the post-Sandinista period) will equally be emasculated and placed into the role of the oppressed. The symbolism of the bank note here is only another example of how readers may interpolate the historical onto the present, in addition to viewing it as diegetic of a sociocultural past, as we can tease out synchronic and diachronic interpretations of the exchange of money for the anus.

The verb *invertir* conjures a dual schema of characterization. On one level, it indicates a changing or substituting of the order, position, or sense of a thing. The cochón would, therefore, be inverting heteronormative sexual practices and expressions. The verb, however, also has an economic definition, wherein it signifies the productive application of capital. Can the sodomee be thought of in terms of economics, as a product of caudillo and neoliberal economics? I will touch on this later when I analyze in closer detail Galich's two novels on post-Sandinista Nicaragua. Returning to the new historical novel, however, the first entry of the verb *invertir* is a central axis in the genre's task of fictionalizing the historical. But does the second entry of the verb reverberate in these rewritings of history? Referencing traditional, heterosexual patriarchal societies, Gayle Rubin theorizes that the system only functions by means of a traffic in the corporal bodies of women within the masculine homosocial. From my analysis of *Margarita, está linda la mar*, it is evident that a trafficking in bodies is taking place. But is it the movement of women as possessions between men that defines Ramírez's reflection on the past through the optic of the present?

CHAPTER TWO

Marketing Masculinities
in Nadie me verá llorar

Cristina Rivera Garza's *Nadie me verá llorar* underlines the substitutive process of inversion as it recounts the life of a woman in the last years of Porfirio Díaz's government and the beginning of the Mexican Revolution. The novel is constructed around an oppositional gender voice to the main narrative, as the photographer, Joaquín Buitrago, provides Rivera Garza with a framing device to the narrative of and about Matilda Burgos, a provincial girl from Papantla, Veracruz, who leaves the house of her uncle in Mexico City after a brief involvement with Revolutionary fighters. Matilda becomes a prostitute, and then later a patient in a psychiatric ward, where she is classified as being mentally ill after she refuses the advances of a group of soldiers. Unsurprisingly, the critical gender work to date on the novel has focused on the feminine/feminist aspects of the transgressive lead, who turns her back on hegemonic masculinity's strategies of societal control.

Upon Matilda's arrival in Mexico City, the reader can easily piece together how her uncle, Marcos Burgos, functions as the axis around which his local society revolves. In a microeconomic sense, he structures and dictates the machinations of the household through a set of rules designed to inbreed hygiene and order. Mexican society at the beginning of the twentieth century and during the last years of the Porfiriato was underscored by the project of modernization. As Maricruz Castro Ricalde explains, society was structured around institutions of law, hygiene, and order that permitted a national project of modernity (viii). The historicized dictator (including the domestic dictator Marcos) further inscribes the importance of

26

hygiene onto his own body. He is obsessively preoccupied with cleanliness, both his own and that of others, and being impeccably dressed.[1] Writing hygienic bodies for these patriarchal men becomes a metonymic inscription of writing codes of hygiene and cleanliness onto society, which, as Ricardo Melgar Bao suggests, is inherent in Latin American projects of modernity (31)—a nation that is, by virtue of the power structures of government, phallogocentric in nature and as a construct.

Keeping this in mind, the hypermasculinity of the political (macro) dictator in *Nadie me verá llorar* within this matrix is an afterthought, as Rivera Garza reorients the axis of power to the domestic dictator in the form of Marcos Burgos, thus posing a case-study system (which is really rhizomatic) in understanding the whole. The reorientation of the dictator may also fall in line with the literary probing of femininity in Mexican society, a connective thread that runs through much of the author's work, inspired no doubt by antecedents such as Rosario Castellanos and contemporaries like Ana Clavel. The author acknowledges this point, stating in an interview that the original title of the novel was to be *Yo, Matilda Burgos* (Macías Rodríguez and Hong), though it was discarded as too similar to testimonio-style narrative produced by female authors in the twentieth century.

Nadie me verá llorar illustrates a narrative: "de desarraigo tanto vivencial como intelectual, de buscados puntos-de-fuga, de estar-en-el-fuera-de-lugar, de una gozosa (aunque también sufrida y a veces violenta y violentada) autonomía, que me gusta mucho, con la que me identifico profundamente y a la cual no voy a dejar escapar" (Macías Rodríguez and Hong). Rivera Garza's own description of her work becomes tangible in the presence of history and the dictator within the diegesis. Women in Rivera Garza's novel gain a level of subjectivity above the simplistic monetary value Rubin suggests.[2] They instead become cogs in a system where "una buena ciudadana, una muchacha decente, una mujer de buenas costumbres tiene que empezar por aprender los nombres exactos de las horas" (119). Marcos's wife, for example, works like an automaton around his schedule and preferences, which are underscored by the necessities of personal (and symbolic) hygiene (within the national imaginary). Conversely, within the novel, and more broadly within the narratives I examine, the lack of personal hygiene is a first physical step in the desubjectification of bodies, which is followed by psychological or physical castration as a final blow.[3]

These acts are, in essence, transgressions of the established matrix of masculine power within the social context of the diegesis. Rivera Garza homes in on transgressions to discursively navigate the social body of masculinity through the feminine character of Matilda, who posits an un-*Santa*-like prostitute. I refer here, of course, to Federico Gamboa's *Santa* (1903), the novel that is a recurrent intertext in *Nadie me verá llorar*. Though Rivera Garza gives a voice to this silenced faction of Mexican society that Gamboa synthesizes into the submissive and sexualized Santa—a type, not a round character—what is really at stake is how this character maneuvers through the historical and the social to unearth the gendered mechanisms of control that remain unchanged, or are perhaps better hidden, in the present.

If the domestic dictator Marcos Burgos is akin to George Mosse's idea of the masculine stereotype (6), then the other men in the text, such as Joaquín Buitrago, Eduardo Oligochea, Paul Kamack, and Arturo Loayza, function as countertypes. For a stereotype to come into existence, Mosse argues, an efficient system and hierarchy of countertypes must first be constructed. The masculine stereotype is to be strengthened by "the existence of a negative stereotype of men who not only failed to measure up to the ideal but who in body and soul were its foil, projecting the exact opposite of true masculinity" (6). Marcos Burgos thus serves as the most stereotypic example in Rivera Garza's examination of masculinity in the text, the written subject most approximated to the Masculine as construct and subject position. He belongs to the new hegemony of knowledge, science, and modernity—the era of the *científicos*—that subverts the traditional emphasis on physical power and aesthetics. This new ethos of science, and by default its discursive elements, defines the strategies of modernization, whether in the latter years of the Porfiriato or during contemporary shifts toward an open market, when westernization and the partaking of the cultural and economic episteme of the Global North define conditions of the modern. Marcos demonstrates an avid interest in the project of modernization when he notes that "si el régimen en verdad creía en el orden y el progreso, . . . los médicos, y no los políticos, tendrían que dictar estrictas legislaciones urbanas" (126). Though some readings of the novel have identified Marcos Burgos as a character who is abjected from the nation due to his provincial heritage, we can conversely observe how "Marcos desarrolló una fe ciega en las posibilidades abiertas del futuro, en el progreso de la nación" (124). He becomes, I argue, a symbol of knowledge-based hegemony, stressing that the Masculine is sociohistorically conscious and evolutionary. His belonging is tied to an unabashed imitation of the stereotype, as "no sólo imitó [la] manera de vestir [de sus maestros] sino que además pudo desarrollar la misma ingravidez de movimientos y la mesura pacífica de sus miradas," and that "todos olvidaron que era de Veracruz y, de la misma manera, todos estuvieron de acuerdo en su brillante futuro" (125). Marcos, though coming from the province, evidences the possibility of simulation and performance of masculinity as a successful strategy of emulating the stereotype. More importantly, the genotype of the subject does not delimit its possibilities in the gendered order, but its phenotypic performances and beliefs elude the corporality (at times) of the body.

The morphine-addicted, failed photographer Buitrago, on the other hand, plays the role of the countertype to the scientific and modernizing stereotype. As a "sissy" in the economy of masculinity, he is both subjugated and ontological to the hegemonic. José Piedra defines "the sissy" in gender relations among men as being a subject that is " 'ultra' feminine, feminized, and/or [whose] effeminate behavior [is] perceived as passive, weak, and forever ready to suit the bully's whims" (370). Other characters, such as the psychiatrist Eduardo Oligochea, who treats Matilda, and Arturo Loayza, who is Buitrago's childhood friend and now lawyer, pose middle grounds between the stereotype and the subordinate masculinities that populate Rivera Garza's novel. They slip into the crevices, or gray spaces, between the gender and subject positions of dominant and subordinate.

As an example, Eduardo Oligochea is a man who places utmost importance on the precision of science as "tanto en su escritorio como dentro de su cabeza los objetos y las palabras se mueven con ritmos metódicos, siguiendo patrones rigurosos pero nimbados de armonía" (103). These "patrones" suggest a connection to Marcos Burgos's rules of hygiene and the imitation of his own "patrones": the professors on whom he modeled his behavior and countenance. Rivera Garza effectively contrasts his fixation on language and certainty with the self-narrative of a patient, Roma Camarena. When asked by Oligochea about her parents, she responds, "¿mis padres? Las putas lo vuelven loco" (101). She sidesteps his questioning and instead focuses on the philandering husband she blames for her condition. Eduardo's medical evaluation of the subject is of interest, as he notes that "su delirio era polimorfo, destacándose con más claridad la idea de que el marido la había hecho guaje, y que ella, a su vez, lo había engañado para vengarse de él. Tenía un delirio de ideas por asociación" (101). His evaluation concludes, "le quedó sólo el resentimiento hacia su esposo al que no le perdona las faltas que según ella le ha cometido. *Locura intermitente. Violento celosa. Acceso maniaco. Libre e indigente*" (102). His precision of language contrasts sharply with Camarena's self-styled narrative. Furthermore, an implicit doubt is placed on the woman, who by being interned in La Castañeda, is now an unwanted societal element. If anything, then, the female body is abjected in the novel, not the man of science. Oligochea's official report places doubt on her husband's actions but strongly asserts

Camarena's transgressive actions of adultery, which break the code of order and hygiene. The narrative further notes that "entre las palabras y el olor, él busca uniformidad, exactitud. Un método científico. Una manera de explicar la vida del cerebro y la conducta de los hombres basada en experimentos" (39). The novel, borrowing from Rivera Garza's doctoral dissertation, *The Masters of the Streets: Bodies, Power and Modernity in Mexico, 1867–1930*, specifies how in 1917, a small group of doctors got together to (re)configure "el lenguaje de la psiquiatría" (104), so much so that conditions such as "la verborrea incomprensible de los mayores de cincuenta años," now "se convierte en demencia senil" (103).

Science becomes a hegemonic textual strategy defined by its economy of verbiage and the epistemological cache it places on descriptive accuracy, which in turn permits a definition, separation, and purification of the national imaginary. Scientific discourse as a hegemonic text is, quite expectedly, contrasted with the voice of poetry and poets, returning us to Ramírez's juxtaposition of the father of modernismo with the contemporary political strife of competing modernizing agents. Eduardo affirms that though some "psiquiatras todavía son poetas, hombres subyugados por las profundidades ignotas del alma" (39), he is instead what he wants to be, "un profesional sin poesía" (39). Marcos Burgos adds his two cents that "los bohemios, como denominaban a los poetas, eran tan peligrosos como los mismos pobres" (129), who were, and still are, a societal element defined by the "stain" that Melgar Bao describes as contrary to the construct of a nation.

This fixation on the word, both spoken and written, is specified in Oligochea's most worrying dream, which is centered on "palabras equívocas" (105). These "wrong words" are evoked by a relationship the doctor had in his youth with a young girl from provincial Jalapa, Mercedes Flores, who, after making love for the first time, tells him "I'm your man. . . . You're my woman, Eduardo" (105). The statement displaces the male subject from the emulation of the Masculine and destabilizes the market of masculinities that the novel constructs, emphasizing that the linguistic and the symbolic are ontological to any episteme of gender. Language, therefore, not only becomes imperative in the discourse of nation, as seen in Marcos Burgos, but is also primary in the construct of the self, a theme developed in Rivera Garza's *La cresta de Ilión* (2002).

Oligochea, furthermore, is completely dependent on the approval of the homosocial mass in his self-justification as a mature member of society. Subjectivity and belonging are essential, and he makes this most clear when he shows a photo of his fiancée to Joaquín, who notes "la necesidad de aprobación en los ojos de su confidente" (52). Eduardo gains subjectivity not by means of the scrotal sack, like Ramírez's males, but through homosocial approbation, reminiscent of Eve Kosofsky Sedgwick's postulates of homo-erotic desire. Sedgwick describes the homosocial as "a word occasionally used in history and the social sciences, where it describes social bonds be-tween persons of the same sex; it is a neologism, obviously formed by anal-ogy with 'homosexual,' and just as obviously meant to be distinguished from 'homosexual'" (1). The reference to homosexuality corroborates an ap-plication of the countertype/stereotype model, for the term homosociality "is applied to such activities as 'male bonding,' which may, as in our soci-ety, be characterized by intense homophobia, fear and hatred of homo-sexuality" (1). Eduardo's moment of castration, though political and not physical, occurs when Buitrago sees that "de repente éste parece un perro amaestrado o un mozalbete de apenas diecisiete años, ambos con el ho-cico abierto como si aguardaran palmas en el lomo o regalos" (52). The climax of the castrating scene, which is to say the metaphorical flaccid penis or the swallowing of the testicles, occurs when Buitrago chastises Eduardo: "Vamos Eduardo. No te hagas pendejo. Esto ni siquiera es una mujer. Cecilia es tu boleto para entrar por la puerta grande a la colonia Roma" (53). From this we note how the novel dephallicizes Oligochea through a sustained inquiry into and placement of the relations of power among men, and not necessarily through the manipulation of the male body and its organs that the author of *Margarita, está linda la mar* prefers. Rivera Garza instead foments a discursive space that dialogues not only with historic ideas of Mexican masculinity (Irwin xxviii), but also with the writing of gender into a text that in its new historicity implicates contem-porary positions and constructs of identity.

The novel creates a market dynamic of competing yet variant mascu-linities that upholds a singular structure of power that is the Masculine. Eduardo Oligochea as an example does not conform to the definitions and expectations of the homosocial and belongs instead to what Connell terms "complicit" masculinities, "constructed in ways that realize the patriarchal dividend, without the tensions or risks of being the frontline of troops of patriarchy" (79). Connell further notes that by sheer numbers, complicit masculinity is the most pervasive category observed in Western culture, and "often involve[s] extensive compromises with women rather than naked domination or an uncontested display of authority" (79). Men in this group are by necessity complicit with the hegemonic project and their need for approval from and approximation to the gendered ideal remains unchanged. They are neither Mosse's stereotype nor countertype, instead existing in a crevice between the two. They sustain hegemonic masculinity through their pervasive and unrelenting adulation of the political phallus yet do not function as a symbolic counterposition. As a result, the novel does not displace the focus of power between corporal *sites*, but instead creates a market of masculinities where men are commoditized as symbolic, structural, and fluidly functional *types*. Parting from this framework we can see how Oligochea, for example, belongs to the stereotype in his stubborn yet consistent adherence to the language of science but falls from hegemony as he cannot gain the approbation of a drug-addict photographer who, for the first time, "le habla de tú" (53). Eduardo's slippage, both into the crack between stereotype and countertype and into actions that run against law and order, is punctuated by an encounter with a young drug addict from a seemingly wealthy background, who asserts that "todo el mundo rompe las reglas, doctor, todo el mundo" (97). The speaker belongs to a demographic that "son, por lo regular, aunque no todos, oficinistas, farmacéuticos, estudiantes de leyes o de medicina. Gente como él. Gente a la que puede ver a los ojos sin conmiseración. Hombres jóvenes de traje, corbata y sombrero de fieltro que llegan de la mano de sus padres o sus tutores, con el afán de verlos curados del vicio y el cinismo de las drogas" (98). The youth (like Eduardo) belongs to the hegemonic class and asserts that, though his father (like Marcos Burgos) "cree que el país está destinado a encontrar su propia grandeza" (99), he does not share in the same hope. This disenchantment with the national rhetoric of modernity and progress is made complicit with a usage of drugs as a means of escape, an approach that is in stark discord with the strategies of the dictator Marcos. The theme of drugs and the subsequent escape from reality brings to the fore Joaquín Buitrago, who is the opening narrative element in *Nadie me verá llorar*.

Buitrago at first has the potential of best approximating the stereotype of masculinity (which is in itself a close approximation to the Masculine), as he not only comes from a wealthy family but is also blessed with good looks and education. In his younger days, he could have subscribed to both the discursive and the aesthetic hegemonies of masculinity. Unlike the drugged youth who confronts Eduardo, however, Joaquín shows no semblance of belonging to the modernization project. He evidences first signs of breaking with this rhetoric when, in an almost vampiric state, he observes "la luz de su propia figura en los aparadores. Lo hace con duda, volviendo ligeramente el rostro a la derecha y luego a la izquierda, como si temiera que algún transeúnte se burlara de él" (24). As an insomniac, Buitrago is also located outside the culture of work and order specified by Marcos Burgos, going to bed just as "los demás despiertan y la ciudad vuelve a juntarse en su nudo de ruido y velocidad" (14); away from the markets of

economic progress, his subjectivity falls outside the parameters of gendered positions of power. He shows a precocious fixation on subjectivity
like Eduardo but makes no attempts at reconciliation with the homosocial as he lacks his own Cecilia. Joaquín also evidences a break from the
linguistic economy of Oligochea, when the latter questions the former,
who "rara vez tiene respuestas inmediatas o lineales" (33). Furthermore,
"hablar, para Joaquín, es desvariar. Confunde el tiempo de los verbos y
los pronombres" (33). The fall from norms of work and language place
Joaquín in what Connell calls the category of subordinate masculinities,
which unlike the complicit varieties are explicit countertypes to the
stereotype.

Rivera Garza places Buitrago in a central dialectic that frames the novel,
marked by the question "¿cómo se convierte uno en fotógrafo de putas?"
(19, 186). His profession, at first glance, adheres to the hegemonic norms
of hygiene and order, as photographers were hired by state institutions to
photograph and document prostitutes and patients in mental institutions
(Irwin 75), and to document, categorize, and collect the body maintained
within the discursive limits of power. Buitrago, however, comes to focus
on elements of the photographed subject that go beyond simple scientific
documentation. He notes how the prostitutes he photographs "hacía[n]
esfuerzos entre risibles y sinceros por imitar las poses de languidez o de
provocación de las divas" (19). He is less focused on the practice and order
of codifying gendered bodies and more on the aesthetics and nuances, the
poetics and coming into being of these same subjects. Though the man
controls the gaze of the photographic apparatus, the subject in Buitrago's
photography is the woman, or object of the photograph, as women exist as
independent subjects in the photo. They are conscious of their own movements and are given free rein in the composition of the photo. They
become subjects when the lens becomes a mirroring surface onto which
they model the poses and expressions of vedettes and Hollywood actresses.
Buitrago becomes nothing more than a body holding a camera, a finger
pressing a shutter, displaced from the patriarchal power ontologically im-
posed on the cataloger of bodies. Joaquín is therefore desubjectified and
becomes a portal by which the objects of his photography gain their own
subjectivity, seeing the lens as a mirror. He aims to capture "el lugar en que
una mujer se acepta a sí misma. Allí la seducción no iba hacia afuera ni
era unidireccional; allí, en un gesto indivisible y único, la seducción no
era un anzuelo sino un mapa" (19). This space, or perhaps surface, where
the woman comes to terms with herself recounts a Lacanian mirror stage,
where the subject engages in a Hegelian dialectic with the image in the

mirror (lens). Joaquín is further convinced that it is possible to reach that place. Psychoanalysis holds the opposite to be true, however, which in turn leads to the futility of Buitrago's aesthetic project, annulling him within the dialectic of the lens image.

This futility is further evidenced in his interactions with other members of the photographic homosocial. One member comments upon seeing Joaquín's portfolio, "¿esto es lo que fuiste a aprender en Roma, flaco? Esto es un trabajo muy menor" (23). Aside from belittling his art, the speaker also aesthetically countertypes Buitrago as a *flaco*, separating him from the virile and sensual male body that Héctor Domínguez-Ruvalcaba notes in early twentieth-century Mexican visual and textual culture. Even among the complicit group of photographers, Buitrago embodies a subordinate group, a countertype that serves as the antithesis of what man (or the photographer) should be within the project of modernity.

Instead of populating the novel with a random spattering of men, Rivera Garza establishes a system of comparisons among the male characters in *Nadie me verá llorar* by means of ontological equivalencies that later fragment into the multiplicities of men in her fictive society. Buitrago is tied to Oligochea by working within the world of science but differs from the latter in that his narrative voice is far removed from the structural and lexical precision of the psychiatrist. Oligochea is similarly connected to Marcos Burgos, as both subscribe to the linguistic economy of science. Buitrago is associated with the lawyer Arturo Loayza, who shares a common childhood. Both characters were born into wealth and educated; their parents were also friends. Joaquín demonstrates a calculated adherence to Loayza's belonging to the hegemonic discourse, modifying his speech to mimic the voice of order (as the newly arrived Marcos Burgos once did in copying his "patrones"), as "cada una de sus frases contiene al final un punto y aparte. Un nuevo párrafo" (217). Within this dialectic exercise of comparisons and constructs, Buitrago engages Arturo to secure the patrimony left by his parents. While Arturo by day is the stereotype of the wealthy, progressive, and articulate Mexican man, he shows a slippage into the crevice between stereotype and countertype in the company of Buitrago. We see how "los dos se observan con una delicadeza casi femenina, un cuidado que sólo están acostumbrados a practicar frente a las mujeres" (235). Loayza, in Buitrago's house, seems to break with one of the tenets of the homosocial, the lack of expressing homoerotic desire. This feminization of the lawyer stresses Rivera Garza's project of questioning the male stereotype, a task seen in her other novels and among several contemporaries, such as Ana Clavel, without necessarily mounting an oppositional countertype: Arturo, much like Eduardo, is never discredited from the discursive and professional spaces of science and law.

Connell's strategies of hegemonic masculinity include in addition to science and law—both sources of objectivism—the role of the press in society. Rivera Garza displaces print culture to the realm of the individual, just as she does with the creation of a market of individual masculinities that compete and collaborate in the shaping of the nation. The character of Matilda Burgos is juxtaposed intertextually with the protagonist of *Santa*, as Matilda reads the novel while working among other prostitutes in a brothel. She comments, "sólo las muy atolondradas o francamente estúpidas, como Santa, acudían al registro y pasaban por la humillación del examen médico" (162). Matilda carves out a textual niche characterized by a transgression of this literary tropic figure that *does* subscribe to patriarchal norms and regulations of economy and hygiene. Here we note again the importance placed on cleanliness and hygiene as written onto the body and as written as a marker or signifier of the power enforced by and erected around the Masculine. But the literary model in *Nadie me verá llorar*, much like the model of masculinity, is not without countervoices. Ligia, Matilda's theatrical and romantic partner, follows a Quijotesque reading of *Santa* when she imitates the literary character and finds herself a man who rescues her from the brothel. She comments, "es el sueño de toda puta, ¿no? Tú deberías hacer lo mismo. La Modernidad no va a durar toda la vida" (185). By implication, and not quite accidentally, La Modernidad allows for the performance of independent women, and the transgression of social constructs and regulations.

Gender roles and models within the literary texts interlaced with *Nadie me verá llorar* are not, however, geared only toward the female characters. Men also have a literary tradition of behavior, of performance shall we say, that designates their position within, in complicity with, or outside patriarchy. In the novels Matilda reads in the house of her uncle's friend Columba, she notes that "los héroes son siempre hombres [que] [á]giles de mente y cuerpo, logran vencer todos los obstáculos para rescatar a las heroínas en el último momento" (140). If men are to be men, like the young Revolutionary Cástulo Rodríguez, who initiates her into the world outside the sanitized confines of her uncle's house, then they too must in some way dialogue with these literary models. Following with the effects of the literary in the discursive space and outside it, Jorge Ruffinelli notes an acute sensibility for language and the epistemological paradigms it opens up in Rivera Garza's textual production. He surmises that "Rivera Garza estudia en su ensayo los lenguajes, y en su novela *crea* un lenguaje a la vez que *explora* (a través de sus personajes) el *lenguaje*. Estamos, al fin, en el centro de lo literario" (38). The literary and language provide a model and a playground for identity experimentation and expression, whether it be following the hegemonic system or transgressing it; the displacement of the dictator from the national to the domestic and the role of the hegemonic on more intimate and interpersonal relationships are thus intertwined with the aesthetic exploration of language. Unlike the Nicaraguan poet and politician, Rivera Garza does not write a personal subjectivity of politics but instead dedicates *Nadie me verá llorar* to the consideration of the historical constructs of genders within the tangential process of creating the national (gendered) imaginary.

In comparison to Sergio Ramírez's novel, *Nadie me verá llorar* is seemingly divorced from contemporary Mexican politics, but it inculcates instead an economy of masculinities reminiscent of free market Mexico, with its evident positioning of stereotype versus countertypes as competing brands of the national, and the reconciliation of complicit masculinities with the hegemonic domestic caudillo. Returning for a moment to Rubin's thesis on the commodification of women, it is evident from a structural reading of *Nadie me verá llorar* and *Margarita, está linda la mar* that these writers conversely commodify male bodies within an economy created and perpetuated by the Masculine. Returning to the analysis of the verb *invertir* in Ramírez's novel, it is relatively uncomplicated to identify how the Mexican author alludes to the second entry of the verb, as she creates a market of masculinities that are played off against each other with the end game of providing a dominant model that colonizes and defines the market dynamics of gender in the text.

CHAPTER THREE

Political Masculinities
in La fiesta del Chivo

Keeping with the economic concept of gender, I here direct our attention to Mario Vargas Llosa's much-studied caudillo novel, which explores the role of masculinity within the authoritarian (semantic, social, political, economic) market of Rafael Trujillo's Dominican Republic. Published a year after Matilda Burgos's incursion into the literary, *La fiesta del Chivo* creates a renewed interest in the genre of the dictator novel, no doubt because of the author's notoriety outside the printed page as well as on it. What is of primary interest in this text is how gender(ed) systems are constructed around the allegorical space of the dictatorship, thereby peeling away the superficial layer that covers how power melds the intimate and dynamic relations between subject-bodies. As with the other historical novels studied here, there is, I argue, an implicit reckoning of the present as a temporal referent to any past fictional discourse and exploration. Though these authors chose to write historical novels, the "new" modifier includes an acute reflection on the place of the present as a sociopolitical and chronological site of enunciation and contestation. As Pons rightly notes, the past in *La fiesta del Chivo* "no es un tiempo fijo y concluido, sino cambiante que se conecta con un presente también cambiante, inacabado, en su contemporaneidad inconclusa" (262). Vargas Llosa has often cited "demons" as being the basis of any writing, and as Sabine Köllman has noted, "politics is one of the most persistent 'demons' which . . . provoke his creativity" (1).[1] Keeping with the idea of a textual and structural economy and commodification of masculinities, I contend that Vargas Llosa writes masculinities into a critique of authoritarian government, which controls both economic and social markets, to investigate how the Masculine reverberates in macrosocial constructs that are inseparable from the politics of a particular (though arguably universal) regime.

The novel unfolds through the return of Urania Cabral, daughter of a one-time confidant of the (sanitized and predatory) dictator Rafael Trujillo, popularly known as El Chivo, to the island of her birth. She cannot psychologically explain the drive to return and the need to talk to her father, a father who in a preterit space and time had consented to her rape to regain favor within and in relation to the Masculine. In this sense, as has been noted by several critics, the novel appears to be structured around the implicit and explicit violence toward women and the fear engendered by a patriarchal society that not only commodifies, but also actively barters with the female body. Following this argumentation, Miguel Gabriel Ochoa Santos posits that the corporal body, and in particular the female body, is a discursive site of oppression and transgression (214) in *La fiesta*. Although these critiques are essential points of entry into the novel, I believe that such a gynocentric framework also opens us to the possibilities of examining masculinities in the text, a condition behind, after all, the impetus to open ground in a masculinity studies–based cultural criticism in Latin America. Ochoa Santos, for example, does not pay attention to the many male (non-Masculine) bodies that are routinely and methodically violated over the course of the novel.

Much has been said about the historiographic and metaliterary aspects of *La fiesta del Chivo*, with even a former Spanish head of state claiming that the novel is "más verdad que la verdad" in regard to what happened in the Dominican Republic during Trujillo's government (Lefere 331). While this may be up for debate (in the most banal of academic discussions), the idiosyncrasies of the text reveal a dialogic that goes further than a conversation about terms such as "history" and "truth." What is of greater value resides in the interconnections the author traces between bodies and types that stand in for particular stakeholders in any autocratic system. This web of relations is brought to the reader through another universal—violence—which transcends any national or imaginary barriers that would otherwise localize the narrative. As such, though the violence against women—specifically, the digital penetration of the young girl performed by the impotent dictator—may provide a silenced aspect of state repression and control, I suggest that it simply presents an anachronistic caveat or anecdote, which permits, as a result, the writing of the narrative voice of the dictator and Dominican society during the years of the Trujillato.

The novel is punctuated by violence (both subjective and structural) enacted by the dictator system in textual and linguistic terms to underscore the connection between violence(s) and structure(s) in the novel/Trujillato. Though writing about the Dominican Republic, the author shies away from using the dialect and lexicon of the island, and his characters—all from diverse social and economic classes—speak in a standard Latin American Spanish. Vargas Llosa further writes violence into (and not by means of) the text with the use of temporal jumps between the narrative of Urania and the events of her youth, a narrative technique that readers will recognize from several of his other works, thereby allowing for a broader reading of the novel away from a simple portrayal or study of the Dominican Republic. Taking the transnationality of the text to hand, we can thus collocate it within a trajectory of fiction that questions and decenters macro and microstructures in contemporary Latin America, a process begun with the author's first best seller.

When the protagonist first talks to her invalid father, for example, her voice intermingles with a separate narrative of the past. Mention is made in an impersonal point of view to a celebration in Santo Domingo immediately after Urania addresses her father. Within the objective recounting of the celebration, Urania speaks, correcting the narration (or herself?), noting that the name of the city was changed to "Ciudad Trujillo" (133) during the dictator's regime. This detail adds to the characterization of the dictator's hypermasculinity, if this hegemonic masculinity can be viewed as being synonymous with the Foucauldian concept of power.[2] By gendering the city as a metonymic representation of the oppressive male figure, the politics of the nation are circumscribed in relation to the centrality of the city versus peripheral towns, villages, and regions. The urban is, in effect, gendered along semantic and symbolic lines that dialogue with and are superimposed on its spatial and cartographic lines, crevices, and nuances. By walking through or existing in juxtaposition with the urban gendered space, the subject is given a sense of positionality in the structures controlled and limited by the Masculine. Such a writing of space is nothing new and in fact can describe many a contemporary text that works the urban in as another character or trope. Later on, Urania's first meeting with Ramfis Trujillo is told in the same impersonal style, complete with dialogue that is not part of her diegesis. Thus, the story within the story appears as the author creates a separate narrative space, characterized by a change in narrative voice, one that runs simultaneously and coherently with Urania's return to the republic.

As critics have emphasized, the novel can indeed be framed by her contemporary situation, which in turn compels the narrative of the past to be read as what trauma theory will call a traumatic text or a textual representation of personal trauma (Caruth 24; LaCapra 48). Though this trauma is initially centered on the violence of fear and assault against the female body, a close reading will note that this violence is actually quite secondary in terms of the generalized violence exerted in the plot. Men, in fact, are as much (or even more) victimized by the regime of fear and violence in Vargas Llosa's dictatorship. The revenge exacted by Ramfis after the murder of his father, for example, is brutal and visceral, as he assumes the position of hegemonic masculinity, yet it lacks the suspense and textual detective work on the part of the reader, which is characteristic of the crime perpetrated against Urania. The torture of Román Fernández, for example, is written without the aid of extended metaphors or symbolisms, as is characteristic of Urania's rape. His eyelids are simply sewn shut, and he is periodically electrocuted and even castrated in graphic detail: his testicles are snipped off with a pair of scissors, and he is then made to swallow them. The castration of the male subject in relation to the exertion of phallic power by Ramfis, as in other new historical novels that probe the creation and maintenance of the hegemonic homosocial, underscores the author's position of writing the dictator.

That being said, and though careful in deconstructing the sanitized and erect figure of the dictator by mentioning his incontinence and impotence, Vargas Llosa resists completely doing away with the hypermasculine subject position within Dominican society, perhaps reflective, on the one hand, of his own political assertion in his native Peru, and on the other, of Judith Payne's thesis of boom writers continuing to enshrine the tenets of patriarchy in their exercises of representation (7). The violence exerted against men by men, however, is central to the author's Trujillato; it is axiomatic of the diegesis, where paradoxically what is not tolerated is the violence against women. Antonio Imbert, one of the conspirators in the plot against the dictator, is visibly agitated by the famous murder of the Mirabal sisters, commenting, "¡Ahora también se asesinaba a mujeres indefensas, sin que nadie hiciera nada!" and that "¡Ya no había huevos en este país, coño!" (319). Having "huevos," it seems, implies that one does not kill women, yet testicles are primal to the definition of the male subject in the text, which by definition suggests a subjugation of the feminine. By creating this paradox, the text suggests that the female is peripheral to the plot, and that what is really under consideration is the power structure among men. The emphasis placed on this site, or locus, of the Masculine reiterates the notion that sociostructural constructs of gender are necessarily and semantically linked to the very real Latin American body.

Returning to the torture scenes of Román, he hears (since he has had his eyelids shut) "risitas sobreexcitadas y comentarios obscenos, de unos sujetos que eran sólo voces y olores picantes" (431). By being castrated, Román loses subjectivity in the face of these mocking "sujetos," effectively losing position in the dialectic among males. Román is deconstructed by the agents of the dictator's successor, as Ramfis exercises a phallic masculinity that intriguingly asserts its position by dephallicizing, in the organic and testicular sense, its competitors. Men in *La fiesta del Chivo* are the main players in the text, even though the diegesis is seemingly framed by Urania's trauma process and the need for reconciliatory catharsis.

By giving the fictional Trujillo a voice, however, the author narrativizes the position of the Masculine agent, allowing, as is expected of the new historical novel, a decentering of the normativity of gender. This practice, as penned by a very hegemonic (extratextual) writer, is epitomized by the virile, clean-cut, and nonperspiring dictator figure who engages in a process that feminizes men "cuyos cuerpos no corresponden al estereotipo de la masculinidad hegemónica. Hombres que expresan sus emociones, artistas, de contextura debil, enfermizos, entre otros, tenderían a ser feminizados" (Olavarría, "Hombres" 120). Trujillo survives in a culture and a homosocial body of men who are complicit with his strategies of domination. Their complicity is marked by a silence that is omniscient, as one of the conspirators notes, "en esos años, Antonio no se hubiera atrevido a hablar mal de Trujillo" (111). When the younger Urania spies the dictator visiting their neighbor's house, her father chides her and stresses that she did not see anything. Note here that the silence enforced by the dictatorship is more than discursive, as Urania is not told to remain silent or to tell no one about what she saw. This option would require a textual and symbolic acknowledgement of the action observed. Her father, however, as a complicit drone of the Masculine pushes for an erasure of the action in itself, disenabling language as signifier of the violence and strategies of the hegemonic order, favoring instead a gendered control of reality that runs counter to the observed fact.

Following what I have highlighted in previous chapters, the true signifier of masculinity in this new historical text is the dismembered but all-powerful scrotal sac, which houses the essence of manliness. It is not surprising that an uncooperative penis and a urethral sphincter that has a mind of its own precipitate Trujillo's demise. Reflective of the importance of the testicles within the homosocial, however, Trujillo never really loses his apical position within the hierarchy of power in the novel. Only Urania knows of his impotence, and only his trusted manservant knows of his incontinence—both gendered subjects bound to the contract of silence evoked by the Masculine order to control a malleable social structure. Even after being ambushed, the dictator does not lose his stature as the stereotype of masculinity, as General Fernández fears reprisals and revenge if he were to take hold of the system. Trujillo loses only prestige and dominance in the text, in the discursive interior of the subject that Vargas Llosa pens. Only through Vargas Llosa's imagination of the historical Masculine (figure) can the text undermine its position, underscoring my thesis of the author relocating the novel onto a broader context that focuses on extra-Dominican structures of power, such as modern Peru. To note in this hermeneutic and spatial displacement is the importance given to the male bodies and the testes as inscribed corporal sites; we can thus contend that the economy of masculinities built around the authoritarian Masculine position is ontoformative to the erotics and poetics of a novel that both subscribes to a phallogocentric diegesis and circumscribes a phallocentric society.[3] As such, the writing of gendered bodies and systems in the new historical schema seems to suggest that Dominican (and implicitly Peruvian) society can viably examine the past in relation to the present through the optic of a masculine discursive space.

After having lost political elections to Alberto Fujimori and suffering a phase of self-imposed disenchantment with his native Peru, Vargas Llosa's rewriting of the dictator figure is poignant in its extrapolation of national (Dominican) politics to a transnational poetics of trauma. By structuring the novel around Urania's migration from the cosmopolitan city of the United Nations to the island of her ancestors, the author suggests converse relationships among the dictator's masculinity, actions, and strategies of power toward other social contexts. Vargas Llosa first demystifies the dictator only to later restrengthen the position of the hypermasculine by dephallicizing, in psychoanalytic and physical senses, challengers to Trujillo and his offspring. This exercise, in turn, suggests that under an autocratic regime of violence, history is bound to repeat itself, and those who suffer are the silenced and raped subjects that enable the dictator. The author's gendered and masculine discursive space is reflective of his own position at the moment of writing the novel, as an outcast politician seeking to reestablish his own political agency against the machinations of his rival after suffering political defeat in the year of the novel's first edition. In a response to a not-too-surprising line of questioning, Vargas Llosa addresses the connections between the literary and the social, noting that "Fujimori was quite different to Trujillo—a more mediocre tyrant" (Jaggi 31). The author's position within the commerce of literature is thus strengthened by the novel, an exploration of masculinities vis-à-vis the transgression of the hegemonic, which then surreptitiously introduces Vargas Llosa's own personal position within Peruvian politics.

The matrices of masculine positions in the novel are connected not only to the political (as analogy of other spaces) but also to the economic, exemplifying the effects of current socioeconomic changes on the literary. Vargas Llosa's diegesis is painstaking in its research and inclusion of national economic policy, as the dictator is shown with his aides discussing the country's state of affairs. Faced with low revenues, the fictive Trujillo refuses to reduce his workforce or to cut costs because to do so would cause social tumult and unemployment. One alternative suggested is to nationalize the dictator's industries, thereby shifting the weight of ledger books in the red to the State, a move that Trujillo is stoutly against. Speaking to a group of senators, he observes, "robarías cuanto pudieras si el trabajo que haces para la familia Trujillo, lo hicieras para los Vicini, los Valdez o los Armentero. Y todavía mucho más si las empresas fueran del Estado. Allí sí que te llenarías los bolsillos" (157). Therein we see an implicit critique of non-neoliberal systems; after all, Vargas Llosa presented himself as a right-wing candidate (though Fujimori quickly outflanked him in that direction after winning the elections). Favored over nationalization, then, is its opposite, privatization, which we must remember is a fulcrum of the neoliberal non-state. In a similar fashion, the dictator in the novel creates a market system based on his own position as the dominator, where subordinate positions are understood and commodified by "su conocimiento profundo de la psicología dominicana" (169). This understanding constitutes "trabar una relación de compadrazgo con un campesino, con un obrero, con un artesano, con un comerciante," which results in "la lealtad de ese pobre hombre" (169) to then bring about policies that may otherwise run counter to the laymen's well being.

In another example of the connection between the dictator's body and national policy, Trujillo's virility and phallic masculinity are contrasted with Venezuela's democratically elected Rómulo Betancourt. In a broadcast of the national Radio Caribe, the announcer "poniendo la voz que correspondía para hablar de un maricón, afirmaba que, además de hambrear al pueblo venezolano, el Presidente Rómulo Betancourt había traído la sal a Venezuela" (35). We must remember that Betancourt not only nationalized Venezuela's oil industry, against the precepts of a free market capitalist system, but also held a longstanding rift with Trujillo that resulted in assassination attempts against both rulers. As Trujillo reflects after taking a bath and putting on talcum powder and deodorant, "el mariconazo ese no se saldría con la suya. Consiguió que la OEA le impusiera las sanciones, pero ganaba el que reía último" (35). The hinted homosexuality of Betancourt and the stereotyped penetration that accompanies the condition are juxtaposed with the clean, hygienic body of a man who promises to "ha[cer]

chillar a una hembrita como hace veinte años," when his "testículos entra-
ban en ebullición y su verga empezaba a enderezarse" (236). See here again
the play on the verb *invertir,* as one is suggested to be *invertido* whereas the
other pushes for more *inversion.*

The testicles first and then the penis lay at the heart of any structural
and semantic writing of the Masculine and therefore place the body as a
key discursive site in the dialogues between the present and the past. Returning once more to the notion of a system, structure, and practice in flux
in the politico-economic climate of Latin America in the latter half of the
twentieth century, I suggest after the analysis of Ramírez, Rivera Garza,
and Vargas Llosa's work that these fin-du-siècle caudillo novels engage in
a materialization of the male body that inverts the traditionally held view
that only the female is commoditized. I argue that the male body and its
manifestations are materialized as units of commerce that disassociate and,
at the same time, align male bodies from and with the Masculine. The
authors connect with social and political institutions through an engagement with economic models, as they write masculinities into their narratives to characterize, organize, and place their own authorial thought and
reflections of the past in relation to contemporary crises.

CHAPTER FOUR

Queer(ing) Masculinities
as the Dictator Falls

In keeping with the matrix that interrelates gender, politics, and economics, Pedro Lemebel reimagines the dictatorship of Augusto Pinochet in
Chile through a characteristic narrative and authorial style. *Tengo miedo
torero* is not structured around a wayward prodigal son or a traumatized
victim; in its place, Lemebel probes a failed Communist plot to assassinate
the dictator in 1986. Instead of focusing the narrative on an intimate voice
within the rebels, that is, within the core challenge to the hegemon, he pens
a neighborhood transvestite, La Loca, who not only falls in love with Carlos, a young revolutionary, but whose house becomes the functional center
for the group as they store their weapons and propaganda in camouflaged
boxes. Note that I call the protagonist a transvestite, and not a transgendered person, as the character repeatedly disidentifies with women, suggesting that he/she does not view him/herself as a body in transition.[1] That
being said, my choice of transvestite is perhaps not even appropriate, as I
believe La Loca to elude any Anglo categorizations (Sifuentes-Jáuregui,
Avowal 201). As a caveat, then, I use "transvestite" as a working appella-
tion, though do not assign to it a holistic appropriation of the character's
sexuality.

Lemebel's novel fits into current trends in Chilean literature charac-
terized by a proliferation of the new historical novel by a diverse set of au-
thors from multiple movements and generations, from Alberto Blest
Gana's nineteenth-century stories and twentieth-century authors such as
Carlos Droguett to the more recent Antonio Gil and Francisco Simón or
Fernando Jerez. Lemebel's *Tengo miedo torero* sneaks into this trajectory of

45

the genre by its inclusion of the events leading up to the assassination attempt on Pinochet. But unlike previous Chilean writers, Lemebel is the first to write the dictator from a queer perspective. Furthermore, unlike Vargas Llosa's politically charged extrapolation, Lemebel's writing of the dictator occurs at a time of relative political stability. The novel coincides with the presidency of Ricardo Lagos Escobar, who oversees the democratization of the constitution and the elimination of Pinochet-era oligarchic cronyism. Lemebel's Pinochet therefore lacks some of the metonymic qualities of Vargas Llosa's Trujillo, as Chile undergoes a process of social liberalization in the early 2000s that is unlike the politics of Fujimori in Peru. Conversely, Chile under Lagos Escobar does not suffer from the Fujishock of the early 1990s, or from the delegitimizing effects of the Fujigolpe, a self–coup d'état that destabilized national politics into an autocratic regime very much like that Vargas Llosa opposes in *La fiesta del Chivo*.[2] Chilean society in the early 2000s is instead punctuated by a series of social advances, as the presidency enjoys historic approval ratings, which are reflected in the novel's tongue-in-cheek depiction of a henpecked Pinochet.

In *Tengo miedo torero*, the band of Communist rebels represents a masculinity that is not complicit with the dictator position but that appears to suggest an alternative approximation to the Masculine. They are neither high-ranking generals nor close aides to Pinochet. Lemebel's rebels do not adhere to the same strategies of political domination or economic constructs forwarded by the hegemonic voice, but instead *queer* traditional patriarchal systems of gender and identity, subscribing in some regards to what Connell deems "subordinate" masculinities (*Masculinities* 78). In modern Western society, the most visible case of this relationship is seen in the dominance of heterosexual men and the subordination of homosexual or queer men. As Connell notes, "this is much more than a cultural stigmatization of homosexuality or gay identity" and that "gay men are subordinated to straight men by an array of quite material practices" (78). They are, however, not entirely subordinate; they decenter the traditional types that Connell identifies as being inherent in any patriarchy. They fall outside or queer the system on two levels. First, they are more accepting of the subordinate male par excellence in the plot—La Loca—even if they embody the traditional virilities attributed to fighters. After the assassination plot fails, they transport La Loca to where Carlos is hiding, showing tolerance of alternative sexual practices and expressions. Second, their aim as a group is to topple the patriarch and to establish a (theoretically) nonhierarchical social structure. Strategies of subverting and oppressing women and other men would in theory not apply in this new society. As such, their espousal of non-Masculine strategies places them outside the structures of the Masculine, though they are not completely removed.

In the novel's central romantic axis (which carries the narrative more so than the political machinations of the rebels), La Loca del Frente's Communist lover Carlos is highly sensualized through the furtive and at times explicit glances, comments, and touches of the queer figure. She throws him a birthday party complete with cake, children, music, and a fine tablecloth, and later offers him some liquor in an adult celebration once the neighborhood children have left. Carlos is corporally inscribed as a body of desire when La Loca informs the reader that he extends "sus labios en una sonrisa perlada de licor" (101).[3] His lips become a point of seduction when she asks him to recount something important about his life, a secret, though she does not want to know everything because he must remain an enigma. He tells her about a close friend he had in his youth, growing up poor in the country. Naked and by a reservoir, Carlos and the friend had started rubbing their penises against the warm sand: overcome by an uncontrollable urge, Carlos recounts how "de un salto lo monté" (103); Carlos's confession is a scene repeated in several Latin American films and novels, where the currently heterosexual male recounts a past experimentation, often in a desolate nonurban setting. What follows is a standoff between the young Communist and his friend, with both boys stroking their adolescent genitals and neither one willing to be the *maricón*. Reminiscent of a duel, the boys each charge the other to bend over, until Carlos's friend ejaculates without warning on his leg. The semen stain angers Carlos and becomes a source of, until now, unspeakable shame. Note here that the stain as written onto the body serves a similar function as seen in the other new novels, as the writing of the unhygienic semantically offsets and decenters the gendered body from the Masculine system. The image of the sensual, virile Communist rebel is further sexualized when La Loca returns from getting him a blanket to spend the night in her house. She notes how "una de sus piernas se estiraba en el arqueo leve del reposo, y la otra colgando del diván, ofrecía el epicentro abultado de su paquetón tenso por el brillo del cierre eclair a medio abrir, a medio descorrer en ese ojal ribeteado por los dientes de bronce del marrueco, donde se podía ver la pretina elástica de un calzoncillo coronado por los rizos negros de la pendejada varonil" (105).

The teeth of the zipper opening to his genitalia is the next step in the queering of Carlos, following the description of his pearly lips: the decentering process is oral and centered on the mouth, in both physiological and textual terms. The author's pen sensualizes the macho figure, and in a conscious moment of pause, contemplates the subverted, virile phallus. La Loca "tuvo que sentarse ahogada por el éxtasis de la escena, tuvo que tomar aire para no sucumbir al vacío del desmayo frente a esta estética erotizada por la embriaguez" (105). Note here the descriptions centered on the mouth and its movements; it is primal to her very survival. The novel's self-conscious usurpation of patriarchy is deliberate and focused, as though not only La Loca but also the text and the reader need a moment of pause, as reader/text/subject must stop over the gendered and drunk body to read, evaluate, and position it as object in relation to others. What is highlighted in this triple subjectivity is that though Carlos is allowed to be a macho and to continue his anti-Pinochet activities, he cannot escape the queer pen that sensualizes him.

The pen goes further than simply eroticizing the macho male through a queer gaze; Carlos as subject undergoes a gender-morphing game of meta-phorical transvestitism that will cement the novel's focus on non-Masculine positions. Sprawled on the couch with his crotch open to La Loca's gaze, he is first described as a "puta de puerto" with "tetillas quiltras" (106). The feminized body then becomes "un dios indio . . . un guerrero soña-dor" and finally "un macho etrusco" (106). Lemebel indicates not only how gender is transitory, from female to male within the same gaze, but also how it is culturally coded, suggesting that performativity does hold a criti-cal and tangible place in writing and being gendered in Latin America, even if critics (including me) are quick to dispel Anglo theory as falsely uni-versalizing. The body as a surface or blank slate is written upon by the pen and gaze of La(s) Loca(s) as Carlos comes into being as a sexual subject and object, open and conducive to metahistorical reinterpretation.[4]

After fellating Carlos, La Loca notes how he lies unconscious to her oral pleasuring in a pose "de Cristo desarticulado por el remolino etílico del pisco" (109). Lemebel's juxtaposition of the Communist to the religious fig-ure demonstrates a deftly crafted deconstruction of the patriarchal voice, showing how even the Communist can become a Christlike figure—after being fellated by a transvestite, of course. Lemebel dephallicizes Carlos's mode, or relation to patriarchy (that is, as both challenger and subordinate), not only by reaestheticizing the virile young body (as a paradox), but by also allowing for a queering of Connell's structures and suggesting an alterna-tive (though untested).

The rebel's virile and aesthetic approximation to the Masculine is then called into being by the portrayal of a "guagua-boa, que al salir de la bolsa se soltó como un látigo," that exhibits "la robustez de un trofeo de guerra, un grueso dedo sin uña que pedía a gritos una boca que anillara su amoratado glande" (107).[5] The mouth that the physical phallus begs for is the corporal space or locus where the subject is queered in the novel. This site of utterance and enunciation is also where the Lacanian phallus is negotiated, as the writing of the revolutionaries and their machinations against the dictator occur from the epicenter of the Loca's house and mouth. In a textual sense, since the mouth is the origin of the utterance, song partakes in an oral inscription onto the sexualized male body, as the drunken encounter is structured around the bolero "Tengo miedo torero," which lends its title to the novel. Lemebel sensuously weaves in the lyrics and emotions evoked by the song to sexualize the archetypal Masculine "torero" figure, just as the neighborhood transvestite needs the arms of the young Carlos to satiate and protect her. Music as intertext is dialogic as a queering element, both of the Communist rebel and of the plot, a factor that I analyze in greater detail in part 2.

Lemebel does not stop at simply queering the macho rebel, but also takes his pen to the figure of the dictator, Augusto Pinochet. Unlike Vargas Llosa, who resorts to the textual interiority of the dictator in relation to everyone around him, Lemebel triangulates Pinochet with his wife and her effeminate companion, Gonzalo, to thus relativize each character's gender expression. Though the queer Gonzalo does not appear explicitly in the novel, he provides a homosexual object and foil to Pinochet's homophobia and Masculine assertion. Gonzalo importantly does not have his own voice but speaks by means of the dictator's wife, which compounds the intimacy afforded by historicizing the patriarch, suggesting that a homosexual voice is often silenced and goes unwritten within an episteme of authoritarianism. In a style that does not include the punctuated separation of voices in the text, the wife's criticisms of the dictator echo within and around the interior space of the Masculine subject. Dressed in a bathrobe, she follows him one morning as he leaves the house, yelling:

Tú no me crees, tú piensas que es puro teatro mi dolor de cabeza para no acompañarte. Tú crees, como todos los hombres, que las mujeres usamos la artimaña de los bochornos para no hacer ciertas cosas. Imagínate cómo voy a preferir quedarme aburrida en esta casa tan grande, mientras tú te rascas la panza frente al río, rodeado de árboles, en esa preciosura de chalet que tenemos en el Cajón del Maipo. Porque fue idea mía que se la compráramos tan barata, casi regalada, a esos upelientos que mandaste al exilio. . . . Piensa tú, ¿que haríamos si no tuviéramos todas estas propiedades para descansar? Tendríamos que mezclarnos con la chusma que va al Club Militar a remojarse las patas en la piscina. Qué asco, bañarse en la misma agua donde tus amigotes, los generales vejestorios, se remojan las bolas. (135)

In addition to disqualifying his thoughts on women, she also asserts herself as the decision maker of the household—the chalet they own, among other properties the dictator amassed, are all thanks to her astuteness. She does not shy away from deconstructing the façade of the military man, calling him overweight and noting that the rest of the military is full of "chusma" that goes to the Club Militar. She makes note of their testicles, of what truly codes for power, and then swiftly demythifies them as vulgarities soaking in water, almost like used teabags. The intimacy afforded by Lemebel's narrative queers the hegemonic position of the male within the household, especially when compared with the relationship between the dictator and his wife in *Margarita, está linda la mar*, where the interactions between Somoza and Salvadorita are explored through the proxies of the conspirator Cordelio and the unsuspecting sergeant Domitilo. With Bible in hand, Cordelio wonders aloud why the boat they arrive in is named *Salvadorita*. The increasingly annoyed Domitilo replies that the boat belongs to the First Lady, and that "son sus negocios propios, distintos de los que tiene *el hombre*" (82). The wife is separated from *el hombre*, as Ramírez's focus is not so much on demythifying the dictator as it is on finding a point of contact between the caudillo masculinity and the masculinity of the poet figure, with the end game of constructing a genealogy of the nation based on the latter.

Returning to the years surrounding the publication of *Tengo miedo torero* and *La fiesta del Chivo*, the Chilean "new" novel is not necessarily constrained by a poetics of allegory like that which shapes the work by Vargas Llosa. This is reflected in the almost playful and uncensored depiction of Pinochet as a harassed husband in opposition to the hypermasculine in crisis that the Chivo enacts. In both novels, testicles continue to be an important corporal metaphor of the Masculine neoliberal system, though unlike *La fiesta del Chivo*, there is no deification of them being essential to writing or conceiving masculinities in *Tengo miedo torero*. Instead, Lemebel decenters them from a position of power, depicting them as quotidian and dirty: "huevos" here are not essential to man or necessary for patriarchal position; rather, they seem to be the stain inscribed on the body. Testicles, in fact, become sites of non-normativity in the novel, suggesting that a queer gaze and pen can successfully and seductively resemanticize the male body.

Like the other novels discussed, though, the notion of corporal hygiene as a signifier of socio-gendered positions is further developed in *Tengo miedo torero*. As noted in chapter 3, the soiling of the Dominican dictator's pants was the first step in his eventual personal (and not political) castration. Lemebel, however, queers the idea of soiling oneself as he dephallicizes the act from a physical standpoint, because the penis is not the source of the stain. Instead, the novel plays with the body and its sites, reinscribing onto them a series of metaphors that allow for an evaluation of the organic as a site of definition and defiance of the structural. As Pinochet rests in his car after surviving the plot to dynamite his motorcade, his bodily functions sever him from Masculine subjectivity.[6] In the backseat, "el Dictador temblaba como una hoja, no podía hablar, no atinaba a pronunciar palabra, estático, sin moverse, sin poder acomodarse en el asiento" (174). We learn immediately afterward that his paralysis is voluntary: "más bien no quería moverse, sentado en la tibia plasta de su mierda que lentamente corría por su pierna, dejando escapar el hedor putrefacto del miedo" (174).[7] The patriarch is soiled, but it is not the penetrating phallus that castrates him from hegemony. Instead, it is the uncontrollable anal sphincter—the quintessential site of being penetrated and of becoming and being a maricón—that releases the fecal stain that condemns the dictator, who two years later would concede political power to a newly formed democratic coalition. The inversion of the staining tool from the penis to the anus hints at the political position of the author, as Lemebel, unlike Vargas Llosa, is not engaged in a dialectic of political phallic privation as represented through the Dominican allegory.

Vargas Llosa suggests that Trujillo as the symbolic phallus is broken, thereby emphasizing the writer's own lack and subsequent envy. In opposition to the Peruvian writer, who writes the fall of Trujillo through castration and impotence, Lemebel seems to dip his queer pen(is) in something other than ink to inscribe the body of the failing patriarch. Pinochet faced a controversial return to Chile in 2000 after facing extradition orders from Spanish judge Baltasar Garzón; *Tengo miedo torero* coincides with a period of reckoning for the ex-dictator, as he struggled with repeated indictments related to the oppressive practices committed during his rule. Lemebel's exercise in releasing the character's anal sphincter during a tense moment in the novel hints at the author's own judgment of the fate and culpability of Pinochet. If the courts cannot serve justice, then it is up to the pen to stain and rewrite the figure of the dictator and his legacy.

By relaxing the dictator's anus, Lemebel emphasizes the organic nature of the nation that he envisions in the essay "Censo y conquista." He writes:

De esta manera, las minorías hacen viable su tráfica existencia, burlando la enumeración piadosa de las faltas. Los listados de necesidades que el empadronamiento despliega a lo largo de Chile, como serpiente computacional que deglute los índices económicos de la población, para procesarlos de acuerdo a los enjuagues políticos. Cifras y tantos por ciento que llenarán la boca de los parlamentarios en números gastados por el manoseo del debate partidista. Una radiografía al intestino flaco chileno expuesta en su mejor perfil neoliberal como ortopedia de desarrollo. Un boceto social que no se traduce en sus hilados más finos, que traza rasante las líneas gruesas del cálculo sobre los bajos fondos que las sustentan, de las imbricaciones clandestinas que van alterando el proyecto determinante de la democracia. (n.p.)

Lemebel's social critique does not stop with Pinochet but continues through the democratic era, as the author is particularly critical of neoliberal economic policies and their effects. His disenchantment with neoliberalism calls to mind Sergio Ramírez's own divorce from politics in Nicaragua amid the liberalizing of the nation's economy. Both authors situate their critiques on the textual anus and the digestive tract. One of the conspirators in *Margarita, está linda la mar* notes, for example, that Somoza "caga por la barriga . . . por medio de una válvula de goma. Lo que pasa es que es un secreto de estado" (37). The procedure is then described as a "supresión del tracto rectal y formación del ano artificial por el método de Charles Richter" (37), signaling Somoza's artificial rule in Nicaragua, as he was kept in power by and for U.S. interests. The connection between the anus of the dictator and the nation is stressed at the end of the novel, as Somoza lays on his deathbed after being stripped naked. An omniscient voice intervenes in the narrative and questions: "¿Para eso te hiciste falsificador de moneda, mariscal de excusados? ¿Qué harías con diarrea?" (351). The idea of uncontrolled bowel movements, evocative perhaps of the late capitalist economies of production, is something that the dying dictator never had to contend with, lending another question to the narrative's interrogation. *Margarita, está linda la mar* coincides with the contemporary right-wing government of Arnoldo Alemán, who oversaw several neoliberal policies in previously Sandinista Nicaragua. The final scatological question in the novel hints at the problems faced by Alemán as he increased foreign investment in the country, which resulted in an economic boom. This boom, as a result of short-term neoliberal tendencies, is the seeming diarrhea that the novel alludes to. Such growth comes at other costs and tears away the social fabric of contemporary Central American society. As such, the novel is reflective of a growing corpus of writers, such as Horacio Castellanos Moya, Fernando Contreras Castro, Maurice Echeverría, and Franz Galich, that calls to attention the detritus and stagnation that corrupts and rules Central America in the wake of neoliberal reforms.

Taking the anus as a corporal site of political discourse, much like the usage of the testicles as a signifier for turn-of-the-century economic realities and paradigms of production, we can see how Lemebel queers masculinities and the dictator in *Tengo miedo torero*. The releasing of the anal sphincter in Lemebel's novel results in not only a staining of the dictator but also a staining of the nation as a site of neoliberal practices, because the country must deal with the fecal remnants of not only Pinochet's political rule but also the liberalized policies he instituted toward the end of his regime. Lemebel highlights this problematic in the essay "La esquina es mi corazón," where he writes:

> Herencia neoliberal o futuro despegue capitalista en la economía de esta "demos-gracia." Un futuro inalcanzable para estos chicos, un chiste cruel de la candidatura, la traición de la patria libre. Salvándose de la botas para terminar charqueados en la misma carroña, en el mismo estropajo que los vio nacer. Qué horizonte para este estrato juvenil que se jugó sus mejores años. Por cierto irrecuperables, por cierto hacinados en el lumperío crepuscular del modernismo. Distantes a años luz, de las mensualidades millonarias que le pagan los ricos a sus retoños en los institutos privados. (n.p.)

The future under current neoliberal ideas, borne from the "herencia" of the dictatorship, is sordid and dark according to Lemebel. The scatological connection between the release of the sphincter and the subsequent "hedor putrefacto del miedo," with society's primordial "carroña," establishes a connection between the assassination attempt in the novel and Lemebel's writing of contemporary Chilean society in the first decade of the twenty-first century. In what has come to be known as "El manifiesto de Pedro Lemebel," written in 1986, the same year as the failed assassination plot, the writer acknowledges: "Me apesta la injusticia / Y sospecho de esta cueca democrática" (n.p.). He continues to lambast the status quo, affirming that the present is "como la dictadura / Peor que la dictadura / Porque la dictadura pasa / Y viene la democracia / Y detrasito el socialismo / ¿Y entonces?" (n.p.). The fecal discharge in *Tengo miedo torero*, just as in Ramírez's novel, is the metonymic representation of instituted free market economic policies, suggesting that any evaluation of growth and development must pass the "sniff test," that is, that microbodies and subjectivities must be evaluated for the potential to survive in a climate of economic austerity where the sovereign consumer is king.

Lemebel's sustained assessment of neoliberal tendencies reflects a populist social concern with the purported economic benefits of the free market system. The author's political position is written into *Tengo miedo torero* through and by means of the anus, which has its own placement within the erotics of the author and paradigms of sexuality. The penetrated orifice, which Ramírez hesitates to open yet questions, connects the economic failings of the caudillo with contemporary neoliberal Latin America. Lemebel's aversion of the anus from a strictly erotic perspective calls to attention his stressing of the dictator's anus and its aftereffects, as it is an inverted penetration of the sphincter, not a penetration from outside the body, that leads to the staining of Pinochet. This inversion, again, calls to mind the economic definition of the term, stressing the conjunct between national economics and the anus as a discursive site.

The displacements of the male body in these new historical novels fall under a larger concern with how and when the figure of the dictator is written by contemporary Latin American writers. Sergio Ramírez underscores a trend in commoditizing the male body in economic terms that deviates from the traditional adoration of the phallus. Vargas Llosa builds on this objectification of the male body and relies on a poetics of allegory to suggest that contemporary Peruvian society is under the iron fist of its own hypermasculine dictator. In a recent interview, he affirms that "todas las dictaduras son el mal absoluto" (Forgues 256), suggesting that the diegesis in *La fiesta del Chivo* is representative of plural social contexts. In essence, Vargas Llosa's Trujillo becomes a subject within the demystification of hegemonic masculinity in the novel, though this position of power is never fully challenged in the text. Conversely, Lemebel and Rivera Garza show an interest in uncovering the aura of the hypervirile, hegemonic embodiment of masculinity. On the one hand, Rivera Garza dislocates the political dictator, instead focusing on the domestic and scientific patriarch and how he was able to carve a period of economic growth in Mexico that can be read in parallel to twentieth-century neoliberal moves. Lemebel, on the other hand, seeks to "denounce the amnesia of the Chilean postdictatorship" (Palaversich 102), as he notes in an interview: "A country without memory is like a blank slate on which one can write whatever one wants, reinventing history in agreement with and at the discretion of the powers currently in vogue" (Novoa 29). Though Lemebel successfully takes up the pen to fill in the gaps in Chile's lacunal amnesia, it cannot be ignored that he writes, or "reinvents," with a queer pen, effectively decentering all the masculinities written into the text.

Though the figure of the caudillo has been studied ad nauseum, the new historical novels studied in these pages suggest that the writing of his role within the literary is pertinent to, and formulated by, the economic and political climate of fin-du-siècle Latin America. Though the telos of the continent, in political, literary, aesthetic, and cultural terms, has undertaken a shift toward deterritorialization as a result of broader processes of globalization (and in part, of the Global North reading the South), the novels studied in this part evidence a turn from this thought, as they attempt a territorialization of narratives and bodies by means of a historical contextualization within a national imaginary. Resorting to the past allows for a momentary escape from the transnational nonspaces and non-identities that McOndo fiction and Latin America are built on, as the new historical novel is by necessity a national manuscript.

Secondly, these authors resist the dematerialization of identity vis-à-vis gendered performativity by explicitly locating their sites of discourse on the male body. The testicles, the mouth, and the anus all operate as tableaux of inscription, deviating from the physical phallus as signifier of power and the malleability of performance as the apical practice of being and writing gender. They function and dysfunction as metonymic representations of greater and extratextual processes that can be sustained and encapsulated only by the corporeality of the (male) body.

The four novels studied in this part share this common trait and praxis as they challenge fiction's ability and power in writing and negotiating the Masculine. As such, they fabricate polydimensional matrices of textual masculinities that explore contemporary themes of power, gender relations, and national identities. As can be expected, these new masculine textualities rely on the authority and flexibility of the word and discourse, resorting to several and varied registers and systems of representation to codify gender. One such semantic field is popular music, which Lemebel carefully and studiously employs to recalibrate gendered approximations to the Masculine in *Tengo miedo torero*. Let us next examine how music and musicality are direct dialectic and dialogic systems and practices in the construct of contemporary masculinities.

PART TWO

Lyrical Readings and the Deterritorialization of Masculinities

The new historical novels sampled in the previous section undertake a re-writing of both the dictator figure in Latin America and the male body in a traditional genre that exemplifies the phallic power of men. Though the authors have been internationalized to some extent—through their relationships with the theoretical Generation Alfaguara and subsequent involvement in the triad of publisher-academic-writer—they territorialize their narratives within a nationally historical framework, resisting the urge to universalize or Orientalize their fictions (see the plethora of Latin American writers who now situate their texts in the Far East), just as contemporary economies are being deterritorialized. These new historical novels, furthermore, arise at a time when masculinity is in supposed crisis, or to be more specific, at a time when masculinities are being renegotiated away from the centric and apical position of the Latin macho, in part because of the vast social and demographic changes brought about by neoliberalism.

The new novel's reaction to this second crisis, however, establishes two distinct characteristics: masculinities in these texts are not simply dominated by the textualized depictions of the Masculine but are instead fluid entities and dialogisms that circulate within the interstitial fluids of the greater construct that is gender in Latin America. Furthermore, keeping in mind an economic episteme, they circulate coding the body as a site of reference, and are therefore ontologically varied and spatially elusive.

Such a trajectory is evidenced when studied alongside another literary trend in Latin American fiction: the intertextual and paratextual use of musical registers and lyrics to expand on what the text can say and where, within the cultural field, it can operate. Though the use of music in fiction is nothing new, there is a studied focus in recent fiction on the potential for popular musical and lyrical genres to explore the importance of culture and culturality as fields of gendered contact when identity seemingly becomes deterritorialized onto the global space. In what has been called "la narrativa de la música popular latinoamericana," Enrique Plata Ramírez comments that "a partir de la articulación entre la literatura y la música popular, alterna y paradójicamente se sacralizaran y desacralizaran, tanto la música como la literatura" (53). The critic further writes that the point of connection between music and literature produces "más un encuentro erótico, pulsional, que cultural" (53). Music is more than a textual leitmotif in these works: it establishes parallel planes of discourse that elucidates richer interpretations of the erotics of any given text, allowing for plural epistemologies and processes of reading. It functions as a Barthesian semic code that triggers a receptive hermeneutic practice of intertextuality, which is appropriated and reworked by these authors, who function as bricoleurs that undertake a Lévi-Straussian enunciative practice, where the "signified changes into the signifying and vice versa" (21), lending the text, instead, to a process and a practice of simultaneous flights of reception, cognition, and inscription. The inclusion of music as a mutually exclusive medium to narrative establishes a system of multiple codes, where these codes are not "added to one another, or juxtaposed in just any manner; they are organized, articulated in terms of one another in accordance with a certain order, they contract unilateral hierarchies," thus producing a "system of intercodical relations . . . which is itself, in some sort, another code" (Metz 242). This other semiotic code, a mixture of both narrative and lyrical registers, houses a tangential cognitive system of meanings where the musical and narrative signifiers are resemanticized, thus permitting a fruitful perambulation into intercodical erotics. It is this other plane, where the axes of narrative and lyric connect, that I am interested in.

This connection is privileged by the inclusion of music into the written narrative text, which follows three poetic schemata, each with its own distinct structures, constructs, and results. On one level, music serves as a textual channel of sexual objectification. The subject of desire resides in the diegetic singer who evokes the song and its lyrics. Popular song characterizes the enunciator and structures his or her interactions. The corporality of the subject is called into question as the mouth functions as a bodily site of discursivity that is not limited to the actual text of the music, instead becoming a position by which gender is written onto the literary bodies extant in the text. This is evident, for instance, in *Tengo miedo torero,* when the neighborhood transvestite's mouth represents the diegetic locus of popular music and the physical pen that inscribes gender onto her lover's (unconscious) body.

Yet popular music as an intertext does not always benefit from an intra-textual subjectification. It appears at times as a passing song overheard on the radio, or as a recurring memory that is evoked and formed around a particular tune. On this second level, Music as a textuality is evocative of Mikhail Bakhtin's thesis on language in the novel: as a dialogic element, it partakes in what the Russian thinker terms polyphony and heteroglossia. The latter circumscribes the collision of multiple languages and registers within the text, whereas the former points toward the many voices inherent in an utterance and within a text, as "each word tastes of the context and contexts in which it has lived its socially charged life; all words and forms are populated by intentions" (*Dialogic* 293). A provocative example of this schema can be found in Horacio Castellanos Moya's *Baile con serpientes* (2002), where the radio playing in the background of the old yellow Chevrolet fills out the interstitial semantics of the exploration of Central American masculinities in the wake of peace accords and diminishing economic opportunity, that is, as textual gendered bodies that are stained by the diarrhea of neoliberalism. Diegetic music, in this schema, functions as a secondary stream of discourse that is directly related to and builds on the primary plot line. It is not necessarily a parallel plane of discourse, but it has a parasitic relationship with the text, existing only as an example or illustration of the narrative.

The third poetic schema, when music is present as a dialogic element, is that it may be extracted from the corporal and diegetic body and become a body of its own—as an intertextual referent that allows a candid reading into the matrices of power, gender, and race that are extant in contemporary fiction. I am thinking particularly of Enrique Serna's use of song in *Fruta verde* (2006), or Mayra Montero's *La última noche que pasé contigo,* where music at times appears as a side note, chapter heading, or epilogue to the main plot. As a result, readers are forced to stop in their tracks, take an inferential walk away from the printed page, and pause, process, and digest the musical and lyrical referent as a parallel plane that may or may not intersect directly with the diegesis. As Wolfgang Iser emphasizes, music exists as a literary and social repertoire (69), though each set of verses forms a schema, which elucidates the reader's involvement, as "the text mobilizes the subjective knowledge present in all kinds of readers and directs it to one particular end. . . . It is as if the schema were a hollow form into which the reader is invited to pour his own store of knowledge" (143), to read together and separately as another plane that the author appropriates as tangential to the primary text.

The narrative text is, therefore, dialogic with the musical referent and its lyrics, genre, interpreters, and receptors. The use of particular musical genres territorializes this fiction within a sociocultural context, just as the device of the historical novel roots the works of Cristina Rivera Garza, Pedro Lemebel, Mario Vargas Llosa, and Sergio Ramírez within a topographic and imaginary boundary. Musical texts and rhythms appear both as intertexts and paratexts in this third model, cajoling the reader forward to unwrap the visible elements of textuality and to undertake a heuristic reading that juxtaposes the affective intensity of the lyrical with the tactile sensuality of the erotic.

CHAPTER FIVE

Defining the Literary OST

The use of music in *Tengo miedo torero* is unsurprising if we take into account that Lemebel is not only an accomplished writer but also a controversial visual artist who experimented with various video and photography art projects, performance pieces, and plastic sculptures. Those familiar with his multifaceted work—especially given his recent death—know that Lemebel is notorious for kissing men in theater pieces and has publicly displayed a television set with pornographic images over his genitals. This explicit exploration of the scandalous and the taboo as epistemologies of challenge and resistance to the Masculine explain in part his use of music in *Tengo miedo torero* as a semantic queering device. Working on the place of language and orality in Latin America, Sonia Montecino notes that "la oralidad es la forma en que el ethos latinoamericano ha trasmitido su historia y su resistencia frente a la expansión del texto. La oralidad es también el lenguaje que . . . desencadena un habla que se resiste a cierta economía porque sus tiempos no son los de la producción en serie" (164). Lemebel, as we have seen previously, restructures the erotics of the male revolutionary through a contextualized understanding of Montecino's latter observation. His text is polyphonic in the Bakhtinian sense, leading Berta López Morales to characterize *Tengo miedo torero* as an expression of multiple ventriloquist voices.[1] The critic notes that the text substitutes for the real body and permits a reading that allows a penetration of the body from various angles: "Por un lado, la fruición del lenguaje, gustado y degustado por la lengua que al tocar el paladar repite la fricción, el contacto de los fluidos corporales; por otra, el placer voyeurista, el ojo voraz que mira aquello dicho, susurrado, murmurado por la voz otra, voz ventrílocua, contradictoria y contrahecha que oculta, se sobrepone y borra la Voz oficial" (121).

She further argues that the protagonist's register and diction are a reflection of her own physical body, commenting that "cuplés, baladas, boleros, tangos, música del recuerdo, del ayer, le prestan su registro y hacen de su voz un collage, un pastiche de sonidos donde el sentido se fuga, haciendo de la voz de la Loca del Frente una voz travesti, excedida en la modulación de lo femenino" (127).[2] Music indeed frames the figure of the Loca in the novel, but I argue that it goes further than being a mere novelistic recourse of characterization; it holds a structural function in La Loca's interactions with Carlos and lends itself as a textual soundtrack to the plot. The text, in this particular reading, evokes music as an analogous filmic recourse, much like the songs sung by actors of the celluloid space, and much like the extradiegetic tunes that were made popular in Hollywood cinema, especially with the advent of original soundtrack compilations sold to satiate film aficionados.

Cinema as a narrative medium serving as an aesthetic referent to these Generation Alfaguara novels comes as no surprise considering that film's poietic past is structured around adaptations of popular narratives.[3] Pop cinema today is, from a marketing standpoint, arguably as much about its actors and off-screen stories as its musical scores and soundtracks. The use and popularity of music in cinema creates a tangential trajectory of meaning, as "increasingly, it seems, we think in soundtracks" (Knight and Wojcik 1). This is perhaps a result of a shift in the industry in the 1950s, when Hollywood began to market compilation albums labeled as "original motion picture soundtrack," which was later contracted to "original soundtrack," or OST.[4] Contemporary OST recordings include a mix of diegetic popular songs, nondiegetic lyrical and acoustic compositions, and cast-sung numbers, which are often versions of well-known songs, inscribing the filmic image with a sociocultural and historical context for the viewer/listener who identifies with the affective and haptic traits of the musical-lyrical register. What occurs, then, in this dialectic between composition and watching/listening is that "as a result of adhering to classical conventions, this kind of scoring works hard to encourage the audience to surrender to the film and fully engage with the emotional worlds and action depicted on the screen" (Davison 3). Music, therefore, peels away the visual skin of the moving image or printed text and encourages an affective process and reaction in viewers/readers, who must disentangle their own sociocultural relations to the interlaced lyrical text. As such, the musical moves us from the realm of the semantic to the field of the affective, thus positioning the reader at a phenomenological point of entry into Masculine systems.

Adding to the theorization of an affective intertextuality between sound/ song and the narrated plot (whether visual or textual), music enters the novel just as it does the cinema, through a variety of mediums and textual strategies, including the nondiegetic score, character performance, radio and sound devices, and diegetic singing, indicative of the plurality of composition in cinematic OST albums and representative of the three-schema model I propose in the introduction to this part.[5]

The original soundtrack to *Tengo miedo torero* begins with the title song, when the protagonist is first introduced and sings, *"Tengo miedo torero, tengo miedo que en la tarde tu risa flote"* (10). The novel's OST album (which, I predict, Generation Alfaguara will soon sell as MP3 downloads accompanying their novels or as embedded hyperlinks in e-book editions) begins with a diegetically sung piece, which would be referenced as a cast-sung number. Critics have mistakenly pegged this tune as that of the popular Spanish singer Sara Montiel, but Lemebel clarifies that the title of the book comes from a meeting with an old transvestite friend, who told him of her performances as Montiel and how she sang "El último cuplé" and "Tengo miedo torero." A laughing Lemebel asks her what follows, to which she replies, "tengo miedo que tu risa, a la tarde, flote," which is repeated by the Loca singing in the novel. The author then unveils that the song does not exist and that "la travesti mintió" (Interview).[6] Inadvertently, Lemebel's appropriation of the transvestite's lie comes to form the structural, literary, and lyrical axis mundi to the novel. From a structural standpoint, the song establishes a positionality of power, with the singer, the torero, and some unseen danger forming a triangulation of potential erotic dynamics in the novel. This triangulation, in essence, situates bodies and positions in reference to the Masculine, where the off-screen danger can be read as the hygienic and oppressive position of hegemonic masculinity. The off-screen position thus situates the torero in relation to or in complicity with the ideal: saving the singer will only add to his relative cache.

Though the author's appropriation of the song is ontological to both the poiesis and the reception of the text, it does create a literary side effect, for by using a fictive song, the text escapes the sociocultural sphere of reading that comes with positing a musical register. The novel, then, asks the reader to reference a register that is not really there, lending a tone of uncertainty to the narrative, suggesting that not everything is as it seems (or as it is historically represented). This is evident in the broader evaluation of the text, as a new historical novel that deviates heavily from the traditional dictates of genre by queering its tone, tenor, and to an extent, use of musicality by emphasizing the disconnect between the diegesis and its real-world historical and lyrical referents.

Immediately after the purported title piece, the narrative segues into Consuelo Velázquez's "Bésame mucho," which is the only song explicitly mentioned by title but never sung by La Loca, heard on the radio, or included as transcriptive lyrics. Instead it is mentioned in passing, as La Loca is described as "tosiendo el 'Bésame mucho' en las nubes de polvo y cachureos que arrumbaba en la cuneta" (10). "Bésame mucho" is never uttered, never located in the enunciative mouth (as a discursive site), and therefore evades a positioning vis-à-vis the desire, identity, and gender of La Loca; instead it posits a heuristic process in the reader, who may or may not identify with its cultural significance. This caveat hints at the connection between the title of the song and the titular "Tengo miedo torero," suggesting that Velázquez's song functions as the real secondary level of discourse that music brings to the text. A closer examination of the lyrics of both songs shows how "Tengo miedo torero" borrows heavily from the final lines and tropic places of the first and last stanza of "Bésame mucho," as what is expressed is the fear of losing love and the loved one. La Loca's interpretation of the song, however, subjugates her voice to a domineering, macho, and penetrating matador, when compared to Velázquez's gender-neutral lyrics. This genderizing of the title results in a queering of the subject's speech, which goes beyond the rouge and lipstick to physically contrast La Loca to the normative virile masculinities of the military dictator and the rebel. Music, therefore, creates a secondary level of gender(ed) discourse that is only made possible by being enunciated from the mouth of the toothless Loca when she appropriates the song under the mislabeled title.

Song in *Tengo miedo torero* is queered as a result of the dialectic between "Tengo miedo torero" and "Bésame mucho," which results in gender-neutral pieces such as "Tú querías que te dejara de querer," the popular Juan Gabriel tune that is sung by La Loca as she ponders her one-sided relationship with Carlos, being tinged by the homoerotics established between the initial dyad of lyrical texts and the subsequent modifications that the reader must make to the musical register.[7] The song laments the loss of affection in a relationship as one lover leaves the other, who still yearns for physical intimacy. Not having had relations with Carlos, La Loca's singing of "Tú querías que te dejara de querer" implicates gender structures on a societal level as the plight of the homosexual in Chilean society is put into question. The line between homo- and heterosexuality is not always clear in a context where the depictions of the virile masculine abound. Citing works by Roger Lancaster and Richard Parker (and channeling Robert McKee Irwin and Guillermo Núñez Noriega among others), Oscar Misael

Hernández argues that dichotomies of hegemonic versus nonhegemonic masculinities do not always function in Latin America, as it is normal for married men, who self-identify as heterosexuals, to engage in homosexual sex with various partners (70). The lyrics sung by La Loca thus summon the homoerotics of a system that subordinates the homosexual, yet at the same time uses him to satiate its own desires as an object of outlet for homosociality.

The mouth in *Tengo miedo torero* is the locus of a politically queering discourse that engages the structures of masculinities through song (and, of course, fellatio), but only La Loca's mouth enjoys this privilege; when Carlos attempts to sing, "Contigo en la distancia," his voice "se quebró en un gallo lírico que lo hizo toser y toser, llenándosele los ojos de lágrimas por el ahogo y la risa" (83). His failed attempt at singing, transcribed as the impotency of his mouth, is contrasted with La Loca's oral orifice, where her "lengua marucha se obstinara en nombrarlo, llamándolo, lamiéndolo, saboreando esas sílabas, mascando ese nombre, llenándose toda con ese Carlos tan profundo" (13). Lemebel's text is not only musical in the sense that it engages a literary OST, but also evocative of a symphonics that interweaves the written word, the dressed-up Loca, the listened song, and the hypermasculine virile body of the rebel into an intricate arrangement of enunciations and actions that challenge heteronormative systems and languages. Carlos is called into being through the mouth, as the transvestite pronounces that his name is so strong: "Para quedarse toda suspiro, arropada entre la C y la A de ese C-arlos que iluminaba con su presencia toda la c-asa" (13). La Loca's reflection on his name involves a climax and a decline into silence, which is punctuated by a sigh that is eroticized by her tongue, which calls, licks, and tastes the syllables of his name (and him?). Her mouth is thus the new site of gendered power—displacing the penis or any of its phallic incarnations, capitalized as a site of sexual becoming and of coming into being

The mouth of La Loca comes into play again in a sexual encounter between the two characters. After hosting a Cuban-style birthday party, La Loca surprises Carlos with a bottle of pisco and some music. Lemebel incorporates the lyrics of his phantom song into this scene, as both characters listen to a vinyl recording. Musicality functions here as a cinematic framing register that imposes the erotics of the title track onto the diegetic interplay between bodies (under construction). The transvestite laments the inability for them to have a relationship, and the rebel subsequently consoles her: "pero no por eso vamos a dejar de tomar, reina . . . poniéndole la corona al extender sus labios en una sonrisa perlada" (94). This is the first reference that the reader has to Carlos's mouth, which immediately precedes his confession of a (queering) staining secret to the transvestite. Here he references the homoerotic secret held since his youth, of being asked for only "la pura puntita" (95) by a peer. By bringing Carlos's mouth into being, that is, as a site of enunciation that occupies the archetypal place of the *torero* within the erotics of the song, Lemebel opens a dialogue into the queering of the masculine figure through the allusion of the *puntita* as the quintessential act of penetration that is linguistically disqualified from its erotic core. The puntita is symbolically never really intercourse, sodomy, or the loss of virginity, though in practice it phenomenologically breaks the sanctity of separation, conjoining two bodies in the sexual act. By signaling this epistemological disconnect between signifier and signified, the novel effectively relocates Carlos away from the realm of the Masculine or its approximation as his secret displaces him from heteronormativity and from playing the protector to the weak/feminine singing voice in the song.

It is Carlos's words that queer him, especially after he confides, "no sé por qué yo no me moví cuando le saltó el chorro de moco que me mojó la pierna" (96). This staining of the subject, which I explicate earlier, causes both a sense of shame and an unpleasant feeling of pleasure-disgust in Carlos, so much so that "a los dos nos quedó una cosa sucia que nos hacía bajar la vista cuando nos cruzábamos en el patio del liceo" (96). The source of shame in this encounter is the staining of the semen on his leg and not the desire he felt for sodomizing his friend, of simply introducing la puntita, as this is explained as simply being "cosas de cabros chicos" (96). More so than homoerotic desire, the violation of the Masculine's adherence to symbolic cleanliness and hygiene in his body succeeds in shifting the revolutionary masculine from a position in dialogue with hegemony. Note here that this displacement is written not as a result of desire that breaches the heteronormative contract but through the physical, organic, and corporal staining of the subject through the viscosity of the bodily fluid, a staining only made possible through the subject's telling of the story in the foreground of the title song. Staining and its subsequent desubjectification within the market of masculinities is thus also a haptic phenomenon, as the text evokes the sticky, humid, and "unclean" textures of homoeroticism to sublate the male body, building too on the affective circulations generated by the lyrical register.

After this confession La Loca leaves to find Carlos a blanket, only to discover him asleep and snoring "por los fuelles ventoleros de su boca abierta" (97). His open mouth foreshadows La Loca's subsequent actions, as she undresses him and fellates his erect member. The narrative, partly due to the ubiquitous soundtrack being played through diegetic and extradiegetic speakers, now encourages a scopophilic textual experience, as the reader is guided to gaze at La Loca's real and erotically undressed mouth as it approaches the sedate penis. If bodies do matter, then the ontologically masculine protrusion of the male body enters a site of reckoning as it is placed in the discursive and queering locus of the mouth. The protagonist, furthermore, is referred to as "la boca-loca" (100), suggesting that the mouth is ontological to the queer subject, and that only in and through it can the negotiation of a queer(ing) identity take place.[8]

In the "concavidad húmeda" (99) of La Loca (note again the haptic as a characteristic of this lyrical corporal space), Lemebel evokes music, musicality, and song as he observes that "las locas elaboran un bordado cantante en la sinfonía de su mamar . . . La Loca solo degusta y luego trina su catadura lírica por el micrófono carnal que expande su radiofónica libación" (100). The detoothed transvestite further comments that fellatio "es como cantar . . . interpretarle a Carlos un himno de amor directo al corazón" (100), reflective of the interconnectedness of varying planes of semantic and tactile inscription that come together in the literary OST.[9] The climax to this interplay of gendered bodies and positions is lyrically written and almost poetic—a symbiotic duet between the mouth and the penis that culminates in acts and body movements that renegotiate previously static positions, as "el mono solidario le brindó una gran lágrima de vidrio para lubricar el canto reseco de su incomprendida soledad" (100). Lemebel immediately follows with the lyrics to "Ansiedad," by J. E. Sarabia Rodríguez, which evokes imagery and sentiments that are congruent with the narrated events:

Ansiedad de tenerte en mis brazos,

musitando palabras de amor,

Ansiedad de tener tus encantos

y en la boca volverte a besar. (101)

Readers, importantly, do not know if this song belongs to the diegetic vinyl record that is played at the beginning of their encounter, or if it can be found in the cinematic soundtrack that floats over the narrative, setting the mood of the scene and creating a secondary plane of meaning that runs parallel to the signifiers in the text. Connecting the two narratives together, that is, the scene in the novel with the lyrical register as intertext, we can see that Sarabia Rodríguez's lyrics reveal La Loca's love for Carlos as being rooted in more than physical desire. We can also observe in the song that the evocation of the mouth as a site of desire and of utterance is queered when associated with the character of La Loca, who fellates the young revolutionary, thereby calling into question his positioning within the matrices of masculinity; the anxiety referenced is not solely one of missing the desired body, but also one of dealing with the repercussions of the libidinous event. This process emphasizes the structural erotics that Lemebel undertakes by appropriating and queering the traditional heteronormative bolero.

Though Lemebel's novel is titled with an imagined song, the exploration of the role of popular music as an intertext in writing masculinities is salient and cannot be ignored. The OST of *Tengo miedo torero* is replete with solos, extradiegetic tunes, and diegetic pieces that reflect or tangentially build on the narrative trajectory of La Loca and Carlos; music in the novel is not only a representational practice of desire, but is also arguably desire itself, as it provides a way of knowing gender through the written body. But not all literary soundtracks enjoy the collaboration of the leading lady/man/transvestite. How are masculinities negotiated when the narrative stops short of, or actively resists a representation of, desire?

CHAPTER SIX

Lyrical Epistemologies
and Masculine Desire

Mayra Montero's *La última noche que pasé contigo* is a classic erotic Caribbean text, which inculcates both the notion of geography as being central to the eroticization of its people and cultures and the use of the bolero as a literary intertext, following in the school of other novels, such as *La importancia de llamarse Daniel Santos* (1988) by Luis Rafael Sánchez, *El entierro de Cortijo* (1983) and *Una noche con Iris Chacón* (1986) by Edgardo Rodríguez Juliá, and *El libro de Apolonia, o, de las islas* (1993) by Iris Zavala. The use of popular music by these authors comes as a result of earlier shifts in the telos of Puerto Rican literature, which began to veer from the works and styles of canonical authors and their texts as a means of representing the social and political shifts within the national imaginary, especially in the wake of ever-working globalizing forces and the experience of mass media culture. From a cultural standpoint, the sociopolitical crises of the 1970s and afterward threw traditional family and sexual structures into flux, and then unearthed private and public concerns with gender roles (on the micro and macro level). Emblematic of this turn is *La guaracha del Macho Camacho* (1976), by Luis Rafael Sánchez. The use of music in these texts is symptomatic of a broader feeling of change and crisis, and a study of its tunes permits an unearthing of its many problems by means of a hermeneutic tearing at the fabric of the canonical and high culture. These narratives put forth a lyrical epistemology of change as they explore the quotidian, personal happenings of peoples and situations that open up tectonic crack lines of power and identity in dialogue with nonnational processes. As Enrique Plata Ramírez observes:

La narrativa caribeña se apropia del discurso musical, para dar cuenta del caribeño en cuanto ser pluricultural, de su cultura, su identidad y su perifericidad. Estas apropiaciones discursivas musicales permiten sostener el encuentro de lo heterogéneo y la transgresión de una alta cultura que dará paso a la cultura popular. Esta tradición narrativa es ya larga e intensa y no parece tener punto final en lo inmediato. (61)

In such a light, the sequence of novels I mention as coming from this shift in the 1970s was just another round of the literary channeling and reflecting communal anxieties.

Perhaps most obvious to the reader of this corpus is the presence of the bolero over any other genre. Its use as a narratological fulcrum to explore plural and varied discourses is a result of its own historical development; the bolero is a register that delineates a local (within a global) ethical and philosophical problematic played out over everyday practice (Fleites 2).[1] Practice here is further constituted by practices of gender and sexuality, where the bolero allows for a symbolic and nontextual exploration of desire and libidinal behavior. Bolero music is a highly erotic genre of musical expression, as it proposes "una actitud ante el amor, pero más: organiza a nivel simbólico las distintas situaciones que puede enfrentar el enamorado" (Fleites 8). The inclusion of its lyrics and melodies in the narratives of writers across the subregion and the continent stresses its viability in the exploration and negotiation of identity, because it has become, to an extent, a register for and a repository of many of the questions and polemics that plague identitarian politics in Latin America.

This intersection between the bolero and discourses or representations of identity is explored in Montero's *La última noche que pasé contigo*, a novel that inserts the reader into the marriage and personal musings of a pair of empty nesters (Celia and Fernando), who go on a cruise after the marriage of their only child (Elena).[2] Located in the nonterritorial spatial coordinates of the ocean—a queering space in recent Latin American cinema, such as *El niño pez* (2009) and XXY (2007) by Lucía Puenzo and *Contracorriente* (2009) by Javier Fuentes-León, and a ripe tropic site of erotic interrogation—the couple enters a period of libidinal awakening and marked sexual activity with each other and with others. Celia reminisces about an extramarital affair she had with her sick father's caretaker, Agustín Conejo, and subsequently has another affair during a stopover on their cruise with a (necessarily) nameless Afro-Caribbean man. Fernando, on the other hand, rehashes the feelings and passions he felt during Celia's first infidelity and has his own trysts with the enigmatic Julieta, a mature woman who meets the couple aboard the cruise. Arranging an erotic dynamism that weaves tales and encounters of passion, mistrust, and animalistic sex, Montero places all the cards on the table when at the end of the novel, the reader discovers that Julieta is Conejo's ex-wife, thereby tying up all the loose ends in an act of erotic serendipity. In addition to separating the novel into eight distinct chapters headed by bolero titles, Montero intersperses amidst the voices of Fernando and Celia a collection of nine letters that appear sporadically in the novel. Written between Abel (a pseudonym for a woman, Mariana) and Ángela, these letters we find connect Fernando to Celia in their respective childhoods. The letters also reveal that Mariana leaves Ángela for a younger woman, Julieta, who becomes Fernando's lover while on the cruise.

Structurally, popular bolero music quite obviously composes the OST of *La última noche que pasé contigo*, as Montero organizes her chapters around the genre, triggering Enrique Plata Ramírez to argue that "la letra de los boleros [son] el recurso ficcional que permit[e] instaurar el discurso narrativo, aproximarse hacia el erotismo, la sensualidad y las historias paralelas de los sujetos periféricos que se sienten al borde de sus vidas" (60). Others who have studied the role of song in Montero's pages unsurprisingly follow the critic's observation, arguing that the main female character's relationship with the bolero changes as the novel progresses, with the final chapter showcasing her rejection of patriarchy and phallogocentrism, which is almost intrinsic to the erotics of the bolero.[3] The focus on feminine sexuality is echoed in the assertion that "*La última noche* se suma así a un corpus de ficción hispanoamericano que trata el discurso erótico como otro medio para mellar los códigos sociales rígidos que impiden la autonomía sexual de las mujeres" (López 134). The inclusion of this novel in this chapter, however, follows my interest in teasing out the masculinities in seemingly critically exhausted works (see the reading of *La fiesta del Chivo* in part 1). How are masculinities and the Masculine framed and constructed in a text (and its accompanying criticism) that seemingly focuses only on the writing of femininities? Here I build on the idea that popular music functions as a phenomenological textual resource to write, represent, and discuss masculinities in fiction while inculcating a cognitive awareness of space and spatial tropes, because music as an affective exercise engenders a sense of being and knowing, all within sites of reception (where we listen to and feel the musical/lyrical) or spaces of contact (social, historical, and cultural zones that inherently evoke a topologic reference system).

Curiously, the only critical texts dealing with masculinity in the novel focus on the "lesbianizing" of the male protagonist. Keeping with a practice of gender studies that traditionally analyzes masculinity through othered optics, particular readings argue the latent homosexual desire in Fernando and his sexual fixation on orality to characterize the male as being lesbianized. Masculinity, when it is acknowledged, is approached through the psychoanalytic prism that places a premium on decentering practices away from a male identity; that is, there is an implicit notion and politics of queerness. The problem with such a strategy to tackling gender and sexuality in the novel is that masculinities are thus often relegated to a single ontological category, which is rendered inert by well-meaning criticism, especially in a text rich in its portrayal of hierarchical masculinities in the Caribbean.

Changing our critical lens, we can see that from the onset, the matrices of masculinity are unearthed through the male protagonist, Fernando, as his narrative opens Montero's foray into empty-nester sexuality. Aside from commenting on the redundancy of coitus with his wife, Fernando reveals his friend Bermúdez as a representative of male homosociality, as it is through him that he learns lessons about marriage and about the cruise they are on. The relationship between Bermúdez and Fernando does not reveal per se a dialoguing with the Masculine, in the political or Gramscian sense, but instead reflects on Christine Beasley's reclassification of what hegemony actually means in masculinity studies. The homosocial group in *La última noche que pasé contigo* reflects the usage of the term only if and when it applies to an "empirical reference specifically to actual groups of men" ("Re-thinking" 171). We can infer from this point that the Masculine as an umbrella term in its cultural and political incarnation is implicitly constructed by and through real groups of men, such as the "butcher" homosocial that Bermúdez represents in Montero's novel.

Bermúdez takes on the role of educator to Fernando by teaching him how the homosocial considers life, love, and adventure, akin in a sense to the dynamics of approval between men seen in Rivera Garza's novel. He is a figure full of theories and explanations for the intricacies of gender relations. In one example, he hypothesizes that the open ocean will make Celia into a tigress in the bedroom, because the hot waters of the Caribbean smell of rotten seafood. The novel knowingly seizes popular discourses of "bodies in heat," as though the tropics and their peoples are more likely to be animalized or engage in animal sex, closer to the visceral barbarity of the nonhuman and necessarily separated from the civility of the (northern) urban. Bermúdez argues that "el marisco pasado, ya tú sabes, es olor de mujer" (14). Whether consciously or simply through a process of dialogic osmosis, Fernando assimilates this line of thinking as he discloses that Celia touches his "labios con la punta de su dedo perverso, su dedo sátiro que olía a marisco antiguo, a tierra remojada, a puro mar de las Antillas" (23), reflecting the power of the real and discrete homosocial in discursively shaping approximations to the Masculine. Importantly, the Masculine is not universal or axiomatic, but is constructed through everyday practice, discourse, and tactics.

The homosocial group that influences the male protagonist sets up his relationship with his own and other sexualities, a homosocial that views the sex act as a motion of predation. Reflective of this violent perspective, his language reveals a subtle discomfort with the practice of heterosexual vaginal sex, as he describes it as being "la carnicería" (15). It is an act where the male must penetrate, consume, and ultimately desubjectify the penetrated body, which is then resignified as a defining body to the penetrator; in other words, *I am who I am based on whom I penetrate*. Fernando's hesitance to enter the "carnicería" reveals a deeply intense anxiety about performing adequately for the Masculine gaze, which is focused not only (if at all) on the gushing and pleased female as sign of masculine prowess but also, convexly, on the virile, sensuous, and violently dominating male. In his relationship with Bermúdez, Fernando constructs his expression of gender around an oral dialectic with other men that is rooted in the narration of sexual practices and desires, which are described as violent and bloody. This narrative subjectifies the male as the butcher entering his domain with a phallic knife and anonymizes the woman as a simple piece of meat in the carnicería. This epistemology of the sex act and sexuality is ontological to the homosocial bond that is shared by Fernando, Bermúdez, and others, and is founded on a corporal and discursive phallic, unredeeming violence. This is noted in "las atrocidades" (107) that Fernando shares with Celia in bed at night, which include an anecdote about the fishermen of Mombasa—African men that "subían a bordo los cuerpos moribundos de los dugongos, unas vacas marinas con pechos de matrona, y fornicaban con ellos hasta que las pobres bestias dejaban de existir. Era un sencillo coito anal . . . con el raro aliciente de que el animal, durante el acto, lanzaba unos gritos angustiosos que parecían sollozos de mujer" (107–8). Sex within this group, a discrete and real homosocial experience that the narrative argues to be formative and primordial to masculinity, is limited to the violence exerted by the self over a possessed and violated animal other. It does not take much work for the reader to deduce that the object of libidinal desire among the butcher homosocial is also viewed, albeit tacitly, as an animal.

Returning to Fernando's real expression of sexuality (versus the idealized paradigm of butcher homosociality), we can see that he does not fully satiate the Masculine gaze and its expectations in his relationships with women. Instead, Montero portrays him as a vulnerable, complex, and humanized representation of male sexuality. His fragile, nonphallocentric, and conflictive nature is evidenced when he eats another man's semen from the cinnamon-garnished vagina of a prostitute, and when he kisses Julieta, whose mouth is coated with the ejaculate of an Afro-Caribbean, brutish taxi driver. These incidences, which are intimately linked to the mouth as a (queering) site of sexual expression, are seemingly contradicted when Fernando describes how Celia mounts his mouth after every visit she makes to her father's house to take care of him. The protagonist's oral enjoyment is truncated when "con más firmeza, la empujaba hacia atrás, la obligaba a retroceder, la ensartaba furiosamente en su verdadero trono" (18).[4] Evoking a complex and conflictive sense of self in relation to the female, the male finds a need to emphasize his phallic corporality, to act out what the butcher requires in its approximating to the Masculine, and to deny his own oral impulses, though in later scenes of the novel, he shows an animalistic consumption drive, wanting to devour his lover Julieta and drink her urine.

The textual descriptions of cunnilingus between Celia and Fernando subtly, yet quite perversely, react to the lyrics of the bolero that titles the first chapter, "Burbujas de amor." The song narrates the yearning desire of a subject for his/her lover, who wants to "Pasar la noche en vela / Mojado en ti." The reasons for placing the song at the beginning of the novel are elementary; Montero has chosen a nondiegetic referent that explicates the underlying tensions and desires in the narrative. The bachata as a sensual body-clinging art, after all, is meant to be accompanied by "todas esas cosas salvajes y calientes" (88) that constitute human desire. It is notable that the only character actively described as being "mojado" is Fernando, as he has a "rostro empapado" (18) after Celia spends a good fifteen minutes "remando absorta" on top of his face (18). The contrasts between this initial performance and the subsequent "placing on the throne" are highlighted when Fernando dephallicizes his body by analogizing his face with the dead calm of the sea. He is not the virile male who massacres the female body but is instead composed of a dysmorphic and desubjectified orifice that sexually pleasures Celia. His corporal body is disarticulated into an anonymous shape-shifting mass like the ocean as Celia rows on top of him, effectively breaking, albeit for only fifteen minutes, the power of the Masculine over his gender expression and coital preference.

Though Fernando strives to shift himself away from the butcher mentality of the homosocial (through the resignifying of key corporal sites of desire), it is plain to see that the break is not as acute as criticism would lead one to believe. In those many encounters with his wife where he haphazardly reassumes his role as king (of the carnicería) by placing Celia on her throne, he finds a mark near her breast that confirms his suspicions of her having an affair with Marianito, her father's cousin. Reinforcing his interdependence on the homosocial, Fernando conjures a narrative of how Celia and Marianito engage in a repeated set of trysts that can only be intertextually inspired by the sordid yet serendipitous tales of sexual conquest shared among groups of men or in commercial erotica. Even when possessing, or acting out, the scopophilic Masculine's ideal of the butcher satiating the victimized female, Fernando repeatedly reaffirms the structural binds of masculinities in keeping with Sedgwick's homosocial triangles.

This focus on orality is strengthened by Celia's diegetic singing of the titular bolero in the chapter. *La última noche que pasé contigo* follows the intertextual model of the literary OST, though it is a two-sided album, with the boleros that title each chapter as side A, and the characters who pronounce the lyrics within the narrative as a sort of side B.[5] The effect of this categorization of the musical within and in reference to the novel sets up dual planes that semantically address the plot. Celia repeats the line "mojada en ti" several times, finishing with a languid "oooooh, mojada en ti" (27) that is described by Fernando as being uncouth and off-key. He attempts a reversal of roles by situating Celia within the aquarium that houses the lonesome subject in the lyrics of the bolero, making her the fish that repeatedly exclaims "mojada en ti." The opposite, however, is not simply dissimilated by his narrative but is put into tension by the recurring routine practice of her mounting him. Keeping this in mind, Celia's diegetic singing of the bolero succeeds in decentering, or at least subverting, the butcher masculinity that is subscribed to by Fernando (at times) and his homosocial group. The lyrical referent assumes an explicitly mocking tone because it is the male character that is wetted by the female, either through her coital mounting of his mouth or by her wetting of his lips with her finger, which tastes of "marisco antiguo" (23). There is a succinct and subtle negotiation of the protagonist's masculine identity, as the lyrics of the accompanying songs and their diegetic representations signal for a complication of the male's position in regard to heteronormative gender structures.

The bolero Celia sings seems to deliver the initial blow in defacing the façade that is Fernando's carnal brand of masculinity. He is further deconstructed when he recounts his encounter with a prostitute who mixes cinnamon powder with talcum to freshen her intimate regions prior to servicing clients. The lady asks him to leave as she attends to another customer, a man who spurs envy and violence in the awaiting Fernando when he brushes the cinnamon-laced powder from his clothing after completing his business with the prostitute. The male protagonist, unhinged by the narrative of another man penetrating his object of desire, barges in on the prostitute and saturates her genitals with the cinnamon powder before tasting her. It is unclear as to what motivates him to do so, though the fact that he uses his mouth instead of his penis to probe the previously butchered terrain signals a possible queer reading of his desire. Quite ironically, the violence he feels toward the other gentleman is vicariously first expressed through the use of the mouth and not through the phallic, violent thrusts of the homosocial butcher entering the carnicería. As such, Fernando situates himself outside the subjective position of butcher homosociality, planting another masculinity in the same space and epistemology, as, after all, his principal drive is to consume the prostitute, albeit through his mouth.

The dialectic between belonging to and deviating from the homosocial's narrative is not a simple issue of black and white; it is complicated by Fernando's description of the prostitute's taste: "Adentro sabía amargo, sabía de cerca a concha triturada, y sabía lejanamente, cada vez más lejanamente, a la canela" (30). What can first be considered the essence of the female for the homosocial—Bermúdez's symbologies of the sea and the feminine—is decentered by the prostitute revealing that he had swallowed "la leche de otro hombre" (31). We return here to the haptic nature of queering masculinities, evocative of Lemebel's sticky, humid stain on the body of the young rebel. It is through this scene that Montero sets in motion a series of transgressions that elucidate a reading that moves beyond visible and obtuse binaries of gender, as the reader is reminded of the topographic ocean as a site of constant symbolic and symbiotic restructuralizations of gender, permitted and carried out, in part, by the inviting and heuristic lyrical texts as titles and as sung intertexts. This act of transgression takes on a nostalgic, uncanny tone when Fernando describes his ambiguous relationship with cinnamon: "me repugnaba algunas veces, y había veces en que amanecía con un deseo brutal de saborearla" (31). Where then is Fernando situated in relation to the butcher?

The character's belonging to the homosocial, which is to say, not the group that is "mojado" in the song, is further complicated when he meets the mature Julieta. She notices his hands rubbing suntan lotion on her body, and he makes a direct effort to "hacerlas parecer más fuertes y laboriosas, más hábiles y despiadadas, es decir, más temibles" (34). Though the diegetically enunciated lyrical intertext characterizes a queering of the male body, it shows signs of fighting this process, of somehow reaffirming the body's penetrating, knifelike agency. What we see in this engagement between the male body and the lyrical intertext is an exploration and experimentation of nonheteronormative practices and identities, which are seemingly accessed, or allowed to be accessed, only through the noncon-forming and relative register of the musical.

Popular song as part of a diegetically sung OST decenters the homo-socially dependent Carlos in Pedro Lemebel's *Tengo miedo torero*, though Lemebel's narrative lacks the male countervoice to the queering erotics of the song. The one exception, however, occurs when, imbued with a poetics of inebriation, the rebel Carlos takes over the narrative as his ventrilo-quist voice explains a long-kept secret of homoerotic frolicking at the banks of a river with another youth, who ejaculates onto his leg. *Tengo miedo torero* manages to queer and decenter virile masculinity through song, but only through an exchange in the control of the narrative voice, in this case brought about by copious amounts of pisco, does Lemebel succeed in exposing heteronormative masculinity as a construct depen-dent on its ties to the homosocial, which are in turn woven by a reliance on oral narratives.

The converse, the sexual reliance on orality, has an opposite effect within the homosocial in *La última noche*. The process of sexualized eating queers the male's belonging to the group when the couple and Julieta eat sushi at a local restaurant on one of the cruise stops. Celia assumes the active, violent role that she occupies when mounting Fernando by cajoling the gastronomically conservative Julieta to try the Japanese delicacy. Mon-tero creates an ephemeral yet tangible triangle of desire between the two women and Fernando when he joins in the sushi "no tanto por el apetito como por la necesidad de unirme al culto" (39). His mouth becomes a site of seduction as he physically assimilates the raw mollusks (evocative of the vagina, at least according to Bermúdez) in a slow and sensual fashion that incites Julieta to caress his ankles with her feet. Fernando's oral fixation alludes to the incident with the cinnamon powder and to his subjugation by the rowing Celia over his face, both incidences that disassociate him from the butcher expression. The text as narrated by Fernando, however, shows an awareness of this deviation, as it reverts to the homosocial's animalization of the female body through the transmutation of genitalia with each piece of sushi offered to him, as the aoyagi becomes a "vulva sonrosada, la cresta del clítoris sobresaliendo de su cojín de arroz, palpi-tando intensamente bajo unos polvos misteriosos" (39–40), and the torigai "otra vulva cercenada especialmente para mi exclusivo festín, otro clítoris latiente, esta vez pardo y resbaloso" (40). The nonhuman is not simply reimagined as genitalia but is brought to life as a pulsating organ of female sexuality that is prey for the Masculine gaze and appetite.

The role of the bolero in the process of constructing a gender identity in Fernando is addressed further in the third chapter, when he sings a few lines of "Negra consentida" to Celia as he reminisces about his adventures from the night of the restaurant. The song conjures exotic visions of the Afro-Caribbean as a source of unrestrained, animalistic sexual possibility that is underscored by the mythically large African penis. Fernando wonders if Julieta wishes to "convertirse en una negra procaz, maquinadora, pervertida; una negra devoradora de ardientes negros insaciables" (81). The novel obviously seizes cultural sexual stereotypes as a means to engage in a broader debate of identity politics, returning to the popularity of low-culture registers within the literary at a time of crisis.

The image of animal males devouring the female evokes the carnicería and reverts the reader to the idea that sex is violence. The description of Julieta as a carnivorous sexual subject when she pushes Fernando to perform oral sex on her—that is, Julieta as akin to the "insatiable Negro"—is juxtaposed with the events of the night before, of him eating the sushi. Like Celia, Julieta shifts the emphasis placed on phallic penetration in their relations and subjugates him to the objectified role of giving her pleasure through his mouth, analogous to the pieces of meat/sushi that are consumed in the homosocial's metaphorical butchering. The movement between epistemological corporal sites returns us to the writing of masculinities in the new historical novel, though the use of the musical intertext seemingly places more value on the mouth than on the testes. Julieta desubjectifies Fernando within the erotics of cunnilingus by reversing the narrated actions of the restaurant—she is now devouring him instead of the reverse, her vagina now as mouth eating the feminized male. She appropriates the erotics suggested by the bolero sung by Fernando and impregnates sushi/female genitalia with the butcher's sexual power, responsible now for devouring and carving out the relegated male body.

The use of popular music in *La última noche que pasé contigo* is not limited to the negotiation of masculinities in Fernando; it is also developed as a narratological strategy by Celia when she describes how she would masturbate during her engagement to Fernando, listening to Lucho Gatica's rendition of "Amor, qué malo eres." Montero problematizes female desire through Celia's description of the masturbatory act: "No era exactamente que me masturbara, no era así, tan burdo, la expresión exacta era 'reconocerme'" (103). The bolero is used as a parallel yet tangential schema to engender a hybrid trajectory that runs counter to heteronormative models of sexuality. As Jorge Rosario-Vélez judges, "Celia polemiza la apropiación del bolero como medio de enunciación de estos deseos porque los sujetos carecen de la capacidad lingüística apropiada para articular lo 'salvaje y lo caliente'" (68). By juxtaposing her masturbation with the song, the text emphasizes the negative connotations placed on female sexual satiation and desire as inscribed by the male gaze that relegates the feminine body to being just a piece of meat to be butchered. Song, therefore, also allows for a coding of feminine erotics in a tangential plane to the demands and expectations of heteronormativity, even within the act of "reconocimiento," which implies a refashioning of the terrain, or at least seeing firsthand what is there and not being solely guided by the homosocial's perspective.

The use of popular bolero music as an OST to *La última noche que pasé contigo* promulgates a literary tradition in the Caribbean that began with authors attempting to subvert dominant writings and writers. In keeping with this movement, Montero creates an epistemology of desire and sexuality emanating from the bolero that cannot be found within the linguistic constraints of narrative fiction. She situates a separate register that includes the sociocultural value of each song in addition to the semantic dialogisms they create when sung in tandem with the erotics of the plot. The writer's resourcefulness echoes Judith Butler's thesis that "desire is manufactured and forbidden as a ritual symbolic gesture whereby the juridical model exercises and consolidates its own power" (76). The idea of a juridical model, however, confines the analysis of power to what is prohibited and held as taboo within the system, without necessarily unmasking the actual operations of power. Without delving into a political critique of Butler's assertion, however, we can still appreciate her putting into a dynamic the source and perpetuator of desire. The legislative branch, so to speak, of this model is language as it is socialized and permissive of certain desires and not others. The use of popular song—semantics outside the constraints of power systems of objective language and high culture—can be considered a strategy of subversion, demonstrating how narrative fiction can engage (through multiple layerings and nonstated actions) in a representation of all that is taboo, unsaid, and secret, unveiling our own sexualities to be vulnerable, social, and phantasmic constructs.

CHAPTER SEVEN

Homosocial Dynamics and the Spatiality of Seduction

Alfredo Bryce Echenique's *El huerto de mi amada* is emblematic of the versatility of a writer often and controversially linked to the commercially viable umbrella term of the Latin American Boom.[1] Focusing on the class struggles in Peru and Latin America as a whole, Bryce Echenique has attempted through fiction to expose the machinations of gender, power, and race in an increasingly unequal context. In an attempt to emphasize this point, César Ferreira observes, "Bryce es uno de los grandes cronistas de la burguesía peruana . . . todas las novelas de Bryce examinan la psicología del sujeto desclasado, antiheroico y solitario" (75). Bryce Echenique, like many authors discussed in part 1 of this volume, works in the tradition of Peruvian contemporaries who assign to the past an aura of privilege, lending a melancholic tone to their narratives (Ortega 237) within a treatment of extant crises and problems. As such, the present is seen in multiple relations to the past, never completely severed as an epistemological other.

El huerto de mi amada is the story of an upper-class Peruvian youth, Carlos Alegre, who falls in love with the much older and much fawned-over Natalia de Larrea. The two escape his bourgeois house in Lima to hide from his family in her country estate, where they are harassed by his father and by the men who want to bed Natalia. The novel recounts Carlitos's love for her, his adventures with the social-ladder-climbing Céspedes twins, and his final and expected reintegration into Limeñan society when he leaves Natalia and marries Melanie (an "approved" partner) after becoming a world-renowned doctor. Julio Ortega observes that *El huerto de mi amada* "es la novela más novelesca de Bryce" (242), given that the author eludes including himself within its pages, and that its plot is purely novelistic. The critic goes on to comment that the novel "ha adelgazado sus referentes a unos cuantos tópicos suficientes . . . que se acompaña de pocos personajes, perfilados por la comedia social esperpéntica y vodivilesca" (242). The novel conforms to Ortega's labeling of a social comedy, because there is no room for tragedy within the diegesis, and the amorous comedy ends with marriage, though Bryce Echenique's pairs are distinctly alternate conjurations of what is permitted under the social code of power.

The novel begins with an epigraph by Felipe Pinglo (1899–1936), the father of Peruvian *música criolla* and a proponent of the *vals criollo*. Pinglo's music has continued to be popular as Los Panchos, Julio Jaramillo, Pedro Infante, and Julio Iglesias, among others, have continued to interpret his music. Included in the epigraph are quotes from the French politician Antoine Barnave, the Duchess of Angoulême, the German philosopher Immanuel Kant, the English playwright William Shakespeare, and the French writer Stendhal (Marie-Henri Beyle). This gathering of eclectic thinkers and writers immediately following Pinglo's lyrics suggests a redrawing of the social and temporal concerns of the novel, as what initially seems a local novel about class renegotiation is really a textual exploration of more universal themes. Here we see an evolution of the author away from the local and territorial to the universal and deterritorial, as the plot and its characters can be dislocated from Lima and replaced by any variation of cultural and spatial referents. The novel, then, can be considered within a trajectory of contemporary fiction that moves towards the deterritorial, even if the diegesis takes place within defined geo-parameters.

Bryce Echenique's reference to Kant is not fortuitous: Stendhal quotes the same passage in the epigraph to the second part of his 1830 naturalist novel *Le rouge et le noir*, which chronicles the life of a young man, Julien Sorel, who attempts to rise beyond his low-class social upbringing yet ultimately fails at the hands of his own passions. The placement of both quotes in the epigraph to *El huerto de mi amada* emphasizes the intertextuality of Bryce Echenique's novel, as his tale of 1950s Limeñan society recycles the social travails of a nineteenth-century French youth. Bryce Echenique also creates a physical point of union between Stendhal and *El huerto de mi amada* in the Kantian quote, but this is a point of contact that is only privy to an active reader willing to trace connections that are seemingly at first not there, akin to the hermeneutics of music within the literary (and filmic).

The first layer of intertextuality, which is to say the connection between the greater works of these snippets in the epigraph and the novel itself, is territorialized in the spatial praxis of Pinglo's song. Though the novel attempts a movement away from national boundaries (Peru) and across temporal frameworks, it paradoxically situates the narrative alongside the parallel text of Pinglo's music, which begins innocently with the lyrical enunciator directing the listener toward the orchard of his lover, where "un florestal que pone tonos primaverales / en la quietud amable que los arbustos dan." There is a "here" and a "there" not necessarily situated within a national space but intrinsic to the characterization of the lover and the beloved, as though space—both physical and semantic—is ontological to the subject. At the very beginning of the novel, through the musical referent, we can begin to underline how song as a narrative device traces a spatial topology that resonates in personal identity markers, such as gender in this particular case.

The second stanza begins with the subject lamenting, "allá dónde he dejado lo mejor de mi vida / ahí mis juramentos vagando han de flotar / porque ese ha sido el nido de amargos sufrimientos / y allí la infame supo de mi amor renegar." The suffering of the subject in the song is illustrated at the beginning of Carlitos's affair with Natalia: immediately after their dance, the other men attending the party scuffle with Carlitos, leaving him to flee with his mature lover to her abode outside the (typical) spatially demarcated Masculine space of the urban. The rest of Pinglo's song continues with the theme of love lost and the lover spurned, which breaks with the paradisiacal tone set in the first stanza and in the first few pages of the novel. The second stanza to Pinglo's tune succeeds in mapping out a textual terrain that establishes a spatial referent to the self, because far from the subject—in the *huerto*—does his happiness reside, creating a before and an after (in temporal terms and spatial movements).

The congruency evidenced between the lyrical and the narrated text is akin to the use of music in Mayra Montero's *La última noche que pasé contigo*, where the artifice of music functions as a cinematic soundtrack that creates plural levels of reception and interpretation. But music also plays a direct diegetic role in Bryce Echenique's piece, as it is through Stanley Black's "Siboney," and with a pinch of magical realism, that the sultry Natalia enchants Carlitos.[2] With the first notes of the song, "Carlitos había sentido algo sumamente extraño y conmovedor, explosivo y agradabilísimo, la sensación católica de un misterio gozoso" (19). We revert here to the familiar magical realist plot point where a character experiences a life-altering realization triggered by a mysterious and unexplained event. The song ends as Carlitos leaves his room to find the source of the music in the garden, though he continues to feel the song in his ears and head, suggesting that though Black's version of the song has ended, a further intertextual relationship is still taking place, both with the song and with magical narratives. The reader, through the lyrical register, is harkened to the generic mode and must read the protagonist's coming actions in the vein of its literary antecedents.

The aesthetic mode foreshadows Carlitos's entrance to a party hosted by his father in the garden, while we expect, and even almost request, a life-altering event to occur. The homosocial mass of doctors at the function is characterized by societal position and faith in science, which is placed in an apical position related to other masculinities in the text. These men are cultured, foreign (in the case of the Argentine cardiologist Dante Salieri), and well-spoken, evocative of Marcos Burgos as the Masculine domestic dictator in Rivera Garza. As the divorcée Natalia and Carlitos get swept away by their passions, the cardiologist destroys the "Siboney" record in anger, suggesting that the song and its romantic affects (as produced by the magical narrative mode) are incongruent with the homosocial body that rules Lima. Who is this young gallant and what right does he have to sweep away the female object of many passions present at the party? The name of the chief antagonist is not fortuitous, as Bryce Echenique sustains the musical interlude by alluding to Mozart's prime enemy, Antonio Salieri.

The breaking of the record, furthermore, establishes the market of masculinities within the microcosmic space of the garden. The protagonist, for example, is distinguished from the Masculine when Natalia calls him a "negro bandido . . . negro atrevido, pero negro ricotón, sí, eso sí" (24), eroticizing and, in a way, desubjectifying the protagonist by comparing him to the animalized African male, as is the case in Montero's *La última noche que pasé contigo*. This textual coding of the male body within the sociostructural market of Masculinity is highlighted when, in a drunken rage, Salieri attacks Carlitos, exclaiming that Natalia belongs to him. This challenge is mounted in juxtaposition to the dance between Carlitos and Natalia, a product of a kinetic interchange that unbalances the stasis of Masculine gender control; Salieri's challenge, then, is a reassertion of the hierarchy salient in the spatial and interpersonal binds that maintain patriarchal systems. The dance and the song—key elements of musicality in the text—create a spatial and diegetic exclusion of the subordinate masculinity from the scientific, modernizing homosocial. After a series of skirmishes, Natalia and Carlitos manage to escape, with the latter successfully fending off his four attackers (the Argentine cardiologist, the doctors Alejandro Palacios and Jacinto Antúnez, and Senator Fortunato Quiroga).

These men of science occupy and perpetuate a discursive space and authority that promulgate notions of hygiene and modernity, situating an imagined national as an extension of Western modernity. Such a political ideology is tangible in several contexts of the Global South, but perhaps more so in Peru, where public intellectuals such as Vargas Llosa have openly questioned the role of native cultures within the modernization process; the latter, of course, is defined along precepts set by the Global North. The last member of the novel's homosocial group is described in more detail than the doctors, as he is a "solterón de oro, senador ilustre, y primer contribuyente de la república" (27). The text here playfully suggests that even within the Masculine, there may be elements of subterfuge, as the "solterón" implies a tongue-in-cheek acknowledgement of the character's nonheteronormative subjectivity: solteróness is a euphemism for homosexuality, though the character maintains a position within the dominant group through the euphemism and an adherence to the other qualities of the homosocial. Quiroga, for example, follows Salieri's naming of Natalia as "la puta" (35), negating her as a (named) person yet reaffirming her commodification as an economic entity that is for sale and that can be bartered between the members of the homosocial.

After Natalia and Carlitos's escape to the diegetic and lyrical space of the huerto, Natalia seeks medical help for Carlitos because he suffers several wounds from the skirmish with the doctors and the senator. Readers pause as the spatial referent activates schemata that interrelate Pinglo's vals to the text, and we remember that the huerto is the other space that characterizes a narrative of division, a before and after within the plot. The young doctor who attends to the protagonist's wounds belongs to the homosocial group of Salieri and the others, and he partakes in the objectification of and assumed ownership of nonheteronormative women, as he describes how he saw Natalia "escandalosamente desnuda" (56). She is not really naked but discursively disrobed by the member of the Masculine who cannot bear for a female body to challenge its normative beliefs, practices, and laws. The doctor explicates how her voice spurs arousal, "porque entre una cosa y otra como si se fuera quitando prenda tras prenda y hasta con música de ambiente" (56). Note here the inclusion of music as a key component of the erotics of the female. He concludes his description of Natalia by swearing, "por lo más sagrado que se le pone a uno la verga al palo con solo verla y escucharla" (57). Also note here the emphasis on the penis as signifier of the Masculine, as its rigidity in traditional terms defines the orthodox homosocial that is really resistant to change. Her body as commodity is thus erected around the corporality of the Masculine, crafted and sensualized through the musical register to produce an almost haptic quality to her nudity. The effect of music here is to create a tactile relationship between the reader and her flesh, to allow us access to her sinews and curves through the sonic mapping of the musical.

The doctor belongs to an educated, urban group and gains Masculine authority "de la vida política y económica del país y la autoridad dentro de la familia" (Fuller 56). The text effectively centers itself on this market of competing masculinities, as the protagonist, in contrast, is described to be effeminate, naïve, and infantile. This dynamic of masculinities, akin to the system of gendered bodies and positions put into play in *Nadie me verá llorar*, implicates society and the nation within the inscription of micro-metonymic bodies.[3] The political institution is explicitly involved in *El huerto de mi amada* as Fortunato Quiroga becomes the country's president. His office is composed of "[una] elegancia suprema. Muebles franceses. Mucho oro y mucha plata por todas partes. Lámparas maravillosas con las bombillas más poderosas del mundo" (64). A tracing of the lines of power that emanate from Quiroga connect him unequivocally with the homosocial and its respective market of bodies. After sitting at his presidential desk for the first time, he announces that he will not work until Lucas, his henchman, kills "la parejita esa" (64). From this we can surmise two things: first, that the Masculine homosocial as embodied by this specific historical group must acknowledge and eliminate challengers as a means to perpetuate its hegemony; and second, that the paralysis to function faced by Masculine character suggests that the challenger, Carlitos, in this situation is more than a simple oppositional entity.

Sedgwick, basing her ideas on earlier work by René Girard, argues that the expression of desire within the homosocial group is often through the use of violence (176), which seemingly corroborates Quiroga's hiring of a hitman to kill Natalia and Carlitos. The statesman instructs his henchmen to "[meter]le todos los plomazos que pueda, en [su] nombre. A ella, en cambio, un solo balazo, y en el corazón" (64). The use of violence as a mediating language among the members of the homosocial (and its challengers) is necessary because the bonds that unite men, that is, the latent threads of homosexual desire, cannot be specified or acknowledged. Violence, therefore, becomes the de facto language of a group that cannot verbalize their own transgressive desires and drives, though in the case of Quiroga, it is telling that he hires a proxy to do so. More telling are the instructions he gives, as perhaps the drive to destroy Carlitos identifies him as the true object of the president's passions and not the woman, to whom he piously designates a single bullet. Perhaps his own violence would reveal something to the group that would then remove him from hegemony?

This group of men in *El huerto de mi amada* is importantly situated in, and ontological to, the urban center (away from Pinglo's huerto) that seems to diffuse into every voice of the narrative. The urban is foundational to the homosocial, so much so that immediately after Natalia and Carlitos make their escape, Salieri repeatedly calls her a whore: "como si empezara a despertar de la peor pesadilla de su vida y estuviese completamente solo y muy adolorido en medio de un hermoso jardín" (35).[4] The noncity (the garden) to the Masculine is a hellish proposition, because it is away from the purported civility of the city that the barbaric and nonheteronormative gain credibility. The urban is left behind in the plot, as in their escape to the huerto, Natalia observes:

> Atrás habían ido quedando barrios enteros, distritos como San Isidro, Miraflores, Barranco, ahora que ya estaban llegando a Chorrillos y torcían nuevamente, en dirección a Surco. Ahí se acababa la ciudad de Lima y empezaban las haciendas y la carretera al sur . . . La idea le encantaba, le parecía simbólica: los distritos y barrios residenciales en los que vivía toda aquella gente, todo aquel mundo en el que había pasado los peores años de su vida, siempre juzgada, criticada, envidiada, tan solo por ser quien era y poseer lo que poseía, y por ser Hermosa, también, para qué negarlo, si es parte de la realidad y del problema, parte muy importante, además; esos malditos San Isidros y Miraflores, y qué sé yo, iban quedando atrás. (39)

The spatial trajectory in the narrative toward the noncity is preceded by a discussion of music, as Carlitos casually calls Natalia's home "el huerto de mi amada" (39). She informs him that the song is an old vals criollo (the same song that appears in the novel's epigraph). Carlitos also wants to listen to "Siboney" when they get to the house, calling it "nuestra canción" (39); more importantly, it is a lyrical testament and vestige of their usurpation of the homosocial. It is by reference to Pinglo's song that Natalia comes to ponder the power structures extant in the city, as she juxtaposes the rurality of the huerto with the phallogocentricity of the urban space.

By resorting to music as a narrative trigger, the author arranges a necessary pondering of the title to Pinglo's song and the novel: as they approach the country house, Natalia asks Carlitos if he knows what the idiomatic "llevarse a alguien al huerto" means. She goes on to explain that "llevarse a alguien al huerto quiere decir engañar a alguien. Y, actualmente, mucha gente usa la expresión solo con el sentido de llevarse a alguien a la cama con engaños" (40). Carlitos's response is unsurprising given his naïveté, as he exalts her to "[darle] el huerto. . . . Todo el huerto que pued[a]" (40). If we were to read between the lines, the change that is noted between the first stanza and the subsequent verses in Pinglo's song comes into play in this scene, as Natalia suggests that the huerto is not as idyllic as it may first seem. The thematic spatial separation between stanzas is furthered in this scene when Natalia hopes that "Lima nos olvide" (41), distancing the events and characters of the huerto from the Masculine cityscape. Paradoxically, however, the two characters later engage in a romantic and carnal relationship that has them erotically recolonizing the city with their kisses and trysts as they return several times to Lima. It is, ironically, also in the city during one of these exercises of spatial redefinition that Carlitos meets his future wife, Melanie. The spatiality of gender that the text evokes through the musical intertext is poignant, as through his return to Lima, away from the huerto, the protagonist slowly reintegrates into the behaviors and expectations of the Masculine (he begins to study medicine, for example). Space, after all, is gendered and genderizing; the subject comes into being in a specific space that is an agglomeration of multiple discursive lines that code for specific relations and nodes of power. The subject inadvertently enters in and subscribes to a spatial contract of gender, wherein actions, expressions, and belongings are intrinsically linked to specific coded topologies.

The gendered nature to space and the city is addressed in the political developments surrounding Quiroga. The old locus of gendered power within the cityscape is challenged by a new participant in the market, Rudecindo Quispe Zapata, a man with indigenous roots from the province, whose pedigree is unclear: "nadie sabía muy bien de dónde había salido . . . [ni] si terminó su secundaria, si realizó algún estudio superior . . . no era miembro del Club Nacional . . . tampoco había viajado a Europa en el *Reina del Pacífico*" (230).[5] More importantly, he does not have real or symbolic ties to the spaces of the Masculine, such as Europe or specific social clubs. Keeping in mind the new political tone of the capital, we observe how Carlitos's once subordinate and rejected masculinity has now become a competing strain within the metropolis that has accepted Quispe Zapata within its milieu. The protagonist cannot assume the apical position of his father's generation, though, especially not through the control of public institutions, because his stay in Lima is truncated by the rise of Quispe Zapata, who metonymically represents the political, economic, and social changes produced in Peru at the end of the 1960s. Quispe Zapata is a new political player in the textual Lima and understandably scorned by the members of the old guard. His rise to fame and power leaves the scientific homosocial incredulous, as he neither belongs to the old aristocracy nor is educated. The plot point coincides with the democratic rule of Fernando Belaúnde Terry and with the military coup by General Juan Velasco Alvarado in 1968. The former represents in many ways the elite, European, and educated class that the Alegre family belongs to, as he was responsible for establishing the Banco de la Nación and for developing key infrastructure—a tangible symbol of centralized progress—during his tenure as president.[6]

The 1960s in Peru, following a larger trend seen on the continent, were also characterized by the rise of Marxist revolutionary guerrillas, such as the Movimiento de Izquierda Revolucionaria, which later splintered into the Partido Socialista Revolucionario and the Movimiento Revolucionario Túpac Amaru. These groups were responsible for the proliferation of guerrilla-style protests and violence in the country, which would serve as a harbinger for the Partido Comunista del Perú, more popularly known as Sendero Luminoso, which I treat in more detail in the chapter 11 discussion of Jaime Bayly's *El cojo y el loco* (including how Bayly writes a local masculinity to confront transnational positions). Their missions and manifestos advocated for greater democracy and transparency, and for an equitable redistribution of national resources that would facilitate the reintegration of indigenous and lower classes into society. Though Velasco Alvarado's government was an illegal one (brought in under a coup), it did foster a spirit of social and economic redistribution commonly known as Peruanismo, restructuring the centralized model of progress. The figure of Rudecindo Quispe Zapata as coming from a poor, non-European heritage and challenging the power-gendered status quo can be read, then, as a fictive pastiche of Velasco Alvarado.

The old guard is estranged from Lima by these changes—Carlitos's father closes his practice and moves the family to San Francisco in the United States, the natural metonymic space for nonleftist policies. Carlitos and Natalia are also displaced as they live the next seven years in Paris, where Carlitos becomes an award-winning researcher and doctor. The shift away from the metropolis resonates in Carlitos's masculinity, as he is not a power-wielding social phallus like his father or Salieri in Lima before him; instead he is described as an absentminded scientist, decidedly unauthoritarian in demeanor. But this personal characterization reflects a larger change in the position of power and authority held by the European man of science and letters that is metonymized by the homosocial group of

Alegre, Salieri, Quiroga, and the rest. This group loses its power as a result of a "democratización de los valores" (Fuller 56) and changes in the political climate, suggesting that the Masculine is evolutionary and defined by contained sociocultural and historical factors.

The relationship between Carlitos and Natalia is also affected by time as she begins to feel inadequate and too old to be with him. If "Siboney" triggered their love, then its replacement cements the end of their relationship. While attending a conference in Baltimore, Carlitos, now known as Carlos Alegre (a naming reference to his maturity and stability in a masculine position), is arrested for leaving the premises with a radio belonging to the dormitory in which he is staying. The young Carlitos, who had been entranced by the maracas of "Siboney," is now enthralled by Ludwig van Beethoven's Seventh Symphony, a piece known for its usage of an Austrian hymn and for its rhythmic balance. We learn after he's arrested and then cleared by the police that he has similarly taken radios in Munich and Zurich, as though his person is lost without an accompanying classical soundtrack. The OST, after all, accompanied all transgressive actions in his youth, and its loss signals a yearning for a previous life or position within the hierarchies of power.

The character's fall from sanity and nonheteronormativity is triggered by the displacement of the vals and "Siboney" from his diegetic soundtrack: "Natalia de Larrea hace el amor frenéticamente con un muchacho casi treinta años menor que ella" (279). Their affair comes to a crescendo when Natalia throws him out of the house and away from the spatial referents created by the musical register, away from the metaphoric huerto that once guided him to happiness. Recovering in the hospital, Carlos is reunited with the young Melanie Vélez Sarsfield, a girl he tutored while in medical school and who is more appropriate for his social stature. She is the polar opposite of Natalia and completes the protagonist's reterritorialization into the spatial center of power in Lima. Natalia, however, comments, "yo siempre dije que Carlitos terminaría casándose con un hombre" (286), suggesting that Carlos's true return is a regression into the homosocial and not as a competing masculinity in the local gender market, as she slyly hints at the homoerotics of belonging to the group. The protagonist's masculine journey is a circular one, guided by and in tune with the text's particular OST.

Perhaps the most important factor to take away from the reading of masculinities in the novel is the studied spatiality of the city and specific territories in the writing of gendered bodies. Space is both gendered and genderizing, as the Masculine city and nationscape are, in tandem with the musical intertext, fundamental in understanding the homosocial.

This spatial movement away from the polis and the power structures of hegemonic masculinity permits a realignment and maturity of the protagonist's gender identity, especially in the face of changing socioeconomics. If anything, then, the novel can be read as an exemplar of how masculinities evolve and are sensitive to key crises; after all, Carlos and not Carlitos now occupies the place of hegemony that he once challenged.

CHAPTER EIGHT

Franz Galich's Managua, Rock City

From a schematic standpoint—and as traditional Latin American music roots the pages within a national imaginary—the use of music in Bryce Echenique's *El huerto de mi amada* creates a topology of masculinities that enables the author to explore further relevant questions of identity and history. The other novels studied in this part also represent historical and deterritorialized diegeses and as such employ music within an imperme-able textual space that houses an examination of the many matrices of power, gender, and race from a relativist perspective, historicized by the moment narrated in the plot. But what happens when this constraint is removed and the narrative is rooted in the present and within a tangible social reality? What becomes of this narratological strategy when the text reacts to an increasingly globalized world where jumping borders is an everyday reality and necessity? How does music compensate for the writing of these glocal masculinities, especially when the familiar terrains of (urban) civilization and (rural) barbarism are blurred by polynodal cityspaces and nonbound urbanities?

The importance of music in constructing a Central American regional ethos is well known and chronicled in a twentieth century rife with crisis after crisis. Beatriz Cortez argues that "durante la segunda mitad del siglo veinte y a medida que se fueron desarrollando los procesos revolucionarios en Centroamérica, la música pasó a desempeñar un papel importante en la resistencia a los procesos colonizadores de la música popular norteam-ericana, así como también en el reto a la construcción de la identidad na-cional." Though it was important in the dissemination of revolutionary movements (really as a substitute for the printed text, given the logistics of distribution in guerrilla terrains, and to compensate for illiteracy among many rural populations), its presence is perhaps most poignant when read as a reaction to homogenizing processes. In Nicaragua, for example, music is formulated in concordance with broader changes that are centralized in the political and literary landscapes that are "no solamente . . . efectos de la guerra, sino que también de las políticas neoliberales que han reforzado la exclusión social y la marginación de las personas . . . han establecido el predominio de la economía financiera y comercial sobre la productiva que ha generado una cultura de consumo" (Ugarte).

From this tumultuous period of political ennui and social malaise, a border-hopping (deterritorialized) author took up the task of understanding and representing Central American society within the ashes of the sociopolitical revolutions of the 1970s. Born in Guatemala, Franz Galich spent the greater part of his life living and working in neighboring Nicaragua. His first novel, *Huracán corazón del cielo* (1995), deals with the 1976 earthquake that wreaked geological and social havoc in Guatemala as it laid bare the many fissures between social groups and hierarchies in the country. His latter work, including *Managua, Salsa City (¡Devórame otra vez!)* (2000) and *Y te diré quién eres (Mariposa traicionera)* (2006), was the beginning of an incomplete tetralogy of novels portraying a Nicaraguan society that is bullet and poverty ridden by civil and economic wars.[1] In the series is the posthumous *Tikal Futura: Memorias para un futuro incierto* (2012), which builds on the narrative worlds constructed in the two previous novels. There is a marked move toward the outside, as the borders of the national and the regional are contested in *Managua* and *Mariposa*, which culminates in *Tikal* taking place in a dystopic future in a hard-to-identify place, vaguely Guatemala, though one could argue that it takes place in any of the Central American capitals. The author describes his work as not bound by physical borders, opining that "de alguna forma ya me he integrado al proceso productivo nicaragüense pero prefiero hablar en términos generales de un proyecto centroamericano, es decir de una literatura centroamericana" (Martínez Sánchez). Part of this transspatial belonging (or perhaps more accurately, unbelonging) can be seen symbolically in the author's oeuvre when characters and plot lines move between the boundaries of the given text, existing polytemporally in multiple narrative diegeses. Characters in one novel, whether principal or secondary, can reappear without warning in another text, moving laterally and without restraint. We can thus collocate Galich among a group of peers, such as Horacio Castellanos Moya, Rafael Menjívar Ochoa, and Rodrigo Rey Rosa, who propagate and perpetuate particular narrative universes that trespass the literary bounds of their individual texts, deterritorializing, in a way, the traditional novel from the printed page.

Galich (like his peers, though this list is by no means exhaustive) places his narrative universe within "tiempos de la cólera neoliberal" ("Tanda"), and in his writing, keeps in mind the migratory nature of literature and culture in the late twentieth and early twenty-first century.[2] Y *te diré quién eres (Mariposa traicionera)* differs from the other works studied and mentioned in this chapter in that it incorporates contemporary, globalized popular music and not traditional tunes. The novel is the immediate sequel to *Managua, Salsa City,* which recounts the meeting of the prostitute La Guajira with the lower-class ex-Sandinista Pancho Rana. An analysis of Y *te diré quién eres* can only be contextualized by an initial probe into the role of music and gender in *Managua, Salsa City,* as the later text builds on the gendered constructions and interactions of Rana and La Guajira and how they partake in a particular market and commodification of masculinities.

The earlier text sets in motion an inquiry into the relationship between the neoliberal episteme and masculinities, as it weaves a spider's web of male characters, factions, and political interests, with La Guajira sitting in the middle as the black widow spider that ominously controls the fate of the many men circling the plot. She is a common prostitute and the head of a band of con men—former Contras—that operate out of a taxi. Her prey/client, Pancho Rana, is the chauffeur of a rich family that has left their house in the care of their employee as they travel to Miami on vacation; note the common extraterritorial space of the United States as both a symbol of a particular economic ideology and as a characterizational space of particular social groups within the local (gendered) hierarchy. La Guajira and Rana meet at La Piñata, a popular nightspot in Managua where, hiding their true identities, the two become enveloped in a passionate game of seduction, dance, and music that leads them to Rana's house. Once within the affluent compound, a shoot-out ensues between him, the con men, and two other opportunistic male assailants with designs of robbing the house. The plot, though simple, is evocative of the everyday social violence present in Central America, including the unexplained element (the two men) as a real danger in any politics of social and urban security for the region.

Managua, Salsa City plays out through the desires felt by the two protagonists as they trade control of their libidinous urges and the text's narrative voice. Galich employs a "popular, oral style—reminiscent of testimonio—in which both the narrator and the characters express themselves" (Kokotovic 20). (Like several novels by Castellanos Moya, the oral style lends the reader towards a tacit critique of testimonio, though I do not engage in any sustained thesis here.) The novel is set in a dark and somber Managua that is written through what María del Carmen Caña Jiménez calls an aesthetics of disgust ("El asco" 220), detritus, and decomposition.[3] Galich's capital is intimately connected to sex: its heat is described as emanating from a collection of multiple unseen vaginas, decentering the traditionally Masculine urban city-text. The dark city evokes disillusionment with the politics of the last quarter of the twentieth century. We can, in fact, read Galich's *Managua* as a spatial and affective critique of neoliberalism and its collateral damage, evocative of the diarrheal metaphor and stain seen in Lemebel and Ramírez. The neoliberal episteme is microinscribed onto local bodies, as narrow individual interests govern the gendered subjects in Galich's text. Money and its gain drive the characters within the market as they jockey for social and sexual position, even though they can never really escape belonging to an impoverished scavenger class that is maintained as the substrate for the rich bosses vacationing in Miami. Most important in this market, the financial impulse of gain is superior to the libidinal impulse of penetration, as one of La Guajira's henchmen notes: "Era más importante la alianza económica" (45) than any sexual prowess or conquering.

This consumerist culture is further reflected in the textual depictions of the body, as the novel succeeds in both animalizing and commoditizing male and female specimens. The examples of the animalized male abound: La Guajira's henchmen display the pack mentality of wolves, Pancho's last name is Rana, the lone male assailant who survives the final shoot-out is described as being rat faced, and so on. A male gaze similarly objectifies the female body as Rana and others deconstruct the curves and mounds of the female form according to their own personal desires, emphasizing each corporal site not as part of a whole but as individual semantic erogenous zones primed for the consumption of the butcher homosocial.

Music is intrinsic to the mapping of these matrices of bodies, economies, and gender, as popular salsa music provides the OST to the exposition of masculine desire through a detailed and almost ceremonial courtship that passes between Pancho and La Guajira.[4] This courtship involves a lyrical dynamism (created by Galich's strong regionalist diction) and a dancing ritual that is theatric in its performance and reliance on a set of preestablished gender cues, where the male seemingly negotiates the female's body to the tune of salsa in an attempt to cajole and capture her in his libidinal trap, though in reality, La Guajira is the one who is really laying a trap for Pancho in the form of her awaiting henchmen.

Their dance and the act of seduction are choreographed to the diegetic playing of the salsa tune "Devórame otra vez." The lyrics to the song suggest an experiential and haptic approximation to sex that is sensual in its failure to establish a strict ontological base for desire as the bodies within the song are systematically devoured. In a sense, sex and penetration revert to the objectification of the corporal under the butcher homosocial:

> Devórame otra vez, ven devórame otra vez,
>
> Ven castígame con tus deseos más
>
> Que mi amor lo guardé para ti
>
> Ay ven devórame otra vez,
>
> Ven devórame otra vez
>
> Que la boca me sabe a tu cuerpo
>
> Desesperan mis ganas por ti.

The first verses of the song introduce the courtship between Rana and La Guajira, and Galich's transcription of the extradiegetic lyrics, that is, the nonfictive song, are inaccurate, suggesting that the words printed are indicative of a diegetic register and not an overlying OST track that provides ambience to the narrative. Perhaps what is written of the song is what the characters erroneously identify as the lyrics? The narrative meshes Pancho Rana's thoughts with the song lyrics, creating a tangible association between the erotics of both the novel and the lyrics. By alternating the singing of the song between the interior musings of both principal characters, the association reconfigures the strata of power that previously held the female to a position of subservience and consumption by the homosocial; the song, after all, eludes gender identifiers so that the enunciator may be male or female. It is as if only through the lyrical intertext and subregister can competing masculinities and femininities challenge the rules of the Masculine market. The desecration of the body is not a one-way process in the song, for the subject is also guilty of consuming the other, as his/her mouth tastes of the lover. Note the emphasis on the mouth as a corporal site of enunciation and subjectification, repeating itself as a locus of challenge and resistance. Its dialogic and symbolic position is strengthened when La Guajira refers to her own orifices as "mis tres bocas" (37), thereby redefining the vagina and the anus along a lyrical understanding and inscription of the body, as they too can now sing or locate the musical intertext—they too can now consume, actively, the male other.

Masculinities in the novel are written through several stereotypically virile devices and prostheses, such as the automobile and the assault weapon. Owning, displaying, and using these objects is a simple strategy for creating masculine identities. Rana and the group of bandits are thus crafted along a singular axis that makes them interchangeable entities. That being said, they are contrasted with the two assailants who join the onslaught on Rana's residence. These two delinquents (who do not have any role in the plot to rob Rana) are representative of a hybridized Spanglish-speaking masculinity that has lived in the United States and has now returned to the area, products of the civil and economic warscapes that have preyed on the region. Their linguistic traits are noticeably juxtaposed to the very localized diction and idiom of the other men, as they mix with English gestures toward the predatory Global North; they are, effectively, masculine symptoms of the neoliberal episteme, predatory and opportunistic in their attack. The two assailants are furthermore removed from the aesthetics of virility that Galich highlights in writing competing local masculinities, as they are described to be rodent-like criminals who lack ties to the homosocial bonds that are vestiges of the guerrilla wars.

On a symbolic level, the novel ends with the seemingly fatalistic reconciliation between the competing political (and local) masculinities, in bloodshed and mayhem as La Guajira's gang is decimated and Pancho is taken for dead. There is, however, a separate sphere of masculinities that Galich constructs in this ending, as one of the Spanglish speakers kidnaps La Guajira and removes her from the economy previously structured around the ex-guerrillas. The sun begins to rise over Managua as the prostitute and the rat-faced assailant leave on a motorcycle. An extrapolation of the sexualized couple onto the imagining of the nation is not out of place in these pages; Galich suggests a bleak future for the region, as the prized feminine commodity is unattainable for local masculinities, captured instead by the neoliberal position.[5] What the novel suggests, furthermore, is that local markets of gender are no longer enough to set the stage for the dialectics of the Masculine and that a transnational and transterritorial theater of masculinities is instead needed.

I am drawing a separation here between the market and the theater of masculinity. This theater, in contrast to the market, is dominated by subnational actors who perform and practice macrosocial/economic/political processes that, in turn, inscribe on them subjective positionalities that implicate a global(izing) discourse. The former—that is, the market—situates specific local relations and power struggles (as in *Nadie me verá llorar* or *Tengo miedo torero*), whereas the latter is a symbolic and real move into the global, where masculine bodies lose territorial links, are ephemeral and unanchored in movement, and represent the very process of deterritorialization. In the theater of masculinity, subnational bodies perform larger processes as part of their performance of individual gender, cementing onto the body an image of the communal body in flux. The rat-faced villain can be seen as representing or performing the Global North in enforcing an episteme of neoliberalism, as the foreign body that seizes local commodities (and bodies).

Written as a sequel, but perhaps also as a response to *Managua, Salsa City*, *Y te diré quién eres (Mariposa traicionera)* picks up the aftermath of the shoot-out and the escape of La Guajira with El Cara de Ratón. Implausibly, Pancho Rana is found, close to death, by the police, who try to make sense of the attack. The novel develops Rana's search for La Guajira across the region—that is, not solely in Managua—and now involves several homosocial groups, such as the police, headed by Captain Anastasio Cerna, and the equally homosocial press, led by Parménides Aguilar. Note the recurrence of the sociopolitical bodies of the Masculine that Ramírez demythifies in *Margarita* as Galich now enters into a broader critique of gendered power systems (as opposed to simply creating a market of competing bodies, as in *Managua*).

Mariposa revisits the scatological topographies of neoliberalism as it presents a city where "el calor sube hasta el delirio y la gente camina como si acabaran de llegar al Infierno" (7). Galich quickly summarizes the events from the previous book with quick cuts between scenes and the use of an occasional flashback or two to get the reader on pace with the plot, marking a stark departure from the lyrical, baroque style of *Salsa City*. The sequel instead carves out and emphasizes the author's unique narrative universe. The author opens the novel aware of this process and with a note of caution: "Cómplice lector, esta novela se puede leer de varias formas, huelga decirlo: como documento histórico o sociológico. Pero la mejor forma es como si se tratara de una película made in Hollywood" (6). By hinting at the possibility of a written text being read as a sequence of celluloid film, the note emphasizes the role of the OST as a titular and epistemological referent in shaping and reading the erotics of its gendered bodies.

The note does not stop there, however, but cajoles the reader to not "establecer relaciones, semejanzas o comparaciones con países de América Latina, Asia, África" (6). I would suggest that the warning in this second part serves an opposite purpose in that the author actually wants us to move beyond Central America and to understand and read the diegesis as representative of any other context in the territories stained by the neoliberal sphincter. We can thus see this warning to the reader as a linkage to the neoliberal episteme: first, by asking us to view the cultural product through the optic and aesthetics of a homogenizing Hollywood; and second, by suturing the plot and its bodies to a Global South, entrenched in implicit economic warfare with the haves of the North. That being said, though, Galich does not pretend to write a non–Central American work but rather argues that the narrative can easily be relocated to similar sites of neoliberal carnage. The first sentence of chapter 1 sets the stage: "*En Managua, a las doce meridiano en punto, el calor sube hasta el delirio y la gente camina como si acabaran de llegar al Infierno*" (7).

The opening note and the subsequent first lines of the novel stress the need for an active, involved reader who goes beyond the narrated plot, diegetic elements, and seemingly closed set of spaces in the text. Such a relationship between author, text, and reader is evident in the title of the novel, which begins with the response to the idiomatic expression "dime con quién andas, y te diré quién eres." Of note here is the author's choice to use the second clause of the expression instead of the first, thereby requiring the reader to reverse-engineer the phrase and not simply complete it. Such a hermeneutics is active and complex and (like the linkage between OST and narrative) forces the reader to move laterally across semantic fields. This play on words is picked up in a discussion on corruption among the police forces in various Central American countries, with a journalist beginning the expression but not finishing it, forcing an involved reading of the text that contradicts the author's note not to extrapolate fiction to reality. Readers are practically forced to finish the text's sentences, just as they are forced to look for tangible connections between the fictive geographies and real referents to the topography of neoliberalism.

The reference in the introductory note to the North American media goliath—in addition to the title's use of "Mariposa traicionera"—brings to our attention the importance of cultural imperialism as a by-product of neoliberal policy.[6] The systems of popular music production and distribution arc, after all, exemplars of cultural imperialism practices and open market movements. Commenting on the operations of the North American music industry, Ian Biddle and Vanessa Knights observe, "This infrastructure is at once concerned to address itself to a maximum number of addresses *within* its 'own' territory and, at the same time, concerned also to export that process of address maximization to territories 'outside' the West, until such a time (projecting itself into an infinitely occidental future) as the distinction between being 'inside' and being 'outside' that infrastructure will become ever more difficult to recognize" (7). The reflection being made here accentuates the role of identity and music within the politics of location, stressing that current trends in the study of popular culture have tended to sideline the "national (of nationalisms, nation-states, national mythologizing narratives and other manifestations of national or nationalist ideologies)" (1) in favor of a nonanchored infrastructure, which itself is paradoxical because its structures are based in the West.

Keeping in mind Slavoj Zizek's and Fredric Jameson's variations of the Hegelian "vanishing mediator," Biddle and Knights argue that the national can be said to occupy the position of this term in relation to the syllogism, thereby opening up "new critical trajectories for popular music studies" (12).[7] The idea of the national in Galich, however, is based on the Pan-Americanism that the author advocates in his own writings on identity and the role of literary and cultural criticism, and it opens to the reader a critical, albeit tangential, interrogative of the relationship between the lyrical and subjectivity.

What I am getting to here is that though the music of Maná does not strictly adhere to what can be thought of as a national essence in Nicaragua, it does play out Galich's musings on the idea of a Central American identity that is born from the politico-economic disasters of the 1990s.[8] This is a tactical and fragile point of entry into the positioning of music as a cultural referent in identity politics, as "the designation of 'national essence' to particular music is more problematic within modern nation states where tensions between homogenous and heterogenous are often lived out" (O'Flynn 22). In this era of cultural, political, and economic reconfigurations of spatial and symbolic spheres and fields, the use of a popular Mexican band by a Guatemalan/Nicaraguan writer in *Y te diré quién eres (Mariposa traicionera)* does not seem so strange, since both cultural spaces are relegated to the South.[9] The novel does not solely reference one specific band or genre, however; it includes diegetic references to Chente Fernández (Mexico, ranchero), Daddy Yankee (Puerto Rico, reggaeton), Shakira

(Colombia, pop), José Feliciano (Puerto Rico, rock), Carlos Santana (Mexico, rock), La Suprema Corte (Colombia, salsa), and Julio Jaramillo (Ecuador, pasillo), stressing that what is at hand is a relationing of the Latin South versus the West.

The lyrical intertext is not simple adornment or a subtle reference to paratextual erotics that cannot be linguistically expressed by narrative: Galich makes explicit an intratextual association between the listened song and the events of his textual movie. Upon listening to the lyrics "*Ay mujer, cómo haces daño, pasan los minutos cual si fuesen años . . . Mariposa Traicionera*" (51), Rana exclaims "¡no, no, mi Tamara no es mariposa traicionera!" (51).[10] The song is vigorously stirred and mixed into the narrative's centrifuge, and not allowed to simply linger over diegetic ears as an alternative emotive plane of expression, as seen, for example, in Lemebel. By connecting the song to La Guajira, Rana establishes a schema of interrelations between the lyrics and the narrative plot and its characters. The reader, urged again to complete the unfinished refrain, must invariably ask: if La Guajira is not the *mariposa traicionera*, then who is?

The novel renews the narrative spotlight on the detritus left by decades of war and negative economic policy, focusing on the Central American male bodies that are socially unadapted and lacking in direction. This lack on the part of previously hegemonic aesthetics and bodies in Galich's two novels reflects José Toro-Alfonso's assertion that hegemonic masculinity as an organizational referent is no longer a viable discursive and experiential position at the beginning of the twenty-first century in Latin America, and that "si existe diversidad en la representación social de lo masculino entonces es necesario explorar esas formas particulares en que muchos hombres construyen y reconstruyen su hombría" (15). Toro-Alfonso, of course, works with a neoliberal episteme, very much like that which lies behind the poetics of the two novels.

The linkage between the titular song and the plot is evoked prior to its enunciation within the diegetic OST, when La Guajira seduces Cara de Ratón in a motel room where she is being held hostage. She does so after realizing that her body as a sexual commodity gives her the upper hand, calling him a "Ratoncito" (22), making reference here to the verses "Yo soy ratón de tu ratonera, trampa que no mata pero no libera, vivo muriendo prisionero" in the song. The neoliberal male—a conjugation of Toro-Alfonso's new masculinities—is resemanticized as the prisoner and as the subject of the song. At first glance, then, the lyrical subject is the male, the "ratón" in the Guajira's trap, set for prey in the first novel. But this genderizing of subjects is flipped after the final shoot-out and the victory of the neoliberal male—his victory redistributes the axes of power, so much so that the female is now the ratón being held. The narrative initially, then, concretizes the genderizing of the mariposa as a feminine body by holding the male (Cara de Ratón) as the now prisoner to La Guajira's charms. This shift seemingly contradicts Maná's song, which is already genderized, as the mariposa is explicated to be a woman: "Ay, mujer como haces daño. . . . Ay, mujer que fácil eres." The inclusion of the neoliberal Ratón then breaks the semantic associations of the song with the diegesis, forcing the reader to actively recalibrate systems of power that are left as pieces of the puzzle waiting to be put together, akin to the parceling of the idiom in the title. This association is strengthened by Rana refusing to accept his lover as a traitor who has left him to die after the events of the first novel. This subsequent refusal sets the tone for the writing of a theater of competing positions, as the text (and by necessity, the reader) must do the detective work to find the true identity of the traitorous butterfly.

The inversion of the association between woman and mariposa is emphasized when La Guajira takes Cara de Ratón's virginity. She is not the fluttering insect that is "fácil y ligera de quien te provoca" but is instead the predatory aggressor that violently kisses and then mounts the "indefenso Roedor" (53). Following this process of inversion or corporal resignification, the gender of the lyrical butterfly becomes paramount in a reading that is intimately related to the descriptive modifier *traicionera* and its lexeme *traicionar*. The lyrical metaphor, at first glance, evokes a promiscuous lover, though the neoliberal episteme posits that the root of Galich's writing of betrayal and treachery lies elsewhere and not within the intimate boundaries of the amorous. Perhaps betrayal—just like gender, music, and self in the two novels—is also deterritorialized from the intimate to the public, from the anchored to the free flowing. The aggressiveness of La Guajira and her coding of the male as a victim of prey, in addition to Rana's fervent honoring of her reputation, disqualifies her from being the butterfly alluded to in the song. If the prostitute in *Y te diré quién eres* is not the lyrical subject, then who is?

Aside from Rana's exclamation upon first listening to the song, the text reveals a narrative mise en abyme when the male protagonist ponders the results of the Sandinista Revolution. Rana reflects that "lo que se comenzó en el setenta no se ha concluido, esta chochada quedó incompleta, fue traicionada, unos más otros menos, pero en fin, traidores" (61). He is of course referring to the revolutionary government that soon fell into corruption and scandal, replicating (albeit with a social consciousness) the injustices of the right-wing dictatorships that had preceded it. The

Sandinistas and their failure to uphold the ideals of the revolution are seen as an axis of the current discontent with the Left in Central America and with the rise of the neoliberal state, because through their ineptitudes, measures of austerity and privatization are voted in. What is of interest here is Rana's usage of the lexeme *traicionar*, as it begins to hint at a gendered identity to the lyrically juxtaposed *mariposa*. The use of the verb is not accidental, as there is a blossoming connection being made between the historic past, the politico-economic present, and the gendered masculine body as a locus of inscription for these processes and epistemes.

We quickly discover, in fact, that men are the only traitors in Galich's tale. Given that the novel plays a game of lyrical inversion to explore the constructs of neoliberal identity in Central America, it comes as no surprise that the author fashions groups of homosocial masculinities, such as the police, the press, and the group of conniving politicians who are blamed for ransacking the country, in a transnational theater of composite actors, evocative of similar microstrategies seen in the new historical novels. They are all traitors, though the reader is not at first privy to whom they are betraying. Examples of this characterization abound: in an attempt to recover La Guajira, Rana attacks a political gathering with improvised explosive devices, leading one politician to scream "¡traición! ¡traición!" (94). The reader can ask here to whom the politician is referring, as Galich is astutely vague. Are the traitors the ex-guerrillas now waging urban economic warfare? Perhaps the text is referring to the political class that has allowed these societies to be ransacked by foreign interests? Or maybe even it is in reference to the corrupt forces of order that are unable to maintain basic civility?

In a knowing wink toward the role of music as an intertext, the only figures left standing, nonchalantly gathering their instruments after the bombing, are a group of hired musicians that don't stop playing their instruments during the Hollywoodesque action sequence. We see here further proof of the authorial play on words and the requirement of a detective reader, as the musicians and music are directly linked to the title of the novel and to the author's note, as well as to the homosocial actor screaming bloody treason, returning us to the question of who the (gendered) mariposas really are.

None of the male characters are exempt from the parameters of betrayal: Pancho Rana is associated with the trope of the traitorous military male when he suggests that he might be viewed as a turncoat for escaping with jewels entrusted to him by a transnational mafioso known as El Jefe. Such an association is jarring to a reader accustomed to identifying with the protagonist-as-hero schema, a schema thrown into flux in contemporary Central American noir-type fiction that does not operate with ethical poles. If the virile and seemingly righteous (in his pursuit to rescue La Guajira) Rana is also characterized as a traitor, how does the relationship between the verb *traicionar* and the mariposa develop?

The latter term is initially used to refer to prostitutes whom Rana consults when looking for La Guajira. The lyrics of the rock song are evocative of the furtive and flirtatious sex workers, though the reference is glossed over when the "mariposas nocturnas" (63) are immediately after described as a group of "abejitas" (63). The author swiftly capsizes the culturally attuned idea of the gender-female butterfly in favor of a descriptor that better labels them as economic bodies that actively commodify and barter with their own bodies.

Such a renaming invariably returns the reader to the author's repeated usage of the verb *traicionar* with the different groups of men that perform in the gendered theater. They, and not the prostitutes who "float" from car to car, become associated with the lyrical imagery of the floating butterfly that actively goes from lover to lover, and who passively opens her "alitas, muslos de colores." The syntactic association is played out in the case of Cara de Ratón, who is arguably the greatest social and moral traitor when he surprises La Guajira in the motel room where she is held hostage by appearing in her clothing. The author cross-dresses the already feminized male "con su calzoncito bikini, el brasier y sus zapatos de plataforma, y las joyas" (70). Not only is he emasculated by his association with betrayal, but he is further removed from the tenets of the Masculine through his dressing as a female, an anthropomorphic conjugation of the "alitas de colores" that characterize the furtive butterfly.

The playful and ever-changing construction and deconstruction of masculinities in the novel work through the cultural reservoir of gender that the Maná song mints, as Galich skillfully interrelates real gender positions with symbolic gender representations. The implied plurality of masculinities is, furthermore, mentioned in the earlier scene between Pancho Rana and one of the "abejitas," La Chobi-Xaquira, who is described by the protagonist as having an attractive body, though she is a transvestite prostitute. She coyly asks Rana what kind of a man he is: "¿Macho-menos o macho-más, macho probado o macho-macho?" (64). This cataloging of contemporary Central American masculinities is reinforced when Alexa, a prostitute who is gifted to Pancho by the homosocial, shares with him her knowledge of men: "Hay quienes les gusta que la mujer los masturbe oralmente, les gusta la eyaculación bucal. Otros, en cambio, les gusta hacer el beso negro; pero eso es babosada . . . hay otros que les gusta que les besen la roseta, pero hay otros que les gusta que les metan el dedo. . . . Ya no digamos los hombres que les gusta dar y que les den y los que les gusta con dos y tres y hasta cuatro mujeres. O todos contra todos, como en la lucha libre" (144).

The smorgasbord of male sexuality seemingly contradicts anthropological work done on the region that isolates cochón culture as a specific example of the traditional aim versus object-of-desire paradigm that is reserved for discussions about Latin American erotics. El Guapo, for example, a businessman with illicit businesses who agrees to sell the stolen jewels, illustrates the idea of a *macho-menos*. His feminine physicality is contrasted with his sexual tastes, as he has affairs with both La Guajira and Xaquira. El Guapo eludes the cochón label, by both penetrating and being penetrated, and instead queers a male sexuality that is traditionally viewed as compatible with Western heteronormative practices. The agent of sublation is the transvestite who reveals that El Guapo likes to be both the sodomizer and the sodomized. The final queering of the businessman is added when Xaquira calls him a "traidor degenerado" (164), thereby morphing his physical and practical semantics with the lyrical and ontological gender schema captured in Maná's song. El Guapo becomes one of many mariposas that Galich gathers in his neoliberal universe, lacking agency and any semblance of a physical or psychological phallus. He becomes a seductive butterfly that goes from flower to flower, "seduciendo a los pistilos," representative, perhaps, of the market dynamics of liberalism. The novel thus suggests that all who partake in the neoliberal system are themselves traitors who can be identified as mariposas, subverting the writing of neoliberal masculinity to a traditionally non-Masculine position.

This verse of the song—so important to the characterization of economic and amorous promiscuity (or perhaps more accurately, of an economics of promiscuity)—reveals a misidentified genderizing of the lyrical butterfly, as the botanical pistil houses the female and not the male genitalia of the flower. The female-gendered butterfly therefore seduces and goes from female-sexualized flower to flower, suggesting that there is an underlying queer facet to the song, which Galich exploits in his intertext, or that perhaps the mariposas in the song have all along been males. Such conjectures, however, only manage to reinforce the underlying queering of gender positions as fluid and nonanchored sites, decentering any attempt to reconstitute the Masculine in a deterritorialized space.

Following this line of thinking, the reader can note how Pancho Rana is sublated from a position of virile masculinity—the norm in

Managua—to a subordinate position that is brought about by the queering transvestite. In one scene, the protagonist reminisces about Xaquira's "lindas piernas y un culo mejor que el de muchas mujeres" (151). Though Rana never really engages in explicit sexual relations with Xaquira, it is alluded to that he participates in a night of debauchery that includes "bichas" and "bichos" (179), insinuating that even his (previously) hypervirile and competing masculinity (in *Salsa City*) is now queered by its participation in the transnational neoliberal economies and politics of *Mariposa traicionera*. Like the undifferentiated butterfly of the song, the reader is left to guess whether Rana is the penetrated or the penetrator.

The figure of the transvestite further implicitly queers Rana and the other men through the many lexical borrowings he displays as the scenes progress. Xaquira and a homosexual makeup artist are known for their usage of pejorative, homophobic language such as "maricón" and "degenerado." Their first line of defense against would-be attackers and cheating lovers is to appropriate the lexicon of heteronormative discourse; to name the other or to stain them with the labels of the abject counterintuitively gives them power. Rana reappropriates and mimics Xaquira's adoption of homophobic discourse as he escapes capture from a group of men who hunt him, calling them "¡jueputas maricones!" (157). His enunciation is a repetition of the diction and discourse of the nonnormative body, though Rana fails to fully articulate his own positionality versus the homosocial; by using the same rhetoric pattern as the transvestite, the reader, through deduction, may surmise that the protagonist also adopts a subaltern gender position.

The parallelism between Maná's "Mariposa traicionera" and *Y te diré quién eres* succeeds in queering the ex-military masculinity of Rana, though the text resists a full-blown recategorization of the character, suggesting that the ties between the poetics of the text and the social erotics of Galich's post-Sandinista Central America are not firm. After all, the half-written title of the novel evokes the incomplete nature of the connection between language and sexual desire and practice, putting forward an aesthetics of (symbolic, politico-economic, gender) incompletion as a model for representing turn-of-the-century Central America. This is illustrated in a conversation between Rana and an associate who is attracted to Xaquira, when Rana asks, "¿Y por qué si tanto te Gus . . . tavo no te la Jala . . . pa para el Mo . . . motombo?" (184). Though initially linguistically decentered by the mimicry of the transvestite's verbal defense mechanism (that seemingly reinforces heteronormativity), Rana remains an ambivalently heterosexual man who cannot fully express his desire toward Xaquira, as seen by the ellipses and quick renegotiations of the spoken word. The play on words, the theater of syllables uttered and absent, suggests to the reader the inherent difficulty in quantifying and qualifying the masculine position in a society experiencing multiple systems in flux.

Following this observation, it is evident that the other masculinities in *Y te diré quién eres* are similarly precluded from any real approximation to the Masculine, effectively transposing them away from a real competing market and onto a theater space of incomplete performativity. This alternate plane of gender inscription is a theater, as it is merely symbolic of macroprocesses and not really a metonymization of real (albeit textual) competing homosocials or masculine positions in the text. The press, for example, does not support Connell's theory of science and objectivity as a necessary strategy for achieving hegemony but is instead a haphazard group of misfits that exaggerate and speculate on the news, repeatedly blaming the Islamic terrorist group Al-Qaeda for the bombing engineered by Rana, evocative of the same disorganized and gender dysmorphic homosocial in Castellanos Moya's *Baile con serpientes*.[11] The forces of order, represented by the womanizing Anastasio Cerna, are initially characterized as patriotic, masculine, and in control of strategies that promote a patriarchal control of society. Cerna singing "Palomita Guasiruca," a song made popular by the Sandinista Carlos Mejía Godoy, a nationalistic and progressive singer/politician, lyricizes this yet is disqualified from a position of hegemony when he fails to achieve an erection while having an affair with his assistant, Vilma. The police captain's final coup de grâce, however, is saved for Xaquira, who seduces him with her "bello tronco asentadero que tanto le apasionaba" (192), effectively writing him, too, as a mariposa.

Following Xaquira's association with the queering of Rana—based on the syntactic relationship between the mariposa and "to betray"—it comes as no surprise that Cerna, representing the law, is the biggest traitor in the novel. The dying protagonist recognizes the head of the Policía Nacional as an ex-Sandinista who betrayed his group to the Contras, only to betray this other group by reverting to the Frente Sandinista de Liberación Nacional (FSLN). Cerna betrays the power entrusted to him as a member of law enforcement by allowing drug lords to operate and by taking part in a "red de corrupción que involucraba a personas del gobierno, la policía, y particulares" (200). He then executes Rana as one of the many who "se oponen al *progreso* de la patria" (201, my emphasis). If Galich is ambiguous in his characterization of Rana, he leaves no room for doubt in the elimination of Cerna as a symbol of the law within the theater of masculinity, as this position is unable to promote any sense of progress in a system and law already corrupted by the transnational and deterritoriality of neoliberalism.

Cerna's and Rana's deaths ensure that no political extrapolations can be made at the end of *Y te diré quién eres*, as is partially the case in *Salsa City*. As Rana slips into unconsciousness, he leaves the reader with a new model of masculinity that emerges from the chaos left by decades of misanthropic politics and top-serving economics, composed of "hombres dispuestos a cualquier cosa con tal de conseguir siquiera un tuco de lo que ellos [los ricos políticos y poderosos] consiguen sin verguiarse en las calles bajo el nica sol de encendidos lolos" (210). Taking this model, then, as a point of entry into a larger thesis on a postconflict, destroyed-by-neoliberalism Central America, we can note two arguments. First, gender as a socioliterary trope is made malleable and negotiable by the disarticulation of a traditional hegemonic model of masculinity. The novel is noticeably lacking in metaphysical and homosocial Masculinity and instead presents a series of theatrical masculinities that are ontologically impotent when it comes to establishing a functioning strategy of patriarchy. Second, by substituting in a group of men who are mariposas due to their betraying and being betrayed, the author establishes a hermeneutic erotics that is based on popular culture, a cultural infrastructure that is itself a product of globalizing and deterritorialized factors.[12] With that being said, the central axis of Galich's text is the intertextual referent of Maná's transnational yet essentially Latin American brand of rock music, which reminds the reader that any questions of a literary and cultural identity (in an Alfaguara age) can only be systemically interrogated through transnational registers and referents.[13]

The use of popular music as an intertext in the writing of masculinities in relation to societies during and in the wake of the neoliberal tsunami evidences a renewed connection between these texts and their ideas of the national. In these societies, popular music is deified: as Vicente Francisco Torres notes, "la canción popular es una religión; el altar es el aparato de sonido y los sacerdotes los ídolos" (21). The religiosity of song is imbued by authors who are "intermediarios, como los santos u orishas que conectan a los fieles—los lectores—con sus deidades populares" (Plata Ramírez 53). The product of this sacred textuality is a narrative that is rich in cultural referents and by nature polysemantic, which additionally serves as a site of enunciation for political, economic, social, and erotic discourses. The novels examined compound the literary veneration of song, as the lyrics, melodies, and dance of musics open up new hermeneutic entry points into an understanding of desire, and of the role of gender within the representation of the social changes occurring outside the novelscape.

The fixation on borders in the face of cultural imperialism in *Y te diré quién eres (Mariposa traicionera)* is sensitive to the novelistic role of topographic space. What is it about Managua, Lima, or the open waters of the

Caribbean that triggers a discussion of masculinity and power? Is this a renaissance of the age-old binary of center/periphery that structures so much
earlier Latin American political and literary thought? The presentation of
new masculinities that are central to the recovery of the national in the face
of the encroaching and assimilating forces of globalization is contingent
on a spatial demarcation of identity. Galich's new model, after all, becomes
a possibility only through the textual mariposas within the delimitations
of the infernal setting of Managua, Rock City. The presentation of a postwar, anti-neoliberal model suggests that alternative masculinities that do
not necessarily engage with the Masculine are written and alive in the symbolic space of the theater. This writing, furthermore, underlines the possibility of writing types or tropes of the male body and the masculine identity position as real literary metaphors, akin to the mariposa. We see, in
essence, as a result of spaces and topographies of being both genderized
and genderizing, the formation of organic masculinities that rise from the
continent in the face of cultural and economic imperialism.

PART THREE

Novel and Transnational Masculinities

In this section I look at current trends in the writing of masculinities, focusing specifically on works that question the corporality and position of previously structured gendered orders in relation to Latin America. Just as politico-economic systems foster a shift in the telos and how we conceive of culture and place, recent Latin American fiction has posited a trajectory that escapes any sense of the (national or regional) essential. Works by Bolaño, Bellatin, Paz Soldán, Clavel, and Roncagliolo, among others, can be placed in this genealogy (all members, of course, of Generation Alfaguara). I am interested in these fictions that stretch conceptions of Latin Americanness, which in turn suggests an inevitable stretching of the cultural ideologies of gender that are so often attributed to essentialized systems.

This shift in writing coincides with, or perhaps more accurately triggers, a shift in reception, as criticism has opened new points of entry into the gender debate, including ecocriticism and cybercriticism, among other fields. There has furthermore been a surge in inquiry related to the effects on and representations of gender in popular culture, such as comics and film (and music, as examined previously). These critiques question the effects of the influence and infrastructures of the North over the economic industries of culture in the South and the resultant ideals and tropes that this brand of imperialism engenders. Keeping in mind the notion of influence and causality, critics (such as David William Foster, Ben Sifuentes-Jáuregui, and José Quiroga) *and* authors (such as Ana Clavel and Pedro Lemebel) have reflected on the validity and viability of including Latin American gender studies within debates raging in the North, noting the emphasis placed on the body over performance, on the blurred spaces of identity that escape categorizations so popularly and casually thrown around in North American schools of thought. With that being said, however, the points of cultural contact, assimilation, and hybridity cannot be ignored, even if a local, independent notion of gender is to be cultivated. In this section I build on the postulates, theorems, and analyses put forth in earlier pages to examine how masculinities can be rewritten moving forward in the neoliberal age (as is the case of Galich's *mariposas*). I am not so much interested in a textual analysis of each work per se, but instead arrange these texts in a tableau that inculcates broader questions and extrapolations that stretch the boundaries of gender and Latin American fiction. This is not to suggest that each work be included in a canonical array of the state of masculinity in Latin America today. Instead, I propose that each text, in its own right, provides a juicy caveat into what to expect from an increasing corpus that is more and more preoccupied with and reactive to the state of (Latin American) masculinity and men.

The ontological disappearance of referential semantic topographies is rolled over into my study of Hernán Rodríguez Matte's *Barrio Alto* (2004), which is followed in a series by others, such as Alberto Fuguet (*Mala onda*, 1991; *Por favor, rebobinar*, 1998), Jaime Bayly (*No se lo digas a nadie*, 1994; *La mujer de mi hermano*, 2002), and Xavier Velasco (*Diablo guardián*, 2003), that portray a consumerist youth enslaved in the tenets of late economic and cultural capitalism. Though originally included in Fuguet's ambitious anthology *Cuentos con walkman* (1993), Rodríguez Matte has developed a relatively recluse literary career that is punctuated by short stories and regular essays in journals and newspapers. Unlike his countryman Fuguet, Rodríguez Matte's forays into the world of cinema and art-house shorts have garnered more attention than his one novel. In what can be considered a fast-forward of *Mala onda* (much of the structure, thematics, and tropes are evolutions of the earlier novel), Rodríguez Matte's *Barrio Alto* highlights questions of class, globalization, and ennui in contemporary Santiago. But what differentiates this piece from Fuguet's generationally defining work are the seeds and referents to the protagonist's existential crisis. In my analysis of *Barrio Alto*, I call attention to the disarticulation of space in relation to hegemonic masculinity in an increasingly agglomerative urban space. This initial observation is then combined with a discussion of the use of North American comic book superheroes as cultural axes that structure the performance of masculinity in upper-class Chile. The study of nonnational cultural tropes in defining localized gender positions allows for the writing of a global masculine order in Enrique

Serna's *La sangre erguida*, and I argue that any new writings of Latin American masculinity must be dialogued with transnational gendered subjectivities and practices. The process of this, however, is contradicted in my analysis of Bayly's *El cojo y el loco*, where I suggest that any efforts of the academy to differentiate between variants of hegemony are futile, as the real effects and affects of the Masculine remain sociohistorically unchanged.

CHAPTER NINE

Glocalized Masculinities
of the Barrio Alto

Connell's hypothesis of transnational business masculinity as a pole of hegemony on an increasingly globalized gender stage sets the platform for evaluating contemporary writings of Latin American masculinities on a global spatial and literary scale. This theorized gender expression is "led by a hegemonic North Atlantic order" ("Masculinities" 9) currently at the apex of gender relations, controlling definitions and models of patriarchy and, in turn, establishing a system of domination wherein local and regional gender expressions, including masculinities, are subjugated to the normative figure of the male businessman.

The fictionalization of Connell's latest brand of theorized masculinity has been included in texts from the Southern Cone to Mexico, representing on the gender-theater stage a symbol and consecration of the sovereign individual consumer. What is of interest to us, however, is both how this globalized masculinity has been portrayed in fiction and what measures are taken to affront or question its authority over the landscape.

In real spatial terms, the neoliberal turn is accompanied by a project of urban diversification and sprawl, depicted in detail in Rodríguez Matte's *Barrio Alto*, a 2004 reincarnation of *Mala onda* that shares similar ideologies and stylistics.[1] Like Fuguet, Rodríguez Matte frames his text around a pop culture epigraph that embodies the cultural and existential ennui faced by the first person narrator. Adhering to an aesthetics of cocaine and alcohol, the plot develops the same disdain for all things Chilean that Fuguet's protagonist, Matías Vicuña, demonstrates when he identifies himself as "un pendejo de un país que nadie conoce y que a nadie interesa. Un país que

112

se cree lo mejor, como yo aquí" (*Mala onda* 14). The similarities between *Barrio Alto* and *Mala onda* are structural, as the former's chapters are also positioned around specific dates, though it is decidedly apolitical, unlike Fuguet's direct reference to Pinochet's plebiscite. Yet Rodríguez Matte's novel, set in 1999, holds economic and modernist implications as the author questions if and how things will change as Chile enters the new millennium.

The plot is centered on a personal crisis that is triggered by a nonbelonging to a defined social context, which then offsets the stability enjoyed by the protagonist, Benja, as a wealthy youth. We can first note Benja's disdain for the local and an identification with global identities when he emphatically affirms that "esos sofisticados grupos [musicales] les importará un carajo lo que sucede aquí en Sudamérica, en el culo del mundo" (44). He, like Matías, is also critical of a consumerist culture that mimics the Global North, creating local versions of products and brands that, in their emulation, lack the authentic air of modernity. Unlike Matías, though, he is really critical of the capitalist model: as a university student majoring in marketing, Benja states that "más de la mitad del mundo occidentalizado se había dejado seducir por la idea de comprar sin saber que eso no servirá de nada. La televisión, los avisos publicitarios, y la idea de acumular nuevas cosas nos estaba rodeando al punto de dejarnos insensibles y asfixiados" (166). Such a critique provides an existential substrate for the protagonist's negotiation of his own subjectivity in relation to global and local positions.

The idea of manliness and belonging to the urban homosocial has further evolved from the temporal space of *Mala onda* in that the economic power to buy drugs and cigarettes, and not carnal prowess in the brothel, defines the act of "hacerse hombre" (Rodríguez Matte 13). The protagonist is unapologetic in his criticism of neoliberal policies in Chile, which he contends have defined the nation and its people as a vague simulacrum of the United States. The confrontation with foreign influences over a national self takes on a mass cultural angle when Benja observes, "Podía verme a mí mismo tratando de imitar lo que había aprendido toda mi vida en los programas de televisión, en las películas, en la ropa y en la música que escuchaba, en la comida y los artefactos eléctricos, los modismos, los peinados y hasta la manera de quedarme callado, todo había sido aprendido de algún estúpido actor medio drogadicto y medio amanerado de Estados Unidos" (67). Taking as a point of departure the explicit challenge to U.S. cultural imperialism that was lacking in *Mala onda*, Rodríguez Matte shifts the debate over global-local subjectivities onto the space of the city, that tangible and semantic metonym of the neoliberal age. This process can be contrasted with Galich's writing of Managua, though in the latter, the city is characterized as a putrid stage, stained by the diarrhea of neoliberalism. The Santiago in the Chilean text, however, is crafted through a different aesthetic response to the practices of neoliberalism, as the author chooses instead to explore how unmitigated growth results in a desubjectified and transient space.

The disintegration of the spaces of the Masculine (which were central in establishing a mapping of gender in *El huerto de mi amada*, for example) calls to attention the role of the ruling homosocial of the Club de la Unión, a physical meeting point of political, economic, and social strains of hegemonic masculinity. This space is metonymized in the figure of Roberto, an overachieving friend of the protagonist, who comes from a storied line of politicians and businessmen that own the privatized power company, which sustains literal and symbolic shifts toward a notion of progress. The critique of this powerful homosocial is carried out through an unremitting desubjectification of Roberto, who, like others of his generation, is described as having been "tragado por el efecto sedante del sistema corporativo" (70). Similarly, these men who occupy and define the traditional pockets of power within the Barrio Alto are described as "robots esclavizados por la idea de acumular y ganar más dinero" (70). The similarities to Connell's idea of transnational business masculinity are powerful, as Rodríguez Matte contrapositions the libertine protagonist with the mindless dressed-in-gray-suits male bodies that function as minions of the neoliberal cancer slowly infecting the planet. Benja challenges the traditional cartographies of control by refusing to be like Roberto and his countless classmates, who now dress in imported suits and drive expensive cars to brain-draining jobs that can only guarantee economic amassing. His refusal is grounded in the parallel disintegration of the Barrio Alto—the traditional space of the homosocial prior to the deterritorialization of the group during the neoliberal episteme (though one can argue that the new strain of transnational masculinity will only find its own spatial axes, perhaps in first-class airport lounges, chic restaurants, and new gated communities)—as a result of archipelagic urban growth and the rise of the middle class, which dislocate the traditional referents of money and privilege from the mapped-out spaces of the wealthy.

The textual construction of transnational business masculinity is compounded by its collocation with traditionally hegemonic masculinities. Seeing a group of patrolling police officers, the protagonist notes: "no hacían otra cosa que deambular como sanguijuelas buscando una manera de sacarle provecho a su poder. No podía razonar con ellos. Había algo demasiado equivocado en la gente que usaba uniformes" (155). He further includes the military and the clergy in this observation, as "débiles detrás de los uniformes" (155). There is an implied comparison of the enslaved robots (transnational business masculinity) like Roberto within this group, arguing that "los ejecutivos y políticos vestidos iguales, llevando coléricas corbatas como si fuese la única prenda con la que pueden tomarse ciertas libertades. Se esconden detrás de la institución" (155). Note the relationship between the sartorial aesthetics of individual bodies within a group and the institutions of power they code for. Also note that, in this comparison, the businessman seems to be just the latest iteration of the hegemonic.

The dematerialization of the traditional homosocial of institutionalized progress (see Bryce Echenique's writing of masculinities) results in a reorganized or disorganized cartographic theater for the subject who cannot help but assert, "no estoy ni en el centro ni en el exterior. Quizás no estoy en ninguna parte" (24), calling to mind what Fredric Jameson calls a crisis of boundaries, where the borders and categories of space are blurred (86). The conclusion to Rodríguez Matte's bildungsroman is not afforded the sanctity of the Barrio Alto to emerge as a mature adult, akin to Carlos Alegre's return to Lima, as Benja must instead negotiate a masculine identity that is constructed as a product of contact with transnational business masculinity.

The realization that the homosocial has been modified by globalizing and tensile forces, and that the Barrio Alto has ceased to exist as a real and an imagined space triggers a survivalist strategy in Benja. The past is left behind and "se vislum[bra] una oportunidad para reorganizar [su] vida como un computador que se reinicia y logra reordenar todos sus archivos desde el principio" (199). Rodríguez Matte draws our attention to the construction of the male body and its subjectivity, focusing on how and with what metaphors the corporal site so prevalent (and organically scripted) in the new historical novel may be rearticulated.

The author's reimagination of the corporality of masculinity is first gleaned through a dialectic construction of the female in relation to nature. Such a textuality invariably invites the ecocritical angle to our analysis; by giving nature and the natural a voice, we force ourselves into the position of the Other through language, allowing for an understanding of the effects of phallocentrism and andro-domination over the planet as an extension of the same in society. The problem with this line of inquiry, however, lies in its objectives, as they are often obtuse and mythopoetic, seeking to find some long-lost Edenic paradise that holds no real value or

constructive framework, recurring instead to a sort of academic masturbatory practice that stresses the arrogance of the literary critic as potentiating
real and discursive challenges to patriarchy. Ecocriticism becomes at times
a repetitive process without end, simply pointing out the cultural equivalencies of the feminine to the natural.

Though vague aims and methodologies are intrinsically problematic and
often only idealistic in their application, a closer look at ecofeminist models, a subset of the ecocritical, poses a point of entry into the aesthetics of
patriarchy in spatial fictions. Working diachronically, Gloria da Cunha-
Giabbai observes that the genderizing of the natural occupies a central
role in characterization of the feminine natural as a monstrous *barbarie* (53),
which is portrayed in opposition to the masculine civilization in nineteenth-
century texts. The recurrence to the natural as feminine is problematized
by Gretchen Legler when she asserts that "the constructions of nature as
female (as mother/virgin) are essential to the maintenance of . . . hierarchical ways of thinking that justify the oppression of the various 'others' in
patriarchal culture by ranking them 'closer to nature'" (228). This can be
applied to how Ana Clavel portrays female genitalia as a flower that must
be perforated and inseminated in *Cuerpo náufrago* (2005), or to how
Galich assigns to the traitorous a nature metaphor.

Rodríguez Matte recurs to this strategy to thus include the spatial urban
(as symptoms of the neoliberal) in the intimate construction of the protagonist's self. Benja refers to the natural as a gendered tool to characterize his
own masculinity when he contrasts himself with a love interest, Amelia,
described as "una delicada mariposa entre el pastizal, libre y despreocu-
pada y yo en cambio me siento como una mosca sucia y oportunista, vo-
lando entre el alambrado de púas y una bosta de caballo" (24). Unlike the
butterflies in *Y te diré* that copulate with the human singing voice, Benja is
also viewed as a natural metaphor in relation to the feminine. There is an
attempt to resemanticize him along the lines of the natural, but this fails
as the protagonist then equates the natural with the power of the multinationals over Chilean society as they create and feed the mindless disease of
capitalism. Disdainful of the new middle class and the robotic automatons
of transnational business masculinity, Benja realizes that conceiving himself through nature only makes him "otro pájaro sin cerebro" (44), unable
to script an affront to transnationalism. The failure of nature as a referent
for the protagonist's nascent masculinity is put to rest when he affirms that
"a veces trato de hablar con mi naturaleza, pero ella no quiere hablar con-
migo" (60). Therein the reader witnesses the first attempt in the novel to
resemanticize the male-in-crisis: by adopting an ecofeminist perspective

and by aligning the masculine with the natural, the novel explores the (failed) possibilities of emerging as a whole and constitutive subject in the face of overarching neoliberal gender structures.

A second attempt at resemanticizing or reorganizing (if we are to follow the computer metaphor) Benja's masculinity occurs as a direct by-product of the author's incursions into the realm of the natural as the protagonist visits the house of a famed architect during a party. The owner of the house is described as an ecologically conscious designer whose "construcciones se adaptan a la naturaleza y no dañan el ecosistema" (49). The architect's abode is described in great detail by Simone, a Dutch woman who befriends the protagonist in one of his many drug-fueled romps through the bars and discotheques for the privileged of Santiago. She comments that the house "estaba inspirado en el refugio de Lex Lutor" (49), making reference to the comic book hero Superman and his nemesis.[2] The connection between nature and Lex is strategic in that the author juxtaposes the natural as a villainous agent in contrast to the neoliberal apotheosis of cultural and gendered masculinity (in the shape of the virile and benevolent Superman who filled Benja's childhood).[3]

We see in this juxtaposition the creation of a viable alternative plane of masculine construction in the face of multinational masculinity, though it comes ironically as a by-product of the latter's spreading southward in the guise of cultural imperialism. The comic as a medium and its larger-than-life gendered archetypes represent how "graphic narratives such as comics have constituted one of the important media in [the] connection between socio-economic modernization, cultural matrices, and mass-mediatization" (Fernández L'Hoeste and Poblete 3).[4]

What is important to keep in mind when talking about the influence of comics in the region is the understanding that the graphic drawing market is not controlled by a single group but is composed of interdependent spheres and genres. We can discern the sphere of the North American superhero comic; the ironic social commentary of Condorito; the Japanese-style manga comics; and some more adult-oriented offerings.[5] The superhero, however, is particularly useful when discussing masculinity in Rodríguez Matte's novel, as the protagonist declares that when younger he wanted to be Superman or the Green Lantern. The schizophrenic man of steel from another planet (or equally the United States?) posits an ideological quandary for Benja, because he is a tangible product of the consumer-driven culture that he despises. How can he confront a symbolic norm and archetype that is already assimilated into his own cultural DNA? Therein we see a problem of constructing a gendered challenge to transnational business masculinity, as it is not necessarily foreign in totality but exists within current glocal societies, enmeshed in the infrastructures of the self-community.

Returning to the architect's house, Benja engages in a struggle toward masculine subjectivity as he ponders the figure of the superhero as a viable alternative to a potential ecomasculinity. He disassociates himself from the natural as he links himself to Superman and the anti-natural but is unable to live up to the superhuman expectations that come with wearing a red cape. At the party he encounters Montserrat, the older sister of Max (a classmate and another representation of transnational masculinity), and is seduced by her bad-girl airs as they lock themselves in a bathroom and frantically begin to remove their clothing. Benja's sexual prowess, however, leaves much to be desired in the shadow of the man from Krypton as Montserrat takes control of the situation, domineering him into satisfying her fantasy: she fellates him to her own rhythm (and seemingly not to lead him to orgasm, though he does ejaculate) and ignores his pleas for intercourse. The protagonist is further desubjectified when Montserrat asks him to introduce a Grolsch beer bottle instead of his penis into her vagina, spurning the potential for a super-masculine identification. The choice of beer is not a coincidence, as the brewery is owned by a multinational beverage company and was at the center of price-fixing scandals with other companies, such as Heineken and Bavaria, between 1996 and 1999. The Grolsch bottle represents in an extra-corporal way the economic interests of Connell's transnational business masculinity as it replaces Benja's flaccid phallus in impaling the woman. From an anthropomorphic standpoint, the elongated neck and corked spout of the Grolsch bottle replicates the coronal sulcus and glans of the male penis. It easily takes the place of the organ, and in doing so emphasizes the loss, so to speak, of the body in the shift toward a new gendered order aestheticized by homogenous suits. Its presence, furthermore, emphasizes the absence of Benja's (non-neoliberal) body in coitus, as the body, in fact, is replaced by capital.

After his encounter with Montserrat, Benja's life spirals out of control as he increases his alcohol and drug intake and is unable to maintain any relationship with his female or male peers. His isolation and disassociation from the social milieu of Santiago is punctuated by an overnight stay in jail and the death of Olaf, another member of the small group of friends. This death and the protagonist's acceptance of being the father of Olaf's baby and assuming a relationship with the pregnant Javiera only underscore his physical and societal impotence in asserting a phallocentric or patriarchal position.

At first glance the future is dismal and dark for Latin American masculinities that must negotiate alternative positions or challenge neoliberal masculinity. The tropic devices of the natural or the superhero fail, in part because of internal paradoxes of power, patriarchy, and control, as the disenfranchised male is unable to appropriate that which has so successfully subjugated others. By planting the problematic of finding an alternative to transnational masculinities in contemporary Latin American society, *Barrio Alto* succeeds in updating the cultural ennui and impending crises experienced by Fuguet, Bayly, and others in the 1990s; this time, however, the crisis is extant, and the protagonist has no choice but to find new aesthetic and semantic tactics of self-reconstruction.

The writing of masculinity in Rodríguez Matte's novel does, however, substantiate an alternative formation of the male body that demonstrates some, albeit premature, potential for challenge. The body in several scenes and metaphors is coded and imagined as a technological assemblage that is separated from the biological determinism of gendered bodies. The protagonist and his friends ruminate on the symbolic analogies between personal computers and human beings, arguing that some people are like traditional hard drives in that they can store a lot of memory, whereas others resemble random access memory (RAM) chips, which temporary hold information while the central processing unit (CPU) calculates and performs operative functions. It is not surprising that the protagonist imagines himself as a computer, half man and half technology, that is unable to "hablar con [su] naturaleza" (60).

The metaphor is extended in Benja's critique of transnational business masculinity as he insists that his tie-wearing, nine-to-five-working peers all have a "preocupación por ganar y competir. Para eso nos habían entrenado. Para eso habíamos sido programados. Aunque, claro, a todos nos entró un virus en el camino" (99). The inclusion of the virus advances the technical metaphor of the male body and importantly places it within a larger hypertext markup language universe, where subjectivity and location are never set or defined, leading Benja to comment that "no estoy ni en el centro ni en el exterior. Quizás no estoy en ninguna parte" (24). The body is virtualized in *Barrio Alto* beyond the simple textual transmogrification into a bundle of wires, silicon chips, and blinking LED lights; it is a figment assembled in a deterritorialized cloud space of computing that gains local presence when pulled up at a fixed (territorial) terminal. Such a reconfiguration, though escapist in essence, bodes for a claiming of the technological as a space of contention away from the traditional warscapes of the cityspace.

The protagonist recurs to a technological idea of self at the end of the novel, after the death of Olaf and the dissolution of the Barrio Alto, in a novelistic stroke evocative of Fuguet's disenchanted character reassimilating into the homosocial. But unlike Matías, Benja is not hesitant or vaguely pessimistic. He instead accepts the role he must take as "se vislumbraba una oportunidad para reorganizar mi vida como un computador que se reinicia y logra reordenar todos sus archivos desde el principio" (199). The subtle optimism in being able to press the "reset" button evidences a thesis that perhaps a new language or coda of representation must and can be evolved to successfully articulate a challenge to globalizing gender positions, which threaten to subordinate nonconforming bodies that lay extraneous to the neoliberal project. Though the subject has lost his position in society and the city has shape-shifted into an unrecognizable constellation, the male body still houses the potential to discursively reimagine a future, to reimage a hard drive littered with faulty clusters and virus-infected files, to reformat the societal implications of the "robots esclavizados" that infect the arterial veins of the national (wherever and whatever that may be).

CHAPTER TEN

Materializing the Penis

Though the previous chapter suggests that the only viable strategy for challenging masculinities in the neoliberal age must come through rearticulations of the organic body, a separate line of inquiry is posited by writers who aim to renegotiate the extant and literal body to accommodate changing gender(ed) norms; that is, this line of flight resists metaphorical pathways out of the masculine crisis and favors instead a thorough examination of how men and masculinities can systematically evolve to reject the Masculine as an oppressive position. A writer at the forefront of this shift is the Mexican Enrique Serna, whose *La sangre erguida* (2010) portrays the psychological and physiological intricacies of manhood through the intricate telling of the lives of three Hispanic men irreversibly connected by the atomic bonds of $C_{22}H_{30}N_6O_4S$.

Continuing with an examination of not-so-comfortable topics along his narrative biography, Serna pens the lives of three men living in (a symbolically transnational) Barcelona, all connected by the omnipotent dictatorship of the penis and the impending fear and reality of its flaccid fall. In what can be considered a biography, or "viagrafía" (306), of a Mexican, a Catalan, and an Argentine man, *La sangre erguida* interrelates the stories of a man subjugated by a voluptuous Dominican lounge singer (Bulmaro), a businessman who suffers from anxiety-related impotence (Ferrán), and a porn star who can control his penis at will (Juan Luis).[1] These three characters are, importantly, types for the traditional macho, the transnational businessman, and the exemplar of the butcher homosocial. These types, however, are separated from the symbolic theater of neoliberal

121

masculinities that Galich negotiates and are instead substrated in a theater of micromasculinities that problematize the real travails of the masculine subject in the face of erectile dysfunction. Note here that the penis is emphasized as the site of masculinity, moving away from the neoliberal bodies I cite previously that favor either other corporal sites (testes, anus, mouth) or other semantic metaphors (technology, nature) for writing masculinities.

Told through alternating chapters with a liberal use of intertexts, memoirs, and prison documentation, the novel chronicles the lives of three different yet very similar men in a globalized tableau onto which their narrative routes are plotted amid the hustle and bustle of multinational corporations, local chino stores, and the many ethnic neighborhoods that color the cityscape. The city that functions as the textual referent for the subjects' gender is not Latin American per se, but is a displaced city that effectively asks to be forgotten. Barcelona is not the focal point of the narrative or even of a character (as tends to be the case in recent urban fiction), as Serna's plot points could really occur in any global city.

This is important, because by doing away with the spatial referent, the novel replicates the topologic regime of the neoliberal, reflective again of the Generation Alfaguara. That isn't to say, however, that the novel does not capitalize on the traditional spaces of becoming men; the brothel, for example, is evoked as a space of becoming, as Ferrán repeatedly finds himself in a brothel where prostitutes bring him to orgasm only through non-coital stimulation, highlighting his impotence, though he metonymizes Connell's business Masculine. There is a suggestion made here that perhaps the new hegemon is really not all that powerful.

The Argentine Juan Luis has an opposite relationship with his penis, as he is able to control its blood-filled vesicles with the power of his mind. After experiencing an involuntary erection as a child when his mother was taking his temperature, he vows to never be betrayed again and attains the quasi-magical ability to raise his penis on command, leading to his eventual success as an actor in the porn industry. His career is intimately sabotaged, however, by an uncooperative penis that will only rise to the touch of Laia, a woman he serendipitously meets and falls in love with. This particular storyline is reminiscent of the premium placed on the homosocial and its narrative in *La última noche*, where what is most important in defining masculinities is the ability to penetrate and possess through the almighty phallus.

In the plot line of the Mexican, Bulmaro, Serna explores the potentiality of orthodox masculinities to survive in an age of transnationalism, highlighting the relationship with transnational business masculinity as seen in Rodríguez Matte's textual challenge. The character leaves behind a wife and children in Mexico City and is subjugated to the desires and whims of Romelia, a Dominican lounge singer who brings him to Barcelona when searching for her big break in show business. Their relationship inverts the traditional roles of man and woman, as Bulmaro is the househusband who begrudgingly welcomes Romelia after she has a night out with Wilson Mendoza, a music producer who promises riches. Upon smelling alcohol on her breath and another man's cologne, he observes that "lo mismo hacía mi mujer cuando yo regresaba pedo de mis parrandas" (183). Perhaps the greatest inversion from the position of macho Latino comes in the shape of his attitude toward modern women, as he characterizes them as jealous Don Juanas who resentfully rein in the male gaze while unabashedly flirting and fornicating with a bevy of men.[2]

The three plot lines highlight the penis as the true corporal and discursive locus of traditional masculinities resituated in the contemporary. Bulmaro, for example, attempts to recapture his dominance over the female when "la puso bocabajo con bruscas maneras de violador, para cogérsela como lo que era: una perra libidinosa" (190), only to be foiled by "su blandengue instrumento" (191), which refuses to be engorged. The idea of the failing penis has been rehashed by writers attempting to pen a non-hegemonic position, but its inclusion in *La sangre erguida* goes beyond a simple literary artifice of characterization, that is, of the usual maricón, or emasculated male. Serna is acutely aware of the power of the biological phallus from a textual standpoint, knowing full well that sexual impotence is a metaphor for societal impotence. The writer aptly and amply uses literary referents that have historically constituted masculine gender norms, such as Don Juan Tenorio and Martín Fierro, to juxtapose canonical representations of the macho with contemporary men who model their behavior on the masculine figures of literature. The Argentine Juan Luis, for example, exclaims that he must win over his lover "como los gauchos del *Martín Fierro*, que seguían luchando con un trabucazo en la espalda" (198). The relationship between literature as a means and mechanism of doing gender is reflected on in Serna's narrative, highlighting the connection made between the potency of the penis, or lack thereof, in the construction of the diegesis. Just as the writers of the new historical novels focused on the discursive sites of the male body to problematize gender within debates of the nation, Serna appropriates the penis as a symbol and site for writing masculinity, resisting metaphorically blowing the body up or reterritorializing it as a reflection of broader processes.

The novel is centered on the supply and demand of the erectile dysfunction drug Viagra (sildenafil citrate), which caused a seismic shift in talking about male sexuality as it became mainstream to discuss the flaccid problems of age and anxiety, which were previously held at bay by public displays of machismo. The contract of silence that Vargas Llosa pens around the flaccid Trujillo is torn up and handled head on. The theme of impotence in *La sangre erguida* is more than purely physiological, as Serna emphasizes the societal disenfranchisement of his characters through the metaphorical connotations of the noun. Men are not only sexually impotent but also unable to assert themselves as lovers, husbands, and heads of the household. A prime example is the husband of Ferrán's ex-girlfriend, Gregorio Martínez. Upon discovering that his wife is leaving him for the Viagra-popping businessman, he disappears into his studio for half an hour, only to emerge "con las mallas negras de mimo, la cara y las manos maquilladas de blanco. Se había pintado en los pómulos dos lágrimas con marcador negro, y en el pecho un corazón rojo con espinas . . . él quería [gritar] su dolor en el lenguaje que mejor domina. Hizo la pantomima de arrancarse el corazón y pisotearlo en el suelo" (256). The mime evokes the inability to speak and to verbalize the problems of masculinities in contemporary societies (and criticism), lest the enunciative subject be considered non-Masculine.

Faced with the inevitability of a gender-democratic future, Serna's characters retrograde into their own bodies as they attempt to find the answers to the problematization of traditional systems of masculinity that held them to impossible and powerful standards. There is a cognitive separation between the self and the penis, the subject and its libidinal appendage, that drives the narrative forward. All three protagonists maintain extended conversations with their genitalia, isolating their true identities from what their penises force them to do. Bulmaro, for example, comments that he no longer has free will and feels like "el último eslabón en la cadena de mando" (22). A similar separation occurs in Ferrán when he stops to ponder the mental disconnect between the penis and the mind, asking "¿por qué la voluntad puede alzar una pierna o un brazo, y en cambio no tiene control sobre el pene? . . . ¿Qué oscuro poder gobierna el mecanismo hidráulico de la erección?" (31). The separation of the subject from the penis calls to attention the importance of the body in constructing gender, akin to the rewritings and reimaginings seen in previous novels, though here the narrative exercise refuses to decenter masculinities from the traditional heteronormative site of male power.

The penis as a physiological and discursive site is appropriated by Serna as he emphasizes its hold over male subjectivity: though it is textually separated from Bulmaro, Ferrán, and Juan Luis, it is not a separate entity but a controlling force that reigns over their every move. Men in *La sangre erguida* operate under the autocratic regime of a "dictadura de la testosterona" (20), headed by a "caudillo rapado" (147) who orders their movements. It is not fortuitous that the penis is described as a caudillo uncompromising in its power, evoking the portrayal of dictators in the new historical novel. The focus on the penis, furthermore, aligns *La sangre erguida* with Vargas Llosa's Trujillato, as though the penis is problematized and made vulnerable, yet never fully castrated from a position of hegemony. We observe its challenge and reclaimed power in the relationship between Bulmaro and Romelia when she kicks him out of their apartment after a heated argument. Out on the street and smarting from being emasculated by the domineering female, Bulmaro contemplates "hacerse respetar a la antigua, con un par de nalgadas y una buena cogida" (146) but hesitates to follow through because he is conscious of his secondary role in the household (and perhaps of changing norms that do not turn a blind eye to domestic abuse). What follows is a debate with the little caudillo, which encourages him to admit his mistake and climb back in bed with Romelia, but Bulmaro resists, instead opting to pack his bags and leave. He undermines the dictator's wishes and takes the reins of subjectivity, ordering the caudillo to "baja[rse] del trono y entreg[arle] la corona" (149).

His domestic politicking has the desired effect, as Romelia chases him onto the street, where "le bastó forcejear con ella un momento para comprender que había bajado a rendirse" (150). Their bout of make-up sex leaves the two satisfied and fatigued as Bulmaro lights a cigarette and comments to his penis: "te lo dije, compadre, a los dos nos conviene que me dé a respetar" (150). Though at first glance it seems that the subject has overthrown the phallic dictator, upon closer inspection, we realize that nothing has changed; Bulmaro is back in the household and is still the last in command, subjugated by the will of Romelia and the libido of the caudillo. He is removed from his previous position of power afforded by patriarchy and relegated to the role of the subservient housewife, not challenging patriarchal systems of domination or the importance of the penis in determining masculine expression.[3]

The effects of giving complete control to the "little general" are illustrated by the Viagra-fueled Ferrán, who assumes the schizophrenic identity of Amador Bravo: "di por muerto a Ferrán Miralles, el agachado solterón sin agallas para ligar, y adopté como programa de vida el nombre de mi álter ego Amador Bravo" (122).[4] Unlike the dialogue established by Bulmaro, which resists complete control, the penile politician who assumes power overruns Ferrán's identity—splitting his libido from his impotent self. By doing so, Serna modifies the transnational masculine and realigns it with a traditional masculinity that emanates from the butcher homosocial (evoked by the naming of Bravo). There is a melding of two distinct positions within the theater, as the new position now posits the realities of a hybrid Latin American transnational male who is global and local in his gender position. Ferrán/Amador's body becomes a site of converging forces that are artificially put into play by the pirated Viagra he buys from Bulmaro. It seems that Ferrán metonymizes a political discourse of autocracy and the potential failings of giving a single person or entity complete control, that is, of effectively merging the two masculine actors. He routinely seduces and forces women to have sex with him and records them in the act, fueled by a desire of "la contemplación, no de los cuerpos que había poseído, sino de [su] propio desempeño en la cama. Narciso posmoderno, lo que más [le] fascinaba de esa pornografía casera era ver[se] de pronto con el nabo erecto cuando cam[biaron] de postura. Ellas eran un mero instrumento para glorificar [su] pene, para ceñirle la diadema de emperador y pasearlo en triunfo por las calles de Roma" (177). The character's megalomania suggests that this type among Serna's masculinities implies the obsession with the phallus as not so much an issue of knowing the self or individuating the body, but of putting masculinity on display—of asserting a social hierarchy based in and around the penis.

Ferrán's rise (both corporal and societal) furthermore inculcates him within Connell's hypothesized position as seen in his relations with a Pakistani immigrant. He plies her with alcohol and blues music, noting that "el primer paso en corremperla era derribar sus prejuicios contra la civilización europea" (173). His cultural and sexual colonization of the third-world female is compounded by the joy he feels when sleeping with Mercé, a rich Catalan socialite who cuckolds her husband for the young, dashing Ferrán. This second relationship inscribes the economic characteristics of transnational masculinity onto the protagonist when he notes that while kissing his lover, her rich husband "estaba metido entre [sus] lenguas, de manera que [él] besaba también su yate, sus hoteles, su astronómica cuenta bancaria" (171). It is not only the obsession with wealth that drives Ferrán but also a need to assert himself over other men, as he "descubri[ó] que buena parte de [su] placer provenía del daño infligido al esposo engañado" (171). Serna again stresses the confluence of a traditional patriarchal masculine with a transnational masculinity.

This melding of two strains poses the value of the novel in analyzing local reactions to nonlocal gender orders. Escaping, in a sense, the structuralist categorization of masculinities that Bryce Echenique, Vargas Llosa, and Rivera Garza adhere to and play off against each other, the writing of masculinities in *La sangre erguida* is predicated on the importance of the orthodox biological space/site in constructing and identifying gender. By writing, voicing, and usurping the testosterone-fueled little caudillo, the author effectively undermines the façade of power traditionally associated with the penis (exposing it for what it is, a malleable site of contention), creating a textual space where masculinity is problematized, though not necessarily dethroned as a symptomatic expression of the real body. If anything, Serna highlights the inescapability of the body in theorizing the Masculine, which, as Ben Sifuentes-Jáuregui argues, is intrinsic to any notion of gender in Latin America.

CHAPTER ELEVEN

Challenging Novel Masculinities

The impact of acknowledging the inescapability of the body resonates in the landscape of Latin American literatures, where the hegemony of machismo and phallocentric positions has greased the wheels of writing in the transnational position. Though Serna does not explicitly challenge transnationality (he does implicitly ponder its real effects), we see in *La sangre erguida* an evolution of Rodríguez Matte's protagonist, who situates himself in opposition to his peers working in banks and for multinationals. Men and masculinities according to Serna can be dialogued with or belong to the new hegemon—the latter a position that is not impermeable but negotiable and transmutable. Within this discussion arises a need, then, for tropic (and not metaphorical, as is the case of the technological body) figures that confront Connell's also tropic position.

What is poignant in Connell's sociohistorical synonym for the Masculine is the increasing discord it has inspired in the field of masculinity studies. The criticism directed at transnational business masculinity as a concept can be summarized into two rough categories. On the one hand, we find a challenge of the very idea of hegemony when theorizing gender (Coles 32). This line of thinking, however, often fails to accurately understand the fluidity of Connell's original scheme. This fallacy is succinctly treated by Demetrakis Demetriou when he notes that "hegemonic masculinity generates not only external but also internal hegemony, that is, hegemony over other masculinities. In this second sense of the term, hegemonic masculinity refers to a social ascendancy of one group of men over others" (341). This second sense of the term therefore accurately describes the position of transnational business masculinity as a gender expression that ascends above local extant models.

The second debate, though, is more convincing, in that it problematizes Connell's vision of the role of transnational business within a global order. What is posited is that no global position can really be hegemonic in reach (Jefferson 66), because to be so would imply a systemic shutting down of local cultures and normatives. This critique is elaborated by Beasley ("Rethinking" 92) when she notes that Connell fails to engage with literature that contests globalization, or that promotes other notions of the very concept. These points of contention, in harmony with the previous line of critique, force us to pause and ponder the validity of a transnational masculinity that oversees and controls a hypothesized world order.

The transnational figure has already been textually woven into Latin American narrative explorations of the effects of globalization, urbanization, and commercialization, resonating with Connell's notion that "neoliberalism . . . works at the level of organizational life . . . at the level of personal life, re-shaping our understanding of the social agent" ("A Thousand Miles" 247). The inclusion of this neoliberal trope in these different contexts channels Connell's notion that "the gradual creation of a world gender order has meant many local instabilities of gender" ("Masculinities" 16), but that "one response to such instabilities, on the part of groups whose power is challenged but still dominant, is to reaffirm *local* gender orthodoxies and hierarchies" (17). It comes as no surprise, then, that a second panel of masculine tropes permeates these narratives, oblivious at times to transnational businessmen, yet unabashedly phallogocentric. Here we can cite the teenage protagonist in *Barrio Alto*, or the disenfranchised mechanic Bulmaro in *La sangre erguida*, for these reactive agents are often unreactive given their failure to confront the avatars of neoliberalism.

Jaime Bayly, an emblematic figure within Generation Alfaguara, has written a series of novels that are distinctly autobiographical (*No se lo digas a nadie* [1994], *Y de repente, un ángel* [2005], and *El canalla sentimental* [2008] among others) and a second series that follows a separate trajectory, focusing less on the realities of a drug-using polysexual member of the upper middle class and more on systems and relationships of power. This second line can be traced through *La mujer de mi hermano* and *El cojo y el loco*, where characters often go nameless, and the narrative stops to ponder and reflect on philosophical and ethical questions. What we see in the stylistic simplicity of *El cojo y el loco* and *La mujer de mi hermano* is the use of types (akin to Serna) in lieu of developed characters as a metaphor of the times, a structured and systematic mise-en-scène of the vicissitudes of gender, which in the former is a treatise on the state of contemporary Latin American masculinity. A further characteristic of Bayly's type-descriptive narrative in *El cojo y el loco* is the presence of an omniscient narrator who always positions himself at a critical distance, both from the traditional diegetic elite and from the very locus of the narrative, Lima. By doing so, the narrator locates us at a critical distance that permits a further analytic study of the typologies and their intricate relationships.

The challenge mounted against Connell's theorization of a new hegemonic masculinity in the twenty-first century is put into practice in *La mujer de mi hermano*, where the protagonist and his sister-in-law cuckold the brother, who works in a bank. The nuances of transnational business masculinity are not lost on this character, as he spends the majority of the day laboring in a central financial institution in an unnamed Latin American city. He dresses in business suits, bends the definitions of marital loyalty when on business trips abroad, and spends hours on his fitness and physical appearance, reminiscent of Connell and Wood's hypothesis that "treating oneself as an entity to be managed" (356) accommodates within the physical body an economic doctrine of profitability, capital gain, and limited loyalty to any one corporation. The narrative strategy deployed in *La mujer de mi hermano*, however, falls short of positing an alternative to the neoliberal brother and instead focuses on emasculating the figure through the philandering wife and the repeated insinuations of his own repressed homosexuality. The novel ends with the neoliberal male agreeing to father what is surely his own nephew, on the one hand suggesting that capitalism as a model is limited in its sustainability as a viable status quo for future generations, yet on the other, putting forth a more ominous reading of the neoliberal male, as a body that disregards traditional systems and hierarchies in favor of a future based only on profit and the undermining of all other local masculinities, for by assuming fatherhood, he annuls the usurping brother/father of the child.

The figure of the *cojo*, then, appears as a literary motif after Bayly's first engagement with the transnational male, though we can see distinct parallels between the hegemonic order in *El cojo y el loco*'s bourgeois preneoliberal order and the globalized metropolitan space of *La mujer de mi hermano*. What the former suggests, when read against the latter, is that though it is theoretically catchy to postulate cogent and new models of hegemony, the internal structures of domination do not significantly differ, that is, there cannot be any true "new" form of the Masculine, just replications of extant positions. *El cojo y el loco* traces a gendered system in Peru immediately prior to the implementation of globalizing neoliberal moves, which permits a reading of masculinity that connects both epochs, especially given the fundamental demarcation of the business-hegemonic model in *La mujer de mi hermano.*

The cojo as a meditative critique of the times can be traced through earlier narratives, such as Enrique Terán's *El cojo Navarrete* (1940), which reflects on questions of race and social class in Ecuador, and Rodrigo Rey Rosa's *El cojo bueno* (1996), which narrativizes postwar economic systems that foster inequity in Central America. Keeping these antecedents in mind, we can observe the genesis of an indigenous dialogic affront to the positions at the apex of hegemonic structures in Bayly's text. Divided loosely into two different yet intertwining accounts of growing up during the second half of the twentieth century, *El cojo y el loco* posits an archetypal reading as the protagonists are reduced to their physical and temperamental compositions. Through the naming of the cojo, Bobby Jr., and to an extent the *loco*, Pancho, in relation to other competing masculinities, we see a recurrence of the market of masculinities that is (unlike the theater) grounded in a referent sociohistorical and cultural context. It is within its dynamics of challenging positions that the novel is enabled to interrogate cojo and transnational Masculinity.

The Latin American cojo is both an object and an agent within a narrative-reflexive practice, where the narrative objectifies the imperfect male body in relation to other orthodox representations of hegemonic masculinity, yet at the same time imbues the trope as an active agent against the hypothesized axis of a hegemonic position. The position here is that the cojo as a textual mode acknowledges the presence of a hegemonic masculinity that shares many similarities with Connell's model, though the Peru that *El cojo y el loco* uses as a stage is better known for its *non*-neoliberal policies, namely the appropriation of private capital and land by the government and the nationalization of a substantial part of foreign-owned interests. The novel, like Bryce Echenique's musical interlude, includes the presidencies of Fernando Belaúnde and Juan Velasco Alvarado, which roughly coincide with the first stage of rapid economic growth in Peru's national gross domestic product in the twentieth century. This stage, however, remedied a liberal national economic model that allowed the rich to get richer while domestic standards of living declined. The novel, therefore, locates the reader in what can be considered the crisis of the agro-capitalist bourgeoisie. By situating the plot within a period of economic upheaval caused by competing economic strategies, the text is at the center of a historical point of contestation, where the emerging doctrines of privatization, free markets, and austerity measures come into dialogue with government-led economic policies.

The cojo, Bobby, evokes a familiar conundrum of contemporary Latin American masculinity, as "el cojo no nació cojo. Nació jodido. . . . Nació jodido porque su destino era el de ser cojo" (11). This circular logic with no viable exit, perhaps best articulated by Enrique Serna in his essays and in *La sangre erguida*, summarizes the disconnect between traditional and modern representations and ideals of gender, particularly when we note that "cuando nació todo era felicidad porque era el hijo mayor, el que llevaba el nombre de su padre, y porque era robusto, rollizo y varón" (11). The juxtaposition between the traditionally virile aesthetics of masculinity and Bobby's condition points to a narrative preoccupation in *El cojo y el loco* with the construct of masculinity in relation to the body, exemplifying the notion of capital as object and agent. His physical disability, or what can be viewed as a symbolic dephallicization, is something that is acquired, as Bobby loses only eight centimeters from his right leg at the age of eight when he contracts osteomyelitis. Prior to the illness, he is a happy and loved child, described as "un niño mofletudo, moreno de tanto ir a la playa, de anchas espaldas y piernas de futbolista, con la contextura de un boxeador en miniatura" (12). The author proceeds to correlate this traditionally masculine aesthetic with the commercial ethic of Bobby's father, Bobby Sr., thereby connecting the virile youthful body, a symbol of traditional Latin American heteronormativity, with a narrative evocation of the capitalist hegemonic trope: "El cojo, que todavía no era cojo, parecía haber heredado el carácter agrio de su padre, que era un jefe implacable, despiadado, que llegaba a la fábrica de neumáticos a las seis de la mañana y se paraba en la puerta para tomar nota de los empleados que llegasen cinco o diez minutos tarde, a los que descontaba el sueldo por la tardanza, sin escuchar siquiera sus disculpas o explicaciones" (12). The father, a repatriated Irishman, believes that "el cariño excesivo podía ablandar el carácter de su hijo mayor y convertirlo en un pusilánime, un sujeto apocado y abúlico, como le parecía la mayor parte de los peruanos, cuyo país había elegido para vivir y en el que había prosperado rápidamente" (12). His position, both as a foreigner and as a successful businessman who fails to integrate into the local culture (he only speaks English to his offspring), evokes a formative version of transnational business masculinity and questions the validity of rechristening the hegemonic position as such, as its precursors freely ambulated during neocolonial paradigms. The novel begs us to ask, how different is the transnational male from extant capitalist masculinities? This correlation is further anchored in the fact that Bobby Sr. "había triunfado en Lima y acababa de fundar un banco" (15), "[el] Banco del Progreso, el banco más poderoso de la ciudad" (59), connecting him to the emergence of the banking sector, which is a key component in the shift toward a free market.

In *El cojo y el loco* we see the first hints of how Bayly creates a market where an approximation of capitalist masculinity is allowed to come into contact and dialogue with the alternative and culturally indigenous masculinity of the cojo. It is here that we can begin to chip away at the theorization of a transnational neoliberal masculinity as a distinct gender expression (a theme in *La mujer de mi hermano*). Also on this stage, the narrative exposes the figure of the cojo as a textual alternative to the financially obsessed father trope. Within the gender structure of the novel, the cojo is initially an *other*, abjected from the spaces of family and power that traditionally house the social and political nuclei of the imagined community. After the life-altering operation that leaves him lame, Bobby Jr. is exiled to a "habitación al fondo del jardín, donde dormiría . . . acompañado siempre de una empleada doméstica . . . no le dejaban participar de las fiestas, de las comidas, de los cumpleaños de sus hermanos" (14). He is not allowed to attend school like his peers and is considered "una mancha en la familia, un error genético, una molestia para todos" (15). We can thus read the novel as a fictionalization of the crisis of reproduction of the old order, which in turn promulgates the shift toward the neoliberal space, but only if successful, that is, if procapitalist strategies are embraced. The author, through the cojo, succinctly deconstructs the old bourgeois family yet highlights the gendered characteristics of Bobby Sr. as a purveyor of a capitalist model that evolves with the times, especially since he is responsible for branching out into the banking sector. The cojo's exile from the heteronormative enclave of Bobby Sr.'s house and family is heightened when Bobby Jr. escapes from his room during a birthday party and proceeds to urinate on a birthday cake in the company of invited guests. This act of protest is not without authorial intent, for by staining the celebration, Bobby inverts his position as a stained object (*mancha*) to a staining agent, formally establishing a challenger position within the cartography of power mapped out by the Masculine. It becomes evident, then, that Bayly's protagonist asserts himself as a trope that enters the milieu of competing masculinities under the yoke of Bobby Sr.'s business masculinity.

The latter's reaction to the challenge is predictable, as he puts the cojo on a boat destined for an English boarding school so that others may "educarlo y hacerlo un hombrecito y meterlo en vereda" (18). To become a man in this context is to be ingrained within the paternal model, as Bobby

"estaba solo frente al mundo, solo, engominado, con saco, corbata, panta-
lón corto y un zapato con un taco bien grande para emparejarlo con el
otro zapato sin taco" (19). Of note in the description is an effort to super-
impose the aesthetics of business conformity over the cojo's body, evocative
of Benja's mindless consumerist peers in the Chilean text. Bobby Sr.'s attempts to exert his control over the possibility of a challenging cojo masculinity, however, are futile, as "durante esos cuatro largos años en los que el
cojo se hizo hombre, se hizo un hombre malo y vengativo y lleno de odio
contra el mundo" (19). This failed attempt at indoctrination into the new
capitalist order that the father represents is the result of the notion of an
inverted brothel (as the quintessential space of masculine becoming),
where the young male becomes the penetrated body, as "el viaje en barco
se le hizo eterno entre los vómitos por los mareos y los vómitos por las vio-
laciones que sufría cada noche cuando el capitán del barco y sus tripulan-
tes se turnaban sodomizándolo, metiéndole una media en la boca para
que no gritase" (20). The repeated gang rape of the cojo and his subsequent realization that "el mundo se dividía entre quienes rompían el
culo y quienes tenían el culo roto" (20) underscore the hesitation to completely disassociate cojo masculinity from traditional practices of sexuality,
where being active or passive often has more value in gender identification
than the object of desire. Though dialoguing with Connell's axiom of
hegemonic masculinity, the cojo reaffirms local stereotypes of gender,
reminding us that theorizations of a global hegemony, such as the idea of
transnational business masculinity, must be debated, questioned, and
reconceptualized because the local does not simply go away.

The carnal lesson that the cojo learns on the boat is complemented by
a modification of the masculine aesthetic that was superimposed on his
body, as he reverts to the traditional model of the muscular and virile macho, thereby creating a physical referent to the challenge of the businessman. He does not fuse together competing models, as is the case with
Ferrán, but undertakes a different subject position; he affirms: "mi cojera
es una tontería que puedo superar siendo un toro, la verdadera cojera es
cojear porque te han roto el culo tres ingleses borrachos turnándose para
montarse encima de ti y dejarte el resto de la noche cagando leche en el
inodoro. Yo seré de los que rompen el culo" (20). A contradiction in cojo
masculinity arises here, as the position is always defined by being handi-
capped, in terms of both a physical disability and the symbolic emasculation
of the subject. With "las espaldas anchas, los brazos hinchados y fibrosos [y]
el pecho de un atleta" (25), his lame leg is even more noticeable, forcing
him to hide it under clothing. The attempts at reestablishing the muscular

male body as an alternative to capitalist masculinity is met, then, with frustration and increasing violence, as Bobby realizes that hours in the gym and repeated beatings of his colleagues cannot declassify him from the semantics of the body, conditioning the cojo to spiral out of control in his attempts at challenging the father model.

After completing his studies and returning to Lima, the cojo is fully subjectified as a mature and competing force to the father, presenting an alternative thesis to the representation of hegemonic transnational business masculinity. Aware that he will never stop being a cojo, Bobby declares, "mira, soy cojo, pero así cojo como soy te puedo romper la cara y el culo cuando me dé la gana" (34), reiterating the place of the body and its ability to engage in an epistemology of erotics. This affirmation of a local tenet of masculinity furthermore forces us to reconsider just how global Connell's postulate is, supporting, in part, the detractors who argue that no true global masculinity can be hegemonic. The reception the cojo receives attests to this, as Bobby Sr. promptly exiles the mancha to the room at the end of the garden, but this time the son reacts violently, warning, "no me hables así, viejo conchatumadre, que la próxima vez te aviento por la ventana y te meo encima" (35), connecting his newfound power to the event that caused his ultimate banishment and rape. A similar confrontation of the father occurs in *No se lo digas a nadie*, albeit in the semiautobiographical vein of Bayly's fiction, where the protagonist spits in the face of the businessman figure of authority. The challenge posed here is subversive, as the homosexual son refuses to assume the mantle of masculinity in neoliberalizing Lima. We can read the father in the novel as a nontypological interpretation of the transnational trope, unlike the *type* depicted in *La mujer de mi hermano*, and emphasize that what is being contested here is the hegemonic grasp of the transnational male over the queer expression of the son. The confrontation between Bobby Jr. and his father similarly poses a tableau of challenging gender positions, albeit in a prior-to-the-Fujishock context, thereby connecting the gender structures of *El cojo y el loco* to the gendered episteme of transnational business masculinity. The author traces a similar scene and compels the reader to identify the points of contact between the hegemonic positions, centering us on the fact that Limeño approximations to the Masculine do not necessarily distinguish between neoliberal and bourgeois eras.

The cojo further stands in the face of what is expected of him as the heir-apparent to Bobby Sr.'s business masculinity when he refuses to attend university, spitting in the face of convention and asserting his role as a mancha. Bobby, paradoxically, is not against capitalism or the economic doctrines of the bourgeois state, instead asserting himself as an anarchic agent who does not have to comply with extant systems of masculinization, as "[él] ya t[iene] plata, ¿para qué mierda [va] a estudiar huevadas que [le] enseñen profesores culorrotos?" (35). By aligning himself to the importance of capital, that is, by formalizing the economic ties that bind in the construction of the gendered subject, the cojo gains a certain respect from his father, who indulges his passion for guns and motorcycles and pays for his trips to a brothel. The father, therefore, becomes an enabler of the cojo within the latter's assimilation into a capitalist masculinity, mirroring Connell's notion that (transnational) business masculinity does not theoretically liquidate local models of power but instead supplants current hierarchies through the border-transgressing panoptical practices of capitalist doctrine. There is no need for conflict when the challenger is not actively engaged in the system that creates and facilitates the hegemon, or textual incarnation of hegemonic masculinity, as the cojo is only a cog in the machine and not, at this point, a systemic affront. The point to take away from this newfound alliance is that the father's bourgeois masculinity mirrors the theorized practices of transnational business masculinity, furthering the thesis that hegemonic positions in Peru, at least, haven't greatly differed between the bourgeois and the neoliberal states. If anything, the position of hegemony is held in place and proliferated through the common denominator of a reliance on capitalism as an ethos, underlining Bayly's transnovelistic critique of all bodies that domineer.

The friendship between Bobby Jr. and Mario, peers in terms of social status and wealth but not in aesthetic conformity to the virile norm, shows how the latter aligns himself with Bobby against the common figure of the profit-minded father type. Bobby "de verdad quería a su amigo Mario, lo quería porque era como él, un loco de mierda, un loco de mierda que nunca en su puta vida quería trabajar en una oficina ni tener un jefe ni mucho menos ser un jefe" (42). Both characters lead a life of excess, riding loud motorcycles and shooting guns in the hours not spent at the local brothels. This hard and fast brand of masculinity, a throwback to the previous standard of the macho male, echoes Connell's notion that "one response . . . on the part of groups whose power is challenged but still dominant, is to reaffirm *local* gender orthodoxies" ("Masculinities" 17). This strategy, however, falls to the wayside as both Bobby and Mario fall in love with Dora, a girl from a respectable and affluent family. The two men, as can be expected, compete for her affections.

The reaffirmation of a local orthodoxy of masculinities is furthered, in this regard, when both characters are juxtaposed in their positive traits as a potential partner. In Bobby's case, it is revealed that "los centímetros que le faltaban en esa pierna los compensaba sobradamente en la pingaza que se manejaba, veintidós centímetros medidos por el propio Mario" (45). Dora, however, is scared of the cojo's organ (a critique, perhaps, of its previous hegemony?) and chooses the more stable Mario as a partner. Betrayed and taken aback by this choice, Bobby shoots Mario in the head during one of their frequent duels, not before reflecting on what had brought him to this point:

> El cojo vio en su cabeza toda la sucesión de eventos humillantes que el destino le había impuesto con una crueldad y una saña que parecían no tener fin, vio a su padre insultándolo . . . vio a los marineros violándolo, se vio solo en el internado . . . vio a Brian tratando de darle un beso, vio a su padre escondiéndolo de sus invitados . . . vio a su amigazo Mario robándole a Dorita, vio a Mario, su hermano del alma, comiéndole la boca a Dorita como si fuese una puta más. (107)

The accumulation of events that define the genesis of the cojo as a victim by birth and by circumstance forces him to kill and to assert himself once again as a violent and marginalized masculinity. After the killing, the protagonist resumes his courtship of Dora and viciously rapes her in a hotel. What the text elicits is that the cojo only achieves and asserts power when enacting a performance of violent, aggressive masculinity, that is, a variant of the butcher homosocial or the extant ontological model that has, as suggested by Bayly and Serna, been domesticated by the hegemony of late capitalism. Bobby's assumed gender role is not at the apex of the slowly neoliberalizing state and rests below the controlling position of the capitalist father, who has evolved to using other means to procure sexual satisfaction.

The cojo's actions leave Dora pregnant, forcing her parents to rush into a marriage of convenience. A final possibility of integration into the capitalist order is presented at this point when Bobby Sr. finds Bobby a job at the local General Motors factory. The naming of the company is not happenstance, as it reflects postbourgeois free market inversion in Peru's economy, permitted by the doctrines of capitalist expansionism, which laid the groundwork for the neoliberal episteme that characterizes the hegemonic males in *No se lo digas a nadie* and *La mujer de mi hermano*. As expected, the cojo's tenure lasts only a few months as the American CEO is forced to fire him after he repeatedly harasses the women who work at the plant. Bobby's father realizes that his efforts to refashion his son are futile, as "su hijo el cojo no había nacido para trabajar allí ni en ninguna parte . . . ese inútil había nacido para joderle la vida a todo el que pudiera" (141), and decides to exile him to the country. The moving of the cojo from the city to the country is the final stage in the disenfranchisement of the model as a challenging masculinity, because away from the city (that was so cruel to Carlitos in *El huerto*), Bobby is permanently defined as a mancha, a failed genetic bourgeois experiment in regeneration: the runt of the litter unable to find sustenance and therefore doomed to death.

The writing of a challenging model to the hegemonic position proves original and well-structured in *El cojo y el loco*, because in opposition to other contemporary works that write and challenge the transnational male, Bayly's novel brings to the fore a connective tendon between the bourgeois and the neoliberal state. The challenge mounted and the challenging trope are written into the epoch of demise and birth that overlaps in the biographies of the cojo. More importantly, however, is the unchanging position of the hegemon, for the position of control within the gendered structure of the diegesis is regimented not by virile, violent manliness but through a formal and open espousal of capitalist doctrine. The author puts forth the notion that sustainable masculine hegemony, whether bourgeois or neoliberal, is successfully reproduced only by the commitment to economic liberalism, and not necessarily by the defining episteme of globalization. If anything, a gendered reading of *El cojo y el loco* points to the fallacy of theorizing new positions of hegemony, since the transnational business paradigm is only an evolution from the bourgeois capitalist model.[1] The age-old adage that the rich get richer remains in effect, even as the manchas of the cojo and the loco pose a challenge, highlighting a second adage that hegemony is always hegemonic, even if we try to call it by another name.

Conclusion

Of Tropes and Men

In addition to cojo masculinity, several other tropes of resistance in contemporary Latin American fiction bear mentioning as indigenous textualities that challenge a neoliberal gender order. The first figure worth citing is that of the journalist, the pen-in-hand urban chronicler who untangles and decenters the Masculine as a system and a position of oppression and corruption. Note here, for example, the protagonist and his mentors in Alberto Fuguet's *Tinta roja* (1997) or the writer turned detective in Enrique Serna's *El miedo a los animales* (1995). Aesthetically disheveled but intellectually strong and inquisitive, this mode of masculinity relies on the rewriting of history and other official discourses as a challenge to the powers of the hegemonic. The journalist or writer, armed with the queering power of words and fiction, is able to counteract master narratives and decrees, exposing the Masculine for what it is and positing several exit strategies away from patriarchal control. Through the linguistic and mediatic field, journalistic masculinity poses a threat to order, suggesting, in a macro sense, that the work and narratives produced by contemporary writer-journalists are viable strategies to combat the tensile forces of globalization and the subjugation of the local to the transnational.

Another potential for challenging patriarchy is evidenced in recent texts from the science fiction genre and how they question the binary of technology/biology as it relates to gendered bodies. Working with the idea of transnationality, Santiago Roncagliolo situates *Tan cerca de la vida* (2010) in an indeterminate yet futuristic Tokyo. The narrative picks up the story of Max, a logistician working for the multinational company Corporación

Géminis, as he arrives in a postmodern city to participate in a conference on artificial intelligence. The novel develops Max's feelings of not belonging to the identity espoused by the multinational and his subsequent affair with Mai, a hostess at the conference hotel.

Roncagliolo's Tokyo is a carefully constructed site of disconnection and simulation, discursively disconnected from the global network, which Rodríguez Matte alludes to, by the quarantine operations at Narita airport: "Bienvenido a Tokio. Si siente algún tipo de malestar, fiebre o tos, pase a la enfermería" (9). The control enforced at entry points into the city, which is to say a calculated reckoning of those subjects allowed within its discursive walls, suggests that the author has created a space that is not the real Tokyo, but is instead an assembled site of debate. It is a controlled, nonporous city-text (evocative of the center in *El huerto* and *El cojo*) that comes to life as Roncagliolo dialogues with broader questions of technology, masculinity, neocolonialism, and globalization. The city of Tokyo in *Tan cerca de la vida* becomes a series of images and simulacra, as Max spies a succession of images "[que] había visto en otras ciudades, la mayoría sólo en películas: un castillo Disney, un puente de Brooklyn sobre un fondo de edificios, una Torre Eiffel. Tokio parecía infestado de réplicas, como un parque temático de las grandes ciudades" (10). The author suggests that the Tokyo we observe and read in the novel is nothing more than a collage of other metropolises, a pastiche of the modern world that can easily be dislocated to any other global city.

Any allusions to a global space, however, are conflicted by the inclusion of characteristically Japanese vignettes, which the author emphasizes to lend credibility to his simulation of Tokyo. The cemetery-like cubicles that serve as overnight hotels for overworked urbanites who miss a train to the suburbs is not science fiction, though the protagonist's surprise would suggest otherwise. Similarly, the manga-inspired café and the cat brothel, where city dwellers without pets go to get their furry fix, are not figments of Roncagliolo's imagination. This play between veracity and simulation, self and other, subject and object, is a repeated trope in *Tan cerca de la vida*, as emphasized by the Corporación Géminis billboards that dot the city's landscape. Showing closeup shots of frogs and other living and nonliving subjects that are reflected over a clear pool with the slogan "Corporación Géminis, Tan cerca de la vida, Como dos gotas de agua" (116), the narrative proposes a consideration of reality and subjectivity that is rooted in the visual and experiential. Roncagliolo undoubtedly sparks inspiration from Hollywood projects that repeatedly depict those spaces that come together in his vision of Tokyo, but further skims off near-future, posthumanistic celluloid projects like *Blade Runner,* the *Terminator* series, and *Minority Report,* to name a few, which explore the role of humans and their identity/body.

The author's reimagining of Hollywood is not the only filmic source for *Tan cerca de la vida,* as the neohorror scenes between Max and a mysterious girl in the hotel's elevator lend a sly wink to the Japanese horror genre that has enjoyed recent critical and financial success, particularly with Hollywood remakes of cult favorites such as *The Ring* (1998), *The Grudge* (2000), and *Dark Water* (2002). This renaissance in the Japanese horror genre is characterized by the recurrent figure of the demonic zombielike child, which signals a narrative continuity with a horrific and covered-up past. The inclusion of this figure in *Tan cerca de la vida* provides an authorial clue as to the true nature of Roncagliolo's protagonist, adding to the discursive separation of Max and his surroundings from a textually veracious Tokyo or identity.

The development of a distinctly Japanese cinematic referent in the novel, along with the traditional inclusion of Hollywood and Mexican cinema tropes and figures, calls to attention the divide and binary the author emphasizes with the visual cues and propaganda for the corporation, prophetically named after the Zodiac constellation represented by a set of twins, which on a symbolic level enshrine the dialectic of self that Roncagliolo attempts to decipher in the novel. Nonfraternal twins, as we know, are genetically identical. Their genotypes are replicas, with identical genomic expressions at all loci. There is, however, by scientific logic a single source, which is to say that within a pair of identical twins, one is always the replica of the other. The source of origin, even within a seemingly identical sampling of identical twins, is what interests Roncagliolo's investigation into the questions of identity that espouse *Tan cerca de la vida.*

He establishes a point of entry into this quandary by juxtaposing Max to his colleagues and to the larger ideal of the Géminis man put forth by the corporation and its leader, Marius Kreutz. The relationship between the individual and the company, the individual and society, is what propels the narrative forward, as Max's unrest with belonging to the carnivalesque assemblage of men, machines, and automatons establishes a diegetic point of contention that permits an examination of his own identity as it relates to the group, a linkage built in part on the pursuit of the origin suggested by the repeated twin image. The group, composed of educated international men of all shapes, sizes, and backgrounds, is carefully depicted in the narrative, escaping the superficial characterization of transnational business masculinity. Roncagliolo goes beyond diegetically confronting the businessman with subordinate masculinities or female bodies, instead embarking on a thorough examination of how Connell's idea of a global Masculine operates in relation to other competing masculinities.

Transnational business masculinity as a gender expression is intimately connected to the operational capabilities and characteristics of the neoliberal economy, characterized by a lack of allegiance to any particular sociocultural context and an egotistical reliance on the subject rather than other communities and their interests. Men who express this gender configuration are therefore concerned primarily with their own financial well-being, without taking into account the negative effects their financial transactions may have on the environment, women, and local hierarchies. They view corporal bodies as marketable economic units within a global system of production. From a relational standpoint, their position subordinates local masculinities and femininities through the exportation and mechanization of jobs, and through their noncommitment to strengthening local infrastructures and social services.

From an aesthetic standpoint, and perhaps more pertinent to the textualities of fiction, transnational business masculinity is slick, styled, and predatory. The men that work in Corporación Géminis adhere to this mold, as they are meticulous in their gray suits and stylishly coiffed hairdos. The chief executive officer of Géminis, Kreutz, is the bastion of Connell's subject position, as he is quick to define this new breed of masculinity, this new world order that is intent on global domination, and that is very different from previous avatars of phallic power. Kreutz, more importantly, gels together the idea of a unified transnational gender expression, as he always uses the first person plural subject when talking about the corporation and its dealings, "decía *somos una familia. O nos preocupamos por usted*" (66). There is no individual or self within the position of transnational masculinity, calling to attention the paradox between the subject and the group that exists in Connell's theorization. The individual who professes this brand of hegemonic masculinity must be highly self-reliant and self-serving in his behavior but can only attain this position of power through belonging to a larger corporation of like-minded individuals, thereby emphasizing the unviability of the position and its economic model. This paradox, however, simply adds to the critique of neoliberalism as a short-sighted plan for development that does not foster any sense of community or continuity to current systems and structures of power.

The men that populate the convention center are representative of this paradox between self and group that characterizes Connell's theorized position of power. They come from different backgrounds, countries, and cultures but are unified by their uniforms and their adherence to rising within the power structures perpetuated by Géminis. Power within the multinational company (MNC) is created and perpetuated by the executive branch that makes decisions. Therefore, when Max introduces himself to his colleagues as someone who works in logistics, they ignore him and instead wonder if peripheral departments have also been included in the meeting. This is the first in a series of juxtapositions made between Max and the drones of the corporation, emphasizing Roncagliolo's questioning of the hierarchies and hegemony of transnational business masculinity.

The men in the corporation are also subjected to the nature of neoliberal economics, as they are "etiquetados, como productos con códigos de barras" (40), like products in a global supply chain that can always be tagged, located, and accounted for. The detail paid to this masculinity is careful and thorough in *Tan cerca de la vida*, differentiating it from other narratives that simplistically critique the role of the businessman in contemporary Latin American societies and its impact on other gender expressions. By creating Géminis, its workers, and Kreutz, the author textualizes the threat of transnational business masculinity, putting forth a fictive study of its systems, hierarchies, and semantics of power. This is fine and well, as from a literary standpoint, an examination of the trope is needed, but what is the greater purpose of delving into this power structure? Particularly within the petri space that Roncagliolo quarantines, what is the narrative aim of writing the transnational businessman?

The answers to this problematic are rooted in the experiential and experimental protagonist, who infiltrates the convention on artificial intelligence from his seemingly peripheral role as a logistician, which does not belong to the executive order of Corporación Géminis. As evidenced in his rejection by his peers, Max plays a challenger role to hegemonic masculinity. He does not occupy the categories of subordinate or complicit masculinity but is instead involved in a textual work in progress, a narrative examination of how hegemony is constructed and what makes it tick. It is through the corporal body of Max that Roncagliolo attempts to challenge the omnipresent hegemony of Kreutz and company.

This challenge is carried out through a calculated performance of gender on the part of Max, who, after encountering the transnational businessmen of the company, "se dio ánimos mentalmente. Se dijo que todo era cuestión de actitud. Ensayó movimientos naturales, de hombre de mundo" (43). But this performance fails abruptly as his coworkers ignore his standing within the company, because his job description, not his virility or musculature, qualify him for inclusion within the homosocial, as "se dio por vencido en el propósito de codearse con sus colegas. En vez de confundirse entre ellos, trataría de apartarse de ellos" (45). The construction of Max's masculinity fails at performing a viable position against the hegemonic expression of gender, which Connell argues is the dilemma faced by contemporary masculinities; yet Roncagliolo follows Rodríguez Matte's cue of reimagining the male body. Unlike the new historical novels that recalibrate the anus, testes, and mouth as discursive sites of expression, Roncagliolo's futuristic narrative computerizes the male anatomy, but not through a superficial semantic system of equivalencies between the body and hardware as was seen in *Barrio Alto*. In *Tan cerca de la vida*, the distinction between technology and anatomy is blurred, as the narrative confuses what is robotic and what is alive and breathing within a larger matrix of how masculinities subsist under the yoke of hegemonic masculinity.

The fusions between technology and masculinity become a reality in the novel as the company-assigned PDA (personal digital assistant) "evalúa todas sus señales vitales, incluso las físicas" (66). The handheld device becomes the new neural center of the globalized subject, who is connected to other bodies through the global positioning satellite system that plots the minions of Géminis in relation to their desires, whether they be restaurants or brothels and massage parlors. When Max is feeling lonely, for example, the device pops up the following message: "sé de un lugar que ofrece compañía femenina. ¿Quieres la dirección? ¿Información sobre tarifas?" (62). Technologizing the body does not stop at the male characters of the corporation but extends toward all spaces of the novel, punctuated by the convention center, where the latest advances in artificial intelligence are paraded. Mixing in with the groups of international men in suits is a plethora of robotic projects that perform various tasks. The little boy who sings oldies is the first example of cybernetic engineering, though the designers "le habían dejado la parte posterior desnuda" (21) to emphasize the artificial nature of the singing subject, who is merely a glorified jukebox in terms of the tasks it can perform.

Other robotic bodies in *Tan cerca de la vida* are not as clear-cut in their adherence to either side of the binary robot/human. The domestic assistant BIBI, for example, recognizes voices and commands and is designed to perform everyday household tasks. Kreutz summarizes what she is able to do, including "contestar el teléfono (de hecho, ella *es* el teléfono)" (26). Another robotic figure, DEV, is designed to deactivate explosive devices and is marketed as a global necessity for police and security forces. Kreutz notes that "él y BIBI son en este momento nuestros módulos estrella" (29). Note the genderizing of the robotic body, as the domestic, anthropomorphic-ally svelte servant with "labios sensuales" (83) is automatically rendered female, whereas the brutish "cubo metálico con una puerta que se abría y se cerraba, como si fuese a tragarse a alguien, y un solo brazo con una pala mecánica" (27) is necessarily masculine. Commenting on the future of robotics and cybernetics, Michelle Chilcoat affirms that "the obsoles-cence of the body also implied the loss of biological matter, traditionally viewed as the immovable or fixed material upon which to construct gen-der differences and inscribe male privilege" (156). But this promise, we see, is resisted from a linguistic standpoint, as the robotic, nonhuman bodies are still categorized as male and female, based on their performa-tive and aesthetic characteristics. The possibilities of technology in rela-tion to gender are often posited avenues into dislocating traditional bina-ries. As Claire Taylor and Thea Pitman argue, technology and cyberspace have a "contradictory position, in that [they] offer [their] users the oppor-tunity to swap gender at will, but frequently the alternative gender identi-ties chosen have recourse to gender stereotypes" (13–14). The technologi-cal and cybernetic in *Tan cerca de la vida* fulfill this evaluation of a gendered posthuman existence, as the machines engineered, designed, and produced by the company perpetuate the gender structures of Cor-poración Géminis.

Following this line of argumentation, the technological gendered bodies of BIBI and DEV do not pose a challenge to the hegemonic, but they operate instead as a rhetorical tool in the construction of Max as the true challenger to Kreutz and the corporation. Just as he is juxtaposed to the executive branch of Géminis, Max is contrasted with the automatons that exemplify the purely robotic. While riding the elevator with one of the robots, she asks him how his day has been, to which he replies, "no dormí nada. . . . Me emborraché con unos tipos que trataron de atacar a una mujer. Y luego tuve pesadillas" (82). Adhering to the categorization of nonhuman, thereby implying a cerebral inability to produce coherent language, the robot responds, "yo también tengo una buena mañana" (82), emphasizing the disconnect between Max and the alternative to transna-tional business masculinity at the convention.

Before continuing, it bears mentioning that Max's reflections on his own behavior and performance qualify him as robotic and repetitive in his need to categorize and organize information as part of his job, characteris-tics that also appear in his descriptions of his subjectivity, such as his views on love: "Era un dato fuera de su sistema lógico. Un electron libre de su experiencia" (85). By alluding to the body as a machine, Roncagliolo seems to hint that Max is more robot than human, at least more robot than transnational masculinity, but disqualifies this notion through the incoherent dialogism between the protagonist and the robot. By playing the character off against several positions along the masculine and robot-human binary, the narrative calls attention to the problem with conceiving the subject along a twofold system, putting forth instead a theory of continuity that is less drastic in its separation of man from machine, and from power.

This strategy is brought to fruition in the subsequent conversation between Max and Kreutz, as the former notes that BIBI, DEV, LUCI, and the other examples of artificial intelligence are not very intelligent at all. Standing in front of the executive board of directors headed by Kreutz, Max affirms that LUCI is just a machine and lacks the cerebral coherence to be truly intelligent. The CEO surprisingly supports his position, exclaiming that "LUCI es una máquina. Ése es el problema, y no hay nada que podamos hacer para solucionarlo . . . Por mucho que aceleremos sus movimientos, incrementemos su repertorio de frases hechas o la forremos con cuero de cerdo, no conseguiremos cambiar ese hecho esencial" (86). Kreutz's, and by definition, the corporation's aim is to create something more than machine, something "capaz de aprender, de adquirir todas las habilidades que le demande su entorno, de adaptarse a cualquier situación nueva y extraer de ella conclusiones para prever situaciones futuras" (88). The corporation's intentions, however, are not to create a human but to engineer life, placing the onus on the action of programming, designing, and manufacturing gendered bodies that are enslaved to the deified position of the transnational corporation and its particular trope of masculinity.

It is at this juncture that Roncagliolo's novelistic imagination appropriates the clichés and repeated scenarios of science fiction and Hollywood, where man and machine coalesce into a cybernetic hybrid that is neither one nor the other, eliminating the binary and establishing a continuum of being that challenges the hierarchical power of the hegemonic. It takes little detective work on the part of the reader to deduce that Max is not a simple worker in the corporation, as he is invited to this high-level meeting and is favored over the homosocial mass in understanding the corporation's next move. His personal circumstances and the textual cues that point to an unresolved past and domestic situation with his wife furthermore add an aura of suspense and suspicion to his background. This is cemented by Kreutz, as he notes that Max is different than "los miles de mediocres que tenemos en nómina y que se pasan la vida hinchando sus méritos para conseguir promociones" (89). The protagonist is neither robotic nor masculine (in the hegemonic sense) but is instead something else.

This other identity is the mixture of human and robot, the cyborg that Donna Haraway theorizes in her manifesto against patriarchy (38–39). The novel, however, rehashes the narrative recognition of otherness that has characterized neofuturistic Hollywood narratives revolving around a point of self-consciousness that establishes the subject as nonhuman. Akin to Arnold Schwarzenegger's character in *The Sixth Day* (2000), who realizes that he is a clone of his previous self, Max realizes that his current body has been reengineered and reproduced. He used to work for a large business but committed suicide after murdering his family and cutting out the eyes of his daughter. He is reprogrammed and regenerated just as he arrives at the Tokyo airport, emphasizing the spatial separation of the narrative in the simulated space of the Japanese capital. Max's moment of unveiling, or auto-subjectification, occurs just as Kreutz markets the protagonist's body to a group of Japanese investors, commenting that "Max está rediseñando toda la estructura comercial de nuestra corporación. Es un trabajo que debería hacer un equipo de técnicos, ingenieros y abogados, pero él lo está realizando en solitario, ¿no es increíble?" (249). Any doubts that Max is a cyborg are dispelled as Kreutz recalls the Hollywood blockbuster *The Matrix* and its imagined world of artificial intelligence and generated experiences, explaining to Max that he is now a product of the transnational corporation's engineering.

Writing Max as a cyborg body in opposition to the transnational business masculinity of his peers at Corporación Géminis posits a strategic challenge to the predicament of masculinities in the twenty-first century, given Connell's emphasis placed on the overarching power of the hegemonic over previous systems of control, such as the military (we must remember that this new incarnation of masculine power does not adhere to traditional codes or aesthetics of masculinity or phallic power, as Kreutz affirms: "Esto no es el ejército" [68]). The cyborg as a strategy of subverting patriarchy is forwarded by Haraway, who argues that "cyborgs have more to do with regeneration and are suspicious of the reproductive matrix and of most birthing. . . . We require regeneration, not rebirth, and the possibilities of our reconstitution could include the utopian dream of the hope for a monstrous world without gender" (38–39). The power of the cyborg as a body lies in its nonconformity with the process of reproduction, which stresses the anatomic differences that give rise to a semantic, sociological, and theological system of gender. By reneging from the commitment to

the duality of reproduction, the cyborg body resists the genderizing tentacles of patriarchy and can posit a theoretical paradigm for understanding
the self, rooted in the blurring of boundaries and dualities.

What is important to note at this point is Haraway's vision for the cyborg
as a decentering force against patriarchy and its subjugation of women.
The role of women and men in *Tan cerca de la vida* is not nearly as
problematized or problematic as the relationship between transnational
business masculinity and subordinated masculinities. Roncagliolo's text
maintains the domination of man over woman, as evidenced by the sexual relations between Max and Mai, the hostess at the convention who
starts a romantic relationship with him. We learn that Mai too is a cyborg,
a regenerated suicide victim who, given the technological limitations of
earlier models, cannot speak but instead communicates through a silent
language that Max and other cyborgs understand. Sex between Max and
Mai is consensual but always violent and assertive, as the male takes a dominating role over the female cybernetic body. The author is careful, however, in writing these scenes, as he dabbles between the line of rape and
BDSM in describing how Mai lets out "bocanadas de aire que podían ser
tanto de placer como de sufrimiento" (178). The subservience of the female
is not purely coital, as Roncagliolo's narrative condemns the female cyborg
body to an objectified position that appears sporadically in the second person register, seemingly placing the reader within the position of the dominated female. The feminine lacks narrative and narratological subjectivity
in *Tan cerca de la vida*, to the extent that only the male cyborg can actively
stand against Kreutz's transnational business masculinity. Therein lies
Roncagliolo's reinterpretation of the cyborg manifesto, as his foray in the
blurred bodies of the nonhuman and nonrobotic is not necessarily concerned with decentering patriarchy, but is instead a challenge of one masculinity by another.

Cyborg masculinity thus puts in motion a possible escape from the
"inescapable body" that Connell underlines as ontological in the theorization of masculinities. Importantly, Roncagliolo's novel is inserted in
a trajectory that examines the possibilities of the cybernetic in a global age,
as Geoffrey Kantaris observes:

> The Latin American cyborg seems to condense specific anxieties sur-
> rounding the dissolution of collective identities and collective memory,
> anxieties which connect historically to the experience of colonization on
> the one hand and, on the other, to the erasure of the nation as a space of
> collective agency and memory, an erasure which seems to be inscribed

in the very mechanisms which affect the transition from nation-state to global market. (52)

The Latin American cyborg is essential, therefore, in concentrating these subjective anxieties that are reactive to broader processes of change, but it maintains the essential anxiety behind the crisis of masculinity produced by demographic changes in the continent. The Latin American iteration, therefore, is not Haraway's cyborg, which potentiates the dissolution of gender, but is instead a body that, from a literary standpoint, provides a metonymic challenge to the forces of change and the structures of subjugation. The protagonist in *Tan cerca de la vida* is not a condensing of the anxieties of gender change; he is a symbolic coalescing of the anxiety faced by Latin American men at the mercy of transnational business masculinity, which has successfully supplanted and eviscerated traditional metaphors and positions of power. The writing on the body here, unlike Rodríguez Matte's technologically imagined body, is built on the fantastic identity of the cyborg as a symbolic affront and not as a theorized reappropriation of the male anatomy. It is not preoccupied with gender democratization or the ending of patriarchal systems, but is focused on decentering the omniscient power of the hegemonic, which other narratives take as axiomatic. At first glance, it seems that Roncagliolo's writing echoes the words of Claire Taylor and Thea Pitman, who argue that "rather than aping metropolitan literary currents, . . . Latin American writers are feeling the need to think through the implications that global technologies have for the writing of the Latin American experience" (20). Upon further review, however, it is clear that the author is not preoccupied with the local or continental crisis of masculinity; instead he is scripting a transnational, nonspecific text that lacks political, geographic, and linguistic markers of origin, much like the products of a neoliberal economy.

The textual process of writing a challenge to regimes of power is not complete without a mention of the roles of revolutions and revolutionaries. Going back to the earlier years of Leftist upheavals in Central America, to modern writings of revolution, the figure of the *revolucionario* bears mentioning as an axis around which gender systems can be balanced. Gioconda Belli's *La mujer habitada* is useful in understanding and characterizing the figure of the revolutionary who wants to dethrone the caudillo. A contemporary writing of this trope can be found in Cristina Rivera Garza's *Nadie me verá llorar* and Pedro Lemebel's *Tengo miedo torero*, where young groups of men organize urban movements that seek to usurp the Masculine body. In both situations, the figure, or trope, of revolutionary masculinity is characterized by an agile and sensual body, virile and attractive to the female and male gaze, yet carefully separated from the expectations of caudillo masculinity. They are often poorly dressed, unwashed, and sweaty, antithetical to the hygiene of the textual Somozas and Pinochets, yet alluringly sexy in their bad-boy image. The rough but groomed erotic body is combined with a linguistic inaptitude at the moment of formulating sentences or writing memorandums, in sharp contrast to the narrative strategies of journalistic masculinities. As challengers to the Masculine order, their language demonstrates a refusal to adhere to spelling and grammatical norms, planting a challenge to the powers that be in both the form and the content of their manifestos. The trope of revolutionary masculinity is, however, only revolutionary in the political sense, in its stated desire to dethrone the government or the autocrat, and is in no shape or form indicative of a revolution of gender norms, as these movements succeed in perpetuating the evils of homophobia and sexism. The female protagonist in Belli's novel, for example, is made to perform domestic duties and is initially regarded as a mere housemaid to the revolutionary fighters. She does, however, demonstrate that masculinity as a gender expression can also be performative, though it is importantly located in and inscribed onto the body.

The novel has been read as a socially conscious manifesto that poses the idea of a "new woman" in Latin America, structured around the female protagonist, Lavinia, with several men holding peripheral places within the machinations of the narrative. In the fictional country Faguas, a central setting in Belli's narrative universe most recently seen in *El país de las mujeres* (2010), the protagonist finds work as an architect and leaves her parents' house to take up residence in the place left to her by her late spinster aunt. By doing so, she essentially severs herself from the traditional expectations and roles of women in the (barely) fictive Central American country. Part of this separation includes a social shift as she enters into a relationship with a colleague, Felipe, and slowly gets caught up in his underground revolutionary movement to overthrow the military junta. This process of becoming part of the movement is instrumental in understanding the development of the protagonist, for the narrative heavily focuses on her thoughts and behaviors as she assimilates into an actively subversive role against the status quo, a similar process to Matilda Burgos's first interactions with the young rebel Cástulo.

The notion of performativity in relation to masculinity is built in the novel around local (if we are to read Faguas as a poorly veiled Nicaragua) understanding of gender and desire, that is, masculinity "is based on a man's aim . . . of penetrating . . . no matter whether the sexual object is male or female" (Irwin xxiv). For men to assert themselves as hegemonic, they must "assert their masculinity by way of practices that show the self to be active or passive . . . every gesture, every posture, every stance, every way of acting in the world is immediately seen as masculine or feminine, depending on whether it connotes activity or passivity" (Lancaster 114). Masculinity is, therefore, about being active and being the penetrator; penetrating, furthermore, implies a violent and performative gesture.

Lavinia essentially acts out what Judith Halberstam calls female masculinity, a "unique form of social rebellion; often female masculinity is the sign of sexual alterity, but occasionally it makes heterosexual variation; sometimes female masculinity marks the place of pathology, and every now and then it represents the healthful alternative to what are considered the histrionics of conventional femininities" (9). A woman with a vagina who acts and performs a role underlined by the sociohistorically contextualized nature of masculinity is, in effect, performing female masculinity. Therein lies a problem with the thesis of solely placing a premium on the body as a discourse of definition in gender, for how can we then define Lavinia? The answer lies, perhaps, in allowing some flexibility to the construct, and not relying overtly on either side of the dyad. The body and performance are, after all, mutually important components in the construct of Bayly's cojo.

Furthering the assertion that masculinity is produced by an activeness of the subject, we note how Lavinia shifts from a passive stance toward an active performativity within the rebel group. She first cringes at the thought of Felipe bringing the injured Sebastian to her house, noting that "sólo quiero dejar bien claro que yo no comulgo con estas ideas. No tengo madera para estas cosas" (69). Her hesitance gives way to a more active involvement in the politics of the movement, as she slowly assimilates its ideals of revolution and violence, slowly performing their cultural brand of masculinity. The protagonist initially positions herself in opposition to the larger group, acknowledging that "pero ella no era de esa estirpe. Lo tenía muy claro. Una cosa era no estar de acuerdo con la dinastía y otra cosa era luchar con las armas contra un ejército entrenado para matar sin piedad, a sangre fría. Se requería otro tipo de personalidad, otra madera" (69). Note here in addition to her reluctance to be active that she reinforces violence as a signifier within the hegemonic discourse of the regime, bringing us back to the butcher homosocial in sexually symbolic terms.

The doing of gender in the novel reveals a precocious practice of constructing the corporal body that is rooted in the performativity of the female. The body reappears, as masculine performance in Lavinia is antagonistically linked to her corporal femininity. During her morning ritual, for example, she applies makeup "ante el espejo, aumentando el tamaño de sus ojos, los rasgos de su cara llamativa" (12). When arriving at a construction site, she maintains the theatrical costuming of femininity: "El sudor corría por sus piernas ajustándole los pantalones a la piel, la camiseta roja a la espalda. El maquillaje manchaba el kleenex con que se secaba la cara" (27). She is detailed in keeping up this visage—after visiting the construction site and before meeting again with Felipe, she puts on the costume of woman once more: "Ella se metió al baño y se secó con la toalla la piel. El polvo en sus brazos se hacía lodo al contacto con el agua. Se veía pálida en el espejo. Sacó el colorete para recomponerse el maquillaje antes de hablar con Felipe" (29). What is critical in the narrative self-awareness of performance in *La mujer habitada* is the use of reflections, as the protagonist sizes up and modifies her appearance in accordance with the observed image in the spatial referent of the mirror. Interestingly enough, Itzá, the indigenous voice operating in a different time and space, undergoes a similar process involving the mirror, as seen in the epigraph to these pages. Belli weaves together temporalities that explore the connections between an oppressive past and a patriarchal present, a narrative tool already seen in the new historical novels analyzed in part 1 of this volume. Although Itzá does not gaze into the reflective glass to retouch her lipstick or check her cleavage, she does see in the mirrored surface an image of herself. The mirror and the reflected image come to be the Butlerian costuming or images that establish or permit what society deems the proper performance of the subject. Lavinia, for example, is aware of the importance and power of the mirror, stating that "cuando uno menos lo imagina resulta que traspasa el espejo, se entra en otra dimensión, un mundo que existe oculto a la vida cotidiana" (94).

Her development of a masculine position is contingent on her undergoing a textual méconnaissance, which then initiates her into the imaginary order. The fixation on the image in the mirror and the acknowledgement that it exists permits the assumption of the masculine ideal, which leads to her involvement and need for belonging in the revolutionary movement. This movement, as metonymized by Felipe, represents revolutionary masculinity, or the masculinity associated with politically subversive groups. In a sense, it is an Oedipal masculinity, as its primary goal is to usurp the hegemonic variant through a symbolic and ritualistic beheading of Masculine apex. It operates under the same principles of violence and activity, with the exception that it is not grounded or stoic like the father or dictatorial masculinity, as embodied by General Vela in the novel. Other characteristics of this trope include a failure to identify with state-sponsored tentacles of control, such as the law and medical fields, and an avowed deviation from hegemonic linguistic norms that cement the authority of government over the bodies that constitute the nation. Revolutionary masculinity, however, is not a form of complicit or subordinate masculinities, as Connell theorizes (it surprisingly falls outside the otherwise holistic structure), but instead hovers over the sociocultural model, gun in hand, waiting to usurp traditional hierarchies of power.

By beginning to assert herself and her agency in the relationship with Felipe, Lavinia assumes a performance of gender that strays further from the performed femininity of the social cotillion and is, instead, more in tune with the rebels who cautiously organize acts of sabotage around Faguas. By means of this Oedipal masculinity, Lavinia gains agency, progressively becoming more active against the Masculine, as the next day at work after the shooting of a fellow revolutionary, Sebastian, she encounters her own reflection in the metallic walls of the office. At the thought of being found out in her role of the previous night, which included active involvement with the counter-government forces in an operation, she assures herself that "nadie lo va a notar. . . . Soy la misma. La misma de todos los días" (77). We are then told, however, that she "no estaba muy convencida; en su interior, la sangre se mecia de un lado al otro en una tormenta de adrenalina" (77). The internal struggle at this moment symbolizes a break in the character's psyche, as she idealizes and identifies with the challenging trope of revolutionary masculinity.

It comes as no surprise, then, that the dialectic between the character and the reflection is not played out further in the novel: there are no more moments of self-evaluation. Lavinia, who before getting involved with Felipe and the movement was a lost and fragmented woman, has now gained a misrecognized idea of herself, performing and embodying the masculine type. This is evidenced by her renewed affinity for all things violent and a new affinity for assault weapons and bombs, which previously agitated her fragile femininity. She starts assimilating into the homosocial by repeating the performative gestures of its masculine members, such as folding the sheets of her bed neatly, thereby emulating Sebastian and Felipe's diligence and precision, though she is not actively conscious of why she does so, as "se levantó y recogió las sábanas, doblándolas cuidadosamente sin saber por qué" (100). Their attention to detail stresses their military nature as a characteristic of their masculinity, as we must remember that their aim resides in usurping the extant military regime. Lavinia further assumes a linguistic belonging to the group when Flor, another member within the movement, instructs her to "sustituir el 'yo,' por el 'nosotros'" (63).

The change from being a passive object to an active subject is further illustrated by the metaphor of a doll. Lavinia places documents given to her for safekeeping in the empty chest cavity of the figurine and promptly announces that "ahora tendrá corazón" (118). The revolutionary documents buried in the inert female body metaphorically imbue the subject with a joie de vivre, for her heart is made present and palpable as the rhythmic and omniscient soundtrack to the narrative: "aceleró en las calles holgadas de sábado por la tarde; el sonido rítmico de su pecho era la única interrupción en el silencio del miedo" (126). Activity, not passivity, is the performance she strives to capture. Activity and not passivity is what denotes masculinity. From being a primping-in-front-of-the-mirror architect to infiltrating the Somocista's palatial stronghold, Lavinia underlines a performativity of masculinity to engage in the movement and to put ideas into practice, as she "anhelaba el momento de participar más activamente" (199). By reading the protagonist through the optic of masculinity, and not as a(nother) transgressive female, we illuminate a separate critical route establishing Belli's protagonist within a genealogy of subjectivities that actively struggles against the (writing of the) Masculine as a monolithic stereotype, only to be engaged with othered bodies. By doing so, we enter a critical site of unraveling, where action (violence) can be understood as the only way of supplanting political and gender dictatorships.

The example I use here to illustrate revolutionary masculinity opens, in turn, two separate tangents on the writing and state of masculinities in contemporary Latin American fictions. On the one hand, it posits that gender criticism can be read against solely gynocentric routes by focusing on the structural and semantic masculine schema extant in certain novels, such as *La mujer habitada* or *Nadie me verá llorar*, and by reading beyond the archetypal (and quite frankly, overdone) "transgressive female" trope. I say this knowing that it inspires a visceral and almost automatic backlash, as the oppression of femininities and women continues unabated. The argument being made here, however, posits that by avoiding this critical route, and by instead engaging the systems and structures of the Masculine (through a study of all gendered bodies), criticism situates itself as a dialoguing agent that can then potentially trace a way out of patriarchy, instead of overly relying on the act of transgression, which is, of course, effective in highlighting the injustices of patriarchal gender systems, but equally ineffective in actually plotting an alternative epistemology, because transgressive bodies are, more often than not, only allowed to transgress and do nothing more. The second tangent underlines the need for local and culturally attuned models, metaphors, and tropes of masculinity to be written against domineering or transnational gender positions. By doing so, Latin American fiction will resist the (culturally and financially) tempting proposition of solely writing neoliberalized (read, globalized and McOndo-ized) bodies that bend to the imperialistic and homogenizing whims, norms, and cannibalizing practices of the Global North.

Notes

Introduction

1. This analytics of gender, or a study of its implications within a literary treaty of subjectivity and identity in relation to the social and the nation, has been attempted in several critical works from the first decade of the twenty-first century. A useful tome is Héctor Domínguez-Ruvalcaba's *Modernity and the Nation in Mexican Representations of Masculinity* (2007), which adopts an interdisciplinary approach to the study of gender in Mexico. The title of the book presents it as an exploration of masculinity and the homosocial mass before, during, and after the Mexican Revolution. In reading the critic's work, however, it is clear that the author's *punto de partida* is the dichotomy extant in masculinity studies, with heterosexual, or heteronormative, masculinity on one end of the binary, and everything else negated, abhorred, and persecuted by it on the other. This latter group becomes the core of his analysis and focuses on how queer representations are formed and survived by hegemonic masculinity. Domínguez-Ruvalcaba's exercise in itself is fundamental in building an understanding of Latin American masculinity, as it emphasizes the position of control held by the Masculine throughout the twentieth century. In another study dedicated to national identity in relation to masculinity, Robert McKee Irwin diachronically examines Mexican texts from the nineteenth and twentieth centuries to develop a theory of masculinity and its heteronormative constructs that confronts Octavio Paz's traditional take on Latin American sexuality. Citing Paz, Irwin argues that the aim of sexual relations, not the object of desire (as is the case in North American identity politics), is important in sexuality (xxiv). Focusing on how the construct of hegemonic masculinity changes from the noneroticized homosocial of the "hombre de bien" (47) of the nineteenth century to more transgressive relationships in the twentieth century, Irwin develops a theory of queer masculinity that challenges Paz's ideas. Guillermo Núñez Noriega's *Just Between Us* is an anthropological study of interest to readers that follows the queer studies angle to masculinity favored by Domínguez-Ruvalcaba and Irwin.

Unlike the cultural and literary scholars, Núñez Noriega bases his work on case studies and interviews (very much like Raewyn Connell's seminal *Masculinities*) and evidences the tensions of border identities and how cultural osmosis has led to changes in Mexican masculinities. Of note in the study is the author's hesitance to use Anglo terminologies, a move that must be applauded for shying away from implicit academic colonialization.

Another must-read study of masculinity is Rebecca Biron's *Murder and Masculinity: Violent Fictions of Twentieth-Century Latin America* (2000), in which she examines masculinity in the detective novel of the continent, not confining herself to country, period, or movements. Like Domínguez-Ruvalcaba, Biron's text rarely talks about masculinities, focusing instead on the relationship between the Masculine and subjugated femininities. The methodology behind her analysis positions masculinity as a hegemonic, phallocentric entity that dialogues with women, who are in effect the primary concern of her text. Biron's point of departure is the binomial conception of masculinity as being a pole with a necessary opposite, or other, with masculinity and the other mutually defining each other. It is clear that Biron, like Domínguez-Ruvalcaba, views gender as a phenomenological construct, though she sidesteps the ontological questions of masculinity, which are left undiscussed. As an example, we can glean from the text how the novels included in the study "explore the actual erasure of women and its implications for prevailing images of masculinity" (7). According to Biron, masculinity is about violence, about the repression of the other, whether it be queer or female, and the imposition of a heteronormative discourse in the national literary space. This contention sustains a powerful inquiry into the Masculine, as violence is indeed a primal tactic in its establishment and perdurability, an idea seen in the later work of Ana Belén Martín Sevillano and her discussion of recent Cuban narrative.

Reading Connell, Biron notes that though few men meet the normative definitions of masculinity in a given cultural and historical context, "they may nonetheless partake of the power associated with hegemonic masculinity" (8). Biron does not delve further into Connell's structuralizations of masculinity into more categories, however, and instead focuses solely on the violence exerted by men in Latin America who are "in crisis" and who use violence to "simultaneously celebrat[e] and undermin[e] hegemonic masculinity" (8). What I would like to highlight, and develop later in parts 1 and 2, is that these men occupy a paradoxical position, as both perpetrators and victims. Taking this observation in hand, I add to Biron's excellent analysis a study of how violence operates within circles of men, and how the oppressors against women are equally oppressive against subordinate male bodies. Societal violence stemming from and against groups of men, rigidly held in position by hegemonic masculinity, is evidenced in Franz Galich's *Managua, Salsa City (¡Devórame otra vez!)* (2000), where violence is both a fundamental narrative and a linguistic device. The city of Managua as depicted in the novel adheres to Biron's idea of a Latin America whose "contemporary violence points to crisis tendencies" (8), as Galich, by means of a tightly spun narrative focusing on a prostitute and her band of con men, weaves a tale of urban violence and corruption in a city that lays bare at night the open wounds of a bloody civil war. Linguistically, the text is violent in its abrupt changes of narrative voice from the first to the third person and vice versa. The prevalence of colloquialisms, idiolects, and nonstandard syntax in the text signals a violent shift from a normative narrative.

The violence against women of Biron's theories does exist in the novel, but on a fantasized level. The one-time street but now club-going prostitute, Tamara, tells her potential john, Pancho, that she was sexually abused as a child. When asked how many people had raped her, she explains that she was gang-raped. Pancho does not believe her because she later corrects herself by saying her cousin assaulted her and that her parents did not ever discover the rape.

This verbal intercourse plays itself out over a greater game of seduction between the two, as they dance, eat, and converse with the topic of sex for money never openly discussed in the third person narrative, though it is explicated in the first person shifts. Physical violence in the text, however, is only exerted between men. Just as Biron notices an allegory between the men and the nation in the texts she studies, Galich evokes a similar motif in the characters he builds in *Salsa City*. Pancho is an ex-soldier who works as a houseboy for an affluent family vacationing in the United States. Tamara sided with the Sandinistas. Pancho drives a modern Toyota, whereas the group of con men who pursue him around the city drive an antiquated Russian (communist) Lada (15). The Calle Ocho duo, another group of men who get caught up in the con game run by Tamara, are Americanized, speak Spanglish, and do not fit the local model of the "latin lover" (60). One of them is both rat faced and an opportunist who attempts to seize Tamara for himself. Even among Tamara's ragamuffin band of thieves, there are individual characters who subscribe to macro-level subject positions. Mandrake is an ex-soldier who fought against the Contras. Hodgson is a drug dealer of African heritage, who plays the role of the hypersexualized black man, or what Connell calls marginalized masculinity.

With so many male characters populating a microcosm of the nation within Galich's diegesis, the issue of violence cements the struggles between men. In fact, Tamara is treated as sacred and always protected, even at the cost of male lives in the final showdown in Pancho's place of work. Contrary to Biron's claim that masculinity is an assertion of violence against women (who represent the other) to promulgate a new national space within times of crisis, Galich shows how violence and masculinity need not always be formulated with an analytical focus placed on the other. Violence can and is exerted by and against men, who negotiate and define the various incarnations of masculinity within their historical and political context. A clear example of this occurs in Mario Vargas Llosa's *La fiesta del Chivo* (2000), where an impotent and incontinent dictator unleashes physical and emotional violence onto a community of men who live in a constant state of fear. In this particular case, the Peruvian writer (re)writes a historical account of the last days of Rafael Trujillo's dictatorship and examines the symbols and practices of regime-based masculinity.

2. Recent tomes have examined masculinity in nineteenth-century Latin America, while there is also a boom in studies examining masculinity in the medieval and colonial periods.

3. José Quiroga goes to great lengths to underline this disconnect in his seminal *Tropics of Desire*, where he argues against a transnationalism of identitarian politics in reading and writing about Latin American sexualities. His gesture is hopefully echoed throughout these pages, as I strongly resist simply reading the South from "over here."

4. I am not suggesting that hegemonic masculinity is a fixed position, as it is by definition a relative construct. What I am affirming, however, is that its relation to other

variants of masculinity is now placed in contention, as open borders and markets disengage traditional enabling mechanisms.

5. The shift to neoliberal strategies, however, is not a universal in Latin America. I recognize here that "Latin America" itself is often only an academic placeholder, and that any type of generalization tends to run into fallacies and errors. Economies such as those of Cuba and Bolivia in recent years have followed a different trajectory, and the election of socialist-leaning governments in Chile and Uruguay, for example, point toward a rethinking of the neoliberal episteme. In the Cuban case, Ana Belén Martín Sevillano's piece on recent Cuban fiction and the writing of masculinity and violence is an excellent example of how non-neoliberal climates are also prime sites of analysis for masculine relations.

6. See Héctor Domínguez-Ruvalcaba's study of Mexican masculinity. Beyond actively defining the project of nation, "the male body claims its centrality as the hero figure[;] this centrality makes his body an object of desire. . . . On the other hand, if virility is prestigious, effeminacy is dishonorable," thereby placing virility at the center of national aesthetics (65). Men are not only central as political bodies; they are also primordial in aesthetic representations and allegorical constructions of the nation.

7. Guillermo Núñez Noriega reminds us that "cultural and political forces, even in modernity, are complex and contradictory; and the tensions generated by such contradictions can be detected in sexual and gender power relations" (12).

8. This converse process is excellently developed in Domínguez-Ruvalcaba's examination of nineteenth- and twentieth-century Mexican texts, where the masculine embodies a political ideal and position and is potentiated with a corresponding symbolic capital.

9. What I am advocating follows a paradigm established in the field of masculinity studies of placing the critical onus on masculine subject positions to deconstruct patriarchal and heteronormative structures. This perspective, while acknowledging feminist and queer approaches, examines and detangles the positions of the Masculine in relation to other masculinities, instead of solely focusing on the Masculine as a binary position to the Feminine or the Queer. By doing so, we move into a terrain of gender studies that has been lacking in depth, where what is being examined is really the relationship between men, as masculinities are also deemed to be oppressed by the Masculine. The proposed line of inquiry borrows from feminist and queer approaches in that it textually decenters heteronormative and patriarchal positions, but it tends to focus, instead, on textual male bodies and entities as potential positions for this very deconstruction.

10. See my arguments regarding domestication in "*La hermana perdida de Angélica María*" for examples of how domestic subnational actors "perform" the economy.

Part I

1. As Carlos Pacheco explains, the transition to democratic governments on the continent has led to a rise in the writing of novels of and about dictators (7). Commenting on the inefficacy of previous critical work done on the dictator narrative, which established congruencies and disjuncts between novels and reality, Pacheco surmises

that a new branch of study must undertake an analysis of the narrative in itself and examine how and why dictators are written (42). María Dolores Colomina-Garrigós notes that the dictator novels from the nineties evidence a shift from their antecedents in the seventies and eighties. The critic summarizes previous studies done on the genre and establishes three distinct phases. Colomina-Garrigós's addition to the field lies in her identifying a new phase in the genre beginning in the 1990s, when authors leave behind questions of representation and authorial authority in favor of writing about marginalized and alternative versions of history.

2. This investigation follows Norma Fuller's assertion that "la identidad de género masculina debe ser entendida dentro de un marco mayor, como la expresión de un orden sociopolítico, fundado en el control de los medios estratégicos de producción y reproducción, como son el parentesco, los sistemas económicos y políticos y del poder simbólico que igualan al orden patriarcal con el 'mundo real'" (57).

3. Seymour Menton establishes six general characteristics for this genre of novel. First, there is an attempt at probing philosophical ideas, instead of simply mimetically reproducing the past. Second, there is a distortion of history through omissions, exaggerations, and anachronisms. Third, there is a fictionalization of historical characters that differs from the writing of purely fictitious characters. Fourth, Menton mentions the usage of metaliterary devices as authors comment on their own works, exhibiting a consciousness of the process of writing, of putting pen(is) to paper. Fifth, the narratives in this genre are bonded to other texts and discourses as intertexts. Last, Menton notes the dialogic, carnivalesque, parodic, and heteroglossic nature of these new novels (42–45). María Cristina Pons agrees with Menton on most points but further adds that these new historical novels do not pretend to be neutral in their takes on history: they are subjective and stress the relativity of historiography (256). Furthermore, they reject the supposition of historical truth and the notion of historical progress, and put forward new nomos of representation from the margins of the social. Ramón Luis Acevedo, citing Fernando Aínsa, adds to the critical corpus of the new historical novel, noting that the genre promulgates a multiplicity of perspectives and interpretations of the past and a distancing from the mythological hegemony of historiography (4).

4. The use of Connell's theory in dealing with Latin American literature and culture is documented and prevalent. In an excellent anthology on masculinity in Latin America, *Lo masculino en evidencia: Investigaciones sobre la masculinidad* (2009), José Toro-Alfonso repeatedly cites Connell's ideas in his introductory remarks (14–23). Other critics, such as Oscar Misael Hernández, use Connell's ideas on hegemony and its challengers without specific citation. Hernández uses the terms "modelo de masculinidad hegemónica" and "modelo normativo de masculinidad" (68) in "Estudios sobre masculinidades: Aportes desde América Latina" (2008) without referencing Connell's work in *Masculinities* (1995). Hernández further adds that "los estudiosos/as de los hombres en America Latina ha propuesto superar la noción de masculinidad y suplirla por masculinidades, reconociendo la diversidad de experiencias e identidades de los hombres y los riesgos de una perspectiva esencialista que encierre a todos los hombres en una sola identidad" (68). The critic attempts to summarize the state of masculinity studies in Latin America but fails to identify their underlying model. Lastly, Ana Belén Martín Sevillano's essay on Cuban masculinities also relies on Connell's model to theorize a hegemonic position that regiments the praxis of violence in both the domestic and the public spheres.

Chapter 1

1. Keeping with this idea, Vargas Llosa's Trujillo in *La fiesta del Chivo* similarly berates his challengers by removing their testicles. In opposition to local bishops who sermonize against the regime, Trujillo exclaims, "¡Los maldecidos! ¡Los cuervos! ¡Los eunucos!" (32). By figuratively castrating those opposing his rule, Trujillo affirms that the clergy are "traidor[es] a Dios y a Trujillo y a su condición de varón" (32).

2. Readers familiar with the novel and the subsequent filmic adaptation will see echoes here of Arenas's descriptions of cruising and seducing partners by the sea. The aqueous, long a symbol of the feminine, becomes a metaphor for sexual fluidity and the breaking of binaries in Latin American cultural production, perhaps most notably in recent cinema that focuses on gender subversion and same-sex desires. See my article on Javier Fuentes-León's *Contracorriente* for more information.

Chapter 2

1. In a similar stroke, the dictator Trujillo in *La fiesta del Chivo* never perspires in public, and Ramírez's Somoza uses copious amounts of Eau de Vetiver throughout the novel.

2. Women are, however, characterized as simple goods of trade between men in Vargas Llosa's *La fiesta del Chivo*.

3. Trujillo's impotence in *La fiesta del Chivo* is predicated by the spreading stains of urine running down his leg. Similarly, prior to the castration of Román Fernández, the dictator stains him with the putrefying excrement that spews from a burst sanitation pipe around a military camp. The stain, the deviance from cleanliness, is ontological to the nonmasculine. In Pedro Lemebel's *Tengo miedo torero*, the voice of the dictator (Pinochet) similarly mourns the poor masses that come to the valley to wet their backsides in the river (48). In Ramírez's *Margarita, está linda la mar*, the conspirators plotting the assassination of Somoza are systematically stained by ink and grease (148). The stain, or "mancha," that Melgar Bao observes runs contrary to eugenic discourses of modernity. The stained individual becomes an unwanted member of society, or within the paradigm of patriarchy, an effeminate and castrated subject.

Chapter 3

1. Vargas Llosa's own thoughts on writing and being a novelist, including the presence of inner demons, can be found in *Cartas a un joven novelista* (México, D.F.: Ariel/Planeta, 1997).

2. I am referring to the thinker's conceptions of power as outlined in *The History of Sexuality* (New York: Vintage Books, 1990). More specifically, "power must be understood in the first instance as the multiplicity of force relations immanent in the sphere in which they operate and which constitute their own organization: as the process which, through ceaseless struggle and confrontations, transforms, strengthens, or

even reverses them; as the support which these force relations find in one another, thus forming a chain or a system, or on the contrary, the disjunctions and contradictions which isolate them from one another; and lastly, as the strategies in which they take effect, whose general design or institutional crystallization is embodied in the state apparatus, in the formulation of the law, in the various social hegemonies. . . . Power is everywhere not because it embraces everything, but because it comes from everywhere . . . is not an institution, and not a structure; neither is it a certain strength we are endowed with; it is the name that one attributes to a complex strategical situation in a particular society" (92–93).

3. By "phallocentric," I refer to the privileging of the masculine and the male (as semantic sites of containing the psychic phallus) in the understanding and evaluation of meaning and social relations and structures.

Chapter 4

1. During a recent lecture on this novel, I was chided by a member of the audience, who told me (quite brusquely and in an offended tone) to never refer to the protagonist as a transvestite, as the correct term is a transgendered person. I have several problems with this assertion. First, by calling La Loca a transgendered person, we are assuming that she is a woman cognitively "trapped" in a man's body. Sifuentes-Jáuregui asserts otherwise, and I tend to agree with him, as he argues that the transvestite blurs the boundaries of male and female, and that transvestism cannot be confused with wanting to be of the other sex. In his recent *The Avowal of Difference*, he argues that "*loca* cannot be translated as gay, or even as queer" (201). My second problem with my interlocutor's terminology resides in the unabashed application of a North American gender studies term to a very local figure who clearly does not associate herself/himself with women, but instead carves out a separate and very specific gender expression. We can note this separation in her thesis on fellatio, as she argues that "las mujeres no saben nada de esto . . . ellas solo lo chupan, en cambio las locas elaboran un bordado cantante en la sinfonía de mamar" (100). It is through this act of gender disassociation from the binary that I identify La Loca as a transvestite and not as a transgendered person, as she shows no inclinations of belonging to the parameters of woman. The problems faced by critics when talking about trans identities is perfectly novelized in Santos-Febres's *Sirena Selena*, where the only thing we can be sure about is the trans nature of the protagonist, which is to say a state of being that is always in between different positions, without necessarily subscribing to any single role or rulebook, escaping the lingo perpetuated by gender studies.

2. The connections between *Tengo miedo torero* and *La fiesta del Chivo* are various. Society is portrayed in crisis, undergoing a moment of flux when a gubernatorial paradigm shift may or may not occur. Lemebel's novel, however, is politically distanced from the present, unlike Vargas Llosa's narrative, which flows from a poetics of allegory, as his Trujillo is reflective of a certain other Peruvian autocrat. Vargas Llosa evades ambiguity in his recent *Travesuras*, however, in which the voyeuristic, sadistic, and Japanese Fukuda eviscerates the female body. As Oswaldo Estrada has noted, Fukuda undoubtedly is representative of the *japonés* who controlled Peruvian politics for more than a decade (171).

3. José Quiroga provides an equally demythifying anecdote about the quintessential Communist rebel Ernesto "Che" Guevara in an essay on Virgilio Piñera. He recounts how when Guevara "saw a volume of Virgilio Piñera's *Teatro completo* in the Cuban embassy, he hurled it against a wall: 'How dare you have in our embassy a book by this foul faggot!' he shouted" (168). Quiroga explains that this anger "testifies that Piñera has already sexualized the revolutionary hero, he has turned him into a representation, has furnished that representation with a (homo)erotics" (177). I argue that Lemebel has not only sexualized the hero, but also made him a subject within the homoerotics of politics.

4. The author himself never shied away from the public spotlight and frequently dressed in drag. The photograph in the sleeve of the edition I used shows Lemebel wearing a dress, his long hair collected in a disheveled ponytail, his eyebrows carefully manicured, and his face made up with rouge.

5. Lemebel's queering of the Communist Carlos can be contrasted with a Vargas Llosa Communist figure. In *Travesuras de la niña mala*, the protagonist's "niña mala" leaves Paris for Cuba to undergo military training to become part of the rebel forces planning to invade Peru. True to form, and to the chagrin of the narrator, she becomes the lover of Commander Chacón. Though the commander never appears as an active subject within the text, he is imagined and written by the narrative voice as being a virile and moustached macho who struts around with a pair of pistols on his hips (38). Beyond the aesthetics of masculinity, he is sexually superhuman as he sports a dual phallus.

6. In much the same way Trujillo did after digitally raping Urania in *La fiesta del Chivo*.

7. The experience of paralysis following desubjectification is much like that experienced by Trujillo in *La fiesta del Chivo*, who lies crying in bed after being unable to achieve an erection.

Chapter 5

1. Bakhtin argues that the author channels the heteroglossia incorporated into a piece of writing, animating these voices as though they are coherent, akin to the theatrical device of the performer who imbibes life through speech into a mannequin (*Dialogic* 181). Lemebel's narrative speaks the discourses of multiple groups and subject positions within and outside the diegesis in a complex polyphonic register that illuminates the multiplicities of masculine identity. Similarly, Erving Goffman's work in *Frame Analysis* builds on the art of ventriloquism in the novel.

2. See Marilyn Miller's anthology on tango in Latin America for essays on the connection between dance, aesthetics, and culture.

3. For further reading into the history of film vis-à-vis literature, please consult Brian McFarlane (381) and Linda Hutcheon (Introduction).

4. For a comprehensive introduction to the phenomenon of the soundtrack album, see Annette Davison's *Hollywood Theory*.

5. Davison defines classical Hollywood scoring as a set of practices "united in the aim of heightening the fictive reality of a film's narrative" (2), which saw a reemergence beginning with a series of disaster movies in the early 1970s.

6. Lemebel makes no reference to the song "Tengo miedo torero" by Spanish *co-pla* singer Marifé de Triana, who recorded the song in 1964. The song expresses the fear a woman feels every afternoon she sees her adored torero fight a bull. The lyrics are vaguely voyeuristic of the erotic agony of bullfighting and place the female (or homosexual) subject at a place of power, away from the violence of the ring, yet at the same time intimately connected to the blood and death experienced by the male figure and the bull. The verses that La Loca sings, however, do not appear in the song.

7. Born Alberto Aguilera Valadez (1950), Juan Gabriel is a Mexican singer best known for his *rancheras*, ballads, and pop music. Though strongly secretive about his own sexuality, popular opinion holds him to be a quintessentially queer Mexican popular figure.

8. This idea brings to mind José Donoso's La Manuela, in *El lugar sin límites* (1966), who proclaims that "vieja estaría pero se iba a morir cantando y con las plumas puestas" (16). La Manuela, unlike Lemebel's Loca, never succeeds in queering an other and is queered herself when she recounts how La Japonesa, a woman, cajoles her into having sex to win a bet. Donoso, however, does not objectify the male body but instead explores the violence exerted against homosexuals by other masculinities in a rural Latin American village. He does objectify the transvestite's penis, which is described to be enormous, reflecting the importance placed in fiction on the physical phallus to characterize the masculine in early and mid-twentieth-century fiction.

9. The relationship between the heterosexual revolutionary and homosexual bears some resemblances to Manuel Puig's couple of Valentín and Molina in *El beso de la mujer araña* (1976). Their moment of physical engagement and the subsequent queering of the dissident Valentín, however, are mediated through the anus, which I argue is a site of political discourse that is inscribed onto the male body, and which Puig uses to challenge Argentine censorship and oppression during the 1970s.

Chapter 6

1. Jorge Rosario-Vélez provides a succinct yet complete bibliography of the bolero in his article "Somos un sueño imposible."

2. Though born in Havana, Cuba, Montero has lived for over half a century in Puerto Rico. She is politically active and has taken part in proclamations presented by the Latin American and Caribbean Congress for the Independence of Puerto Rico (November 2006). She heavily favors a change toward sovereignty and independence from North American legislative rule. In an interview given in February 2008, she argues that Puerto Rico "es una colonia de los Estados Unidos, y a nadie le gusta vivir en un régimen colonial." In interviews, Montero endorses a distinctively Latin American tradition to her texts instead of a North American heritage.

3. For an excellent structural analysis of the novel, see Robert Lauer's article (1997). The critic organizes his analysis around the perceived speed of narrative versus epistolary text, which allows for an infusion of "ficción sexual" in the novel (46).

4. I resist calling this a moment of homosexual panic, since Fernando does not violently act out but instead firmly reasserts his position of dominance.

5. My musical metaphor is of course in reference to audiocassettes, not modern digital recording technology, which in many ways erased the traditional practice of

placing more commercial and popular tracks on side A and demoted "filler" tracks on side B. In the age of being able to download individual songs instead of whole albums, the concept of a side has grown irrelevant, leading some popular bands and singers to release B-side compilations for the true fans. These compositions tend to be more experimental, less mainstream, and evocative of the singer's true essence as an artist and thinker.

Chapter 7

1. Born in 1939, Bryce Echenique shares some similarities with another great Peruvian author, Mario Vargas Llosa (1936). Their first novels were published in the 1960s (though Vargas Llosa publishes *Los jefes*, a collection of stories, in 1959), and they have continued to write prolifically. In opposition to other writers of their generation, and of their commercial and editorial grouping, the two Peruvians have managed to keep with the times in their fiction. Vargas Llosa, for example, began to explore the feminine world in his recent novels. His highly acclaimed *La fiesta del Chivo*, for example, is structured around textual strategies of trauma, such as sudden flashbacks and the meshing of a past traumatic incident with a superfluous contemporary occurrence. Bryce Echenique, on the other hand, jokingly refers to psychoanalytic theories and methods of reading literature, as when Carlitos and Natalia attempt to psychoanalyze their own relationship. He ponders: "imagínate tú todo lo que se imaginarían los discípulos de Freud, si se enteraran de esto" (212). They then suggest that their case is either characterized by "gigantescos complejos recíprocos de Edipo" or "un caso de predestinación fálico-clitórico-vaginal" (212).

2. The tune was originally composed by the Cuban-Spanish composer Ernesto Lecuona, though Bryce Echenique references Black's version of the song on the album *Cuban Moonlight* from 1969, temporally placing the novel at least after this date, though the text suggests quite anachronistically that the events narrated occur in the late 1950s.

3. Please see the analysis of Cristina Rivera Garza's *Nadie me verá llorar* in chapter 2 of this volume.

4. See Norma Fuller's chapter on masculinities in urban centers in Peru (*Hombres e identidades de género: Investigaciones desde América Latina*).

5. The inclusion of this indigenous character in the novel highlights the problematic of race and power that Bryce Echenique attempts to illustrate throughout his literary production. *El huerto de mi amada* is rife with characters, dialogues, and descriptions that unearth the plight of the cholo in Peruvian society as he seeks a place of belonging in the urban centers of power. For a brief introduction, see Jorge Bruce's excellent psychoanalytic study of Peruvian society in *Nos habíamos choleado tanto: Psicoanálisis y racismo* (2007), including the illuminating epigraph by Vargas Llosa, who argues that racism in Peru "nace de un yo recóndito y ciego a la razón, se mama con la leche materna y empieza a formalizarse desde los primeros vagidos y balbuceos del peruano" (5).

6. Belaúnde's presidency was preceded by the democratically elected government of Manuel Prado Ugarteche, who held office from 1957 to 1962. He too belonged to a

wealthy, conservative, and patriarchal family. The presidencies of Belaúnde and Prado were interrupted by a short military regime that lasted from July 1962 to the same month of the following year.

Chapter 8

1. Born Franz Galich Mazariegos, the author died in Managua in February 2007, not quite a year after publishing his last novel *Y te diré quién eres (Mariposa traicionera)*. This novel, along with its antecedent, was meant to compose the first half of a Central American quartet of novels dealing with the social unrest in the region. Unfortunately, Galich's work is unfinished, and the use of music in the two remaining novels can only be speculated. The void in critical voices on the author is also surprising; aside from a few newspaper articles and web postings, there is hardly any examination of his work from outside the literary circles of Guatemala and Nicaragua.

2. Several critics, including me, have examined the relationship between space, bodies, and the socioeconomic episteme in *Managua*. See Venkatesh ("Towards a Poetics") and Quirós. On *Tikal*, Caña Jiménez's neoliberal critique ("Vida resurgida") opens new points of entry into the author's oeuvre, in addition to aiding the reader in locating his production in contemporary Central American letters.

3. See Caña Jiménez's theorization of an aesthetics of disgust in recent Central American fiction in "El asco: Reflexiones estéticas sobre la violencia neoliberal en Centroamérica." Galich's three novels can all be cataloged under this description that seeks affective, phenomenological, and aesthetic parameters for locating contemporary cultural production.

4. For an excellent reference on the genesis, history, and genealogy of this musical genre, see Lise Waxer's anthology *Situating Salsa: Global Markets and Local Meanings in Latin Popular Music*. Waxer argues that the spread of salsa in the 1970s across Latin America, and in the 1980s and 1990s to Europe, Japan, and Africa, can be thought of in terms not unlike the shift made away from boom literature in Latin America. The critic notes, "Though salsa's diffusion to these places does not quite fall into the category of globalization along the lines of McDonald's, MTV, Microsoft, and Michael Jackson, the distinction between 'transnational' (cutting across national boundaries) and 'global' (truly worldwide) is not always clear in salsa's case" (8). Waxer continues this archaeological mapping of the genre by adding that only with the aid of the Big Five recording companies, such as Sony and BMG, in the 1990s salsa truly achieved a globalized outreach.

5. The use of a sexual imaginary as a blueprint for national identity has been studied extensively, both from Doris Sommer's heteronormative viewpoint (*Foundational Fictions*) and from alternative perspectives. Sexuality as a negative allegory of nationhood has been used in the study of Puerto Rican literature. Arnaldo Cruz-Malavé notes "that unlike those Latin American foundational texts that Doris Sommer has so passionately analyzed, Puerto Rican canonical texts have rallied us and bound us through failure and impotence" (140). He further notes that there exists in these texts "an impotence that has cunningly incited us to close ranks around the father, with righteous indignation or with race" (141), and that "at the center of the author's paternal voice

there's not a subject but an *abject*: the monstrously mangled body of a 'feminized' man that bears, like all figures of gender-crossing, the marks of a 'category of crisis,' of the impossibility of sustaining paternal hierarchies that the discourse of nation identity both spectacularizes and condemns" (141). This Frankensteinian model of a gendered nation is borne from Cruz-Malavé's assertion that Puerto Rico exists in that "queer state of freedom within dependency, of nation without nationhood" (140). It is also argued that Antonio S. Pedreira's novel *Insularismo* (1934) is the founding text of twentieth-century Puerto Rican letters, a text in which the nation's identity is codified in a failed bildungsroman. This founding text, when juxtaposed with José Enrique Rodó's *Ariel* (1900) and José Vasconcelos's *La raza cósmica* (1925), demonstrates a lack of a "voz magistral" (150), or authorial voice that promotes an author's "version of Latin-Americanness" (150). Pedreira's novel instead is characterized by a conspicuous emptiness and lack of inspiration. When Rodó succeeds in galvanizing the continent's youth, Pedreira writes: "atentad al *divino Tesoro*, pues el título más alto se puede convertir en mote" (174).

6. In their groundbreaking anthology *Rockin' Las Americas*, Deborah Pacini Hernández, Héctor Fernández L'Hoeste, and Eric Zolov note that the initial spread of rock music to the southern regions of the hemisphere can be attributed to a process of "cultural imperialism" (7). Not until sociological processes of urbanization and economic growth are in full swing does rock truly become an acculturated phenomenon. Rock at the beginning of the 1970s "was often regarded as a sign of imperialist attack, moral collapse, or worse" (9).

7. Zizek and Jameson have each used this term in their writings on late capitalism, though Zizek argues that late capitalism and feudalism were mediated by Protestantism. Ian Biddle and Vanessa Knights use the latter's theorizations, particularly on how the national has become the vanishing mediator, to pose "a useful model for understanding the ways in which a set of new cultural conditions can hide the operating territory of its inception: it is useful therefore to think about this tendency as part of the mechanism by which the local/global dynamic has sought to obfuscate the fact that the 'birth' of that syllogism can be traced specifically to national ideologies" (11).

8. Formed in 1978 as The Green Hat Spies, Maná's music can be seen as a timeline of the development of rock in Latin America. Their early cover recordings represent a period in Mexican, and to an extent continental, music history when large rock concerts and venues were prohibited. As Pacini Hernández, Fernández L'Hoeste, and Zolov note, rock was nationalized in the 1980s following the popularization of the use of original Spanish and Portuguese lyrics, local slang, and local and national topics. This *rock nacional* coincided with the advent of neoliberal economic policies, which "signaled the collapse of the nationalist projects . . . that had defined the economic policy of Latin American governments since the 1930s" (16). Following this trend, Maná released their first album titled *Sombrero Verde* to reflect the new name of the group. Their rise to international fame in the 1990s was largely due to a series of albums composed of popular love songs, danceable tunes, and socially conscious works, such as the 1992 hit "¿Dónde jugarán los niños?" which continued some of the earlier themes first made popular during the boom of rock nacional in the 1980s. Their 1997 "Me voy a convertir en un ave" famously describes the corruption of the police and the establishment. The group deviated from the apolitical trend in Latin American rock of the 1990s, which was no longer concerned with the politics of

music, but that "enacted a politics of *anti*-politics, repudiating at the level of sound and performance not only the old hegemonic ideology of the socialist Left but the ascendant ideology of neoliberal capitalism" (17).

9. Galich's ideas of the national are circumscribed by the importance he gives to indigenous identities in the region. In an article that questions the existence of a Guatemalan identity, he affirms that "aunque suene como un anacronismo, en estos tiempos de la cólera neoliberal, es más necesario que nunca que la revolución social y para que ésta sea, pasa necesariamente por la revolución de los pueblos indios de América Latina, pues ésta no echará a andar hasta que no marche el indio" ("Tanda"). The importance given to indigenous rights is paralleled in Maná's 2006 album *Revolución de Amor*, where the Leftist track "Justicia, tierra y libertad" advocates natives' rights to democracy and land.

10. Galich's transposition of the lyrics is inaccurate; the song should read "Ay mujer, cómo haces daño, pasan los minutos cual si fueran años." The author later repeats the same mistake in the inclusion of the lyrics of a Julio Jaramillo song, "Nuestro juramento" (206).

11. It can be assumed that Galich is aiming an implicit dagger at the North American press, who repeatedly and unapologetically blamed Al-Qaeda for a series of international terrorist bombings after the attacks of September 11, 2001.

12. I appropriate Jeanette Winterson's coinage of the term in her essay "The Erotics of Risk," where the critic understands hermeneutic erotics to be "those features of narrative form that capture the reader by setting out the diegetic erotics of the story itself" (48).

13. Like Mayra Montero, the members of Maná have publicly supported Puerto Rican sovereignty from the United States.

Chapter 9

1. See my article on the cartographies of the two novels ("Growing up in Sanhattan").

2. The use of North American superheroes as a referent when constructing masculinity is a recurrent tool in contemporary fiction and can be seen in Ana Clavel's *Los deseos y su sombra* (2000) and Enrique Serna's *La sangre erguida* (2010). The former juxtaposes indigenous, poor men to the crime-fighting figures of Superman and Batman whereas the latter describes the man of steel as the apotheosis of masculine virility.

3. It is important to note the omission of popular Latin American superheroes as masculine referents in contemporary fiction. Most notable are the omissions of the ethnically hybridized Kalimán and El Payo as local rebuttals to Superman and the Lone Ranger.

4. See also Ariel Dorfman and David William Foster.

5. Created by Rene Ríos in 1949, Condorito is an anthropomorphic inhabitant of the fictional Chilean town of Pelotillehue and is well known throughout Latin America as a reference to the common citizen. He is somewhat an antihero, unambitious and lackadaisical, who gets caught up in everyday problems and circumstances.

Chapter 10

1. Serna employs tropes and strategies inspired from Hollywood productions, much like Roncagliolo in *Tan cerca de la vida*. The figure of the ghostly girl who serves as a rhetorical interlocutor to Juan Luis in the mental institution evokes the ethereal relationship between phantasm and troubled subject in M. Night Shyamalan's *The Sixth Sense* (1999).

2. Serna mockingly disdains modern magazines that exalt women to have multiple affairs and lovers, claiming that the institution of marriage is nullified and that monogamy is not an option for Mexican men in the twenty-first century (*Las caricaturas me hacen llorar* 19; *Giros negros* 45). See my essay "Androgyny, Football, and Pedophilia" for a deeper discussion on the construct of Mexican masculinities.

3. A system of usurpation connects *La sangre erguida* to the caudillo politics of *La fiesta del Chivo*; in both, the apparent coup only solidifies the phallic power of the dictator.

4. The autoscopic separation of Ferrán from Amador in the novel harkens to Juan Marsé's *El amante bilingüe* (1990), where a similar process defines the neurotic condition of the protagonist, who suffers a psychological break when he spies his wife with an Andalusian lover. He assumes a new personality, speaking and thinking as a Don Juan figure, to reclaim a position of hegemony after being emasculated. Issues of Catalan autonomy, though not explicated in Serna's text, do exist as an underlying layer to the space of Barcelona and are fundamental in Marsé's incursion into the linguistic hierarchies of masculinity.

Chapter 11

1. Irene Meler reminds us that "la feminidad como la masculinidad son construcciones colectivas que condensan la experiencia de muchas generaciones pretéritas, y que contienen una compleja red de prescripciones y proscripciones para la subjetividad y la conducta de cada sexo" (Burin and Meler 150).

Works Cited

Acevedo, Ramón Luis. "La nueva novela histórica en Guatemala y Honduras." *Letras de Guatemala* 18/19 (1998): 1–17.

Aínsa, Fernando. *Reescribir el pasado: Historia y ficción en América Latina.* Mérida: Ediciones Otro, el Mismo, 2003.

Anderson, Benedict. *Imagined Communities: Reflections on the Origin and Spread of Nationalism.* London: Verso, 2006.

Arenas, Reinaldo. *Antes que anochezca: Autobiografía.* Barcelona: Tusquets, 1992.

Ashe, Fidelma. *The New Politics of Masculinity: Men, Power and Resistance.* New York: Routledge, 2007.

Bakhtin, Mikhail. *The Dialogic Imagination: Four Essays.* Austin: University of Texas Press, 1981.

———. *Problems of Dostoevsky's Poetics.* Trans. Caryl Emerson. Minneapolis: University of Minnesota Press, 1984.

Bayly, Jaime. *El cojo y el loco.* Madrid: Santillana, 2010.

———. *La mujer de mi hermano.* Barcelona: Planeta, 2002.

———. *No se lo digas a nadie.* 1994. Barcelona: Seix Barral, 1997.

Beasley, Christine. "Re-thinking Hegemonic Masculinity in a Globalizing World." *Gender Identities in a Globalized World.* Ed. Ana Marta González and Victor J. Seidler. Amherst: Humanity, 2008. 167–94.

———. "Rethinking Hegemonic Masculinity in a Globalizing World." *Men and Masculinities* 11.1 (2008): 86–103.

Belli, Gioconda. *El infinito en la palma de la mano.* Barcelona: Seix Barral, 2008.

———. *El pergamino de la seducción.* Barcelona: Seix Barral, 2005.

———. *La mujer habitada.* Managua: Vanguardia, 1988.

Biddle, Ian, and Vanessa Knights. Introduction. *Music, National Identity and the Politics of Location: Between the Global and the Local.* Ed. Ian Biddle and Vanessa Knights. Burlington: Ashgate, 2007. 1–18.

Biron, Rebecca. *Murder and Masculinity: Violent Fictions of Twentieth-Century Latin America.* Nashville: Vanderbilt University Press, 2000.

Bourdieau, Pierre. *The Field of Cultural Production: Essays on Art and Literature.* New York: Columbia University Press, 1993.

Bruce, Jorge. *Nos habíamos choleado tanto: Psicoanálisis y racismo.* Lima: Universidad de San Martín de Porres, Escuela Profesional de Psicología, 2007.

Bryce Echenique, Alfredo. *El huerto de mi amada.* Barcelona: Planeta, 2003.

Burin, Mabel. "Precariedad laboral, masculinidad, paternidad." *Precariedad laboral y crisis de la masculinidad: Impacto sobre relaciones de género.* Ed. Mabel Burin, María Lucero Jiménez Guzmán, and Irene Meler. Buenos Aires: Universidad de Ciencias Empresariales y Sociales, 2007. 87–120.

Burin, Mabel, and Irene Meler. *Varones: Género, y subjetividad masculina.* Buenos Aires: Paidós, 2000.

Butler, Judith. *Gender Trouble.* New York: Routledge, 1999.

Caña Jiménez, María del Carmen. "El asco: Reflexiones estéticas sobre la violencia neoliberal en Centroamérica." *Symposium* 68.4 (2014): 218–30.

———. "Vida resurgida y neoliberalismo en Tikal Futura de Franz Galich." *Latin American Literary Review* 42.84 (2014): 68–87.

Caruth, Cathy. *Unclaimed Experience: Trauma, Narrative, and History.* Baltimore: Johns Hopkins University Press, 1996.

Castellanos Moya, Horacio. *Baile con serpientes.* Barcelona: Tusquets, 2002.

Castro Ricalde, Maricruz. "*Nadie me verá llorar* de Cristina Rivera Garza: Cuestionando el proyecto de nación." *Revista de Literatura Mexicana Contemporánea* 26 (2005): 1006–12.

Chilcoat, Michelle. "Brain Sex, Cyberpunk Cinema, Feminism, and the Dis/Location of Heterosexuality." *NWSA Journal* 16.2 (2004): 156–76.

Clavel, Ana. *Cuerpo naúfrago.* México, D.F.: Alfaguara, 2005.

———. *Los deseos y su sombra.* México, D.F.: Alfaguara, 2000.

Coles, Tony. "Negotiating the Field of Masculinity: The Production and Reproduction of Multiple Dominant Masculinities." *Men and Masculinities* 12.1 (2009): 30–44.

Colomina-Garrigós, María Dolores. *La nueva novela latinoamericana del dictador: Un estudio de la autoridad discursiva.* Diss. Michigan State University, 2003. Ann Arbor: UMI, 2003.

Connell, Raewyn. *Masculinities.* Berkeley: University of California Press, 1995.

———. "Masculinities and Globalization." *Men and Masculinities* 1.1 (1998): 3–23.

———. *The Men and the Boys.* Cambridge: Polity, 2000.

———. "A Thousand Miles from Kind: Men, Masculinities and Modern Institutions." *Journal of Men's Studies* 16.3 (2008): 237–52.

Connell, Robert [Raewyn]. "El imperialismo y el cuerpo de los hombres." *Masculinidades y equidad de género en América Latina.* Ed. Teresa Valdés and José Olavarría. Santiago: FLACSO-Chile, 1998. 76–89.

Connell, R. W., and Julian Wood. "Globalization and Business Masculinities." *Men and Masculinities* 7.4 (2005): 347–64.

Cortez, Beatriz. "La producción musical en Centroamérica." *Istmo: Revista Virtual de Estudios Literarios y Culturales Centroamericanos* 17 (2008). Web. 11 Sep. 2010.

Cruz-Malavé, Arnaldo. "Toward an Art of Transvestism: Colonialism and Homosexuality in Puerto Rican Literature." *¿Entiendes?: Queer Readings, Hispanic Writings.* Ed. Emilie Bergmann and Paul Julian Smith. Durham: Duke University Press, 1995. 137–67.

da Cunha-Giabbai, Gloria. "Ecofeminismo latinoamericano." *Letras Femeninas* 22.1 (1996): 51–63.

Davison, Annette. *Hollywood Theory, Non-Hollywood Practice: Cinema Soundtracks in the 1980s and 1990s.* Burlington: Ashgate, 2004.

Demetriou, Demetrakis. "Connell's Concept of Hegemonic Masculinity: A Critique." *Theory and Society* 30.3 (2001): 337–61.

Domínguez-Ruvalcaba, Héctor. *Modernity and the Nation in Mexican Representations of Masculinity: From Sensuality to Bloodshed.* New York: Palgrave Macmillan, 2007.

Donoso, José. *El lugar sin límites.* México, D.F.: Joaquín Mortiz, 1966.

Dorfman, Ariel. *The Empire's Old Clothes: What the Lone Ranger, Babar, and Other Innocent Heroes Do to Our Minds.* Durham: Duke University Press, 2010.

Echeverría, Maurice. *Diccionario esotérico.* Bogotá: Norma, 2006.

Estrada, Oswaldo. "Desplazamientos politicos del discurso sentimental en Travesuras de la niña mala de Mario Vargas Llosa." *Mario Vargas Llosa: Perspectivas críticas, ensayos inéditos.* Ed. Pol Popovic Karic and Fidel Chávez Pérez. México, D.F.: Miguel Ángel Porrúa, 2010. 149–80.

Fernández L'Hoeste, Héctor, and Juan Poblete, eds. *Redrawing the Nation: National Identity in Latin/o American Comics.* New York: Palgrave Macmillan, 2009.

Ferreira, César. "La palabra de Alfredo Bryce Echenique." *Letras* 78 (2007): 75–88.

Fleites, Alex. "Canta lo sentimental, o la importancia de escuchar boleros entre los 3 y los 100 años." *Latin American Studies Association, University of Pittsburgh,* 2000. Web. 18 Oct. 2010.

Forgues, Roland. *Mario Vargas Llosa: Ética y creación.* Paris: Mare et Martin, 2006.

Foster, David William. *From Mafalda to Los Supermachos: Latin American Graphic Humor as Popular Culture.* Boulder: L. Rienner, 1989.

Foucault, Michel. *The History of Sexuality.* New York: Vintage, 1990.

Fuguet, Alberto. *Mala onda.* Buenos Aires: Planeta, 1991.

———. *Por favor, rebobinar.* Buenos Aires: Alfaguara, 1998.

———. *Tinta roja.* Santiago: Alfaguara, 1997.

Fuguet, Alberto, and Sergio Gómez. "Presentación." *McOndo.* Ed. Alberto Fuguet and Sergio Gómez. Barcelona: Grijalbo Mondadori, 1996. 11–20.

Fuller, Norma. "La constitución social de la identidad de género entre varones urbanos del Perú." *Masculinidades y equidad de género en América Latina.* Ed. Teresa Valdés and José Olavarría. Santiago, Chile: FLACSO-Chile, 1998. 56–68.

———. "No uno sino muchos rostros: Identidad masculina en el Perú urbano." *Hombres e identidades de género: Investigaciones desde América Latina.* Ed. Mara Viveros, José Olavarría, and Norma Fuller. Bogotá: Universidad Nacional de Colombia, 2001. 265–370.

Galich, Franz. *Managua, Salsa City (¡Devórame otra vez!).* El Dorado: Géminis, 2000.

———. *Huracán corazón del cielo.* Managua: Signo, 1995.

———. "Tanda de sueños, visiones y ficciones." *Istmo: Revista Virtual de Estudios Literarios y Culturales Centroamericanos* 5 (2001). Web. 11 Sep. 2010.

———. *Tikal Futura: Memorias para un futuro incierto.* Guatemala: F&G, 2012.

——. *Y te diré quién eres (Mariposa traicionera)*. Managua: Anamá, 2006.

García-Calderón, Myrna. "'La última noche que pasé contigo' y el discurso erótico caribeño." *South Eastern Latin Americanist* 38.2 (1994): 26–34.

García Canclini, Néstor. *Hybrid Cultures: Strategies for Entering and Leaving Modernity*. Minneapolis: University of Minnesota Press, 1995.

Goffman, Erving. *Frame Analysis: An Essay on the Organization of Experience*. Cambridge: Harvard University Press, 1974.

González, Aníbal. "Adiós a la nostalgia: La narrativa hispanoamericana después de la nación." *Revista de Estudios Hispánicos* 46.1 (2012): 83–97.

Halberstam, Judith. *Female Masculinity*. Durham: Duke University Press, 1998.

Halperin, David. *Saint Foucault: Towards a Gay Hagiography*. New York: Oxford University Press, 1995.

Haraway, Donna. *Simians, Cyborgs and Women: The Reinvention of Nature*. New York: Routledge, 1991.

Hutcheon, Linda. *A Theory of Adaptation*. New York: Routledge, 2006.

Irwin, Robert McKee. *Mexican Masculinities*. Minneapolis: University of Minnesota Press, 2003.

Iser, Wolfgang. *The Act of Reading: A Theory of Aesthetic Response*. Baltimore: Johns Hopkins University Press, 1978.

Jaggi, Maya. "Fiction and Hyper-Reality." *Mail and Guardian* 22–29 March 2002: 30–31.

Jameson, Fredric. *The Cultural Turn: Selected Writings on the Postmodern, 1983–1998*. London: Verso, 1998.

——. *Postmodernism, or, the Cultural Logic of Late Capitalism*. Durham: Duke University Press, 1991.

Jefferson, Tony. "Subordinating Hegemonic Masculinity." *Theoretical Criminology* 6.1 (2002): 63–88.

Kantaris, Geoffrey. "Cyborgs, Cities, and Celluloid: Memory Machines in Two Latin American Cyborg Films." *Latin American Cyberculture and Cyberliterature*. Ed. Claire Taylor and Thea Pitman. Liverpool: Liverpool University Press, 2004. 50–69.

Knight, Arthur, and Pamela Robertson Wojcik. "Overture." *Soundtrack Available: Essays on Film and Popular Music*. Ed. Arthur Knight and Pamela Robertson Wojcik. Durham: Duke University Press, 2001. 1–18.

Kokotovic, Misha. "Neoliberal Noir: Contemporary Central American Crime Fiction as Social Criticism." *Clues: A Journal of Detection* 24.3 (2006): 15–29.

Köllman, Sabine. *Vargas Llosa's Fiction and the Demon of Politics*. Oxford: Peter Lang, 2002.

Lacan, Jacques. *Ecrits: A Selection*. New York: Norton, 1997.

LaCapra, Dominick. *Representing the Holocaust: History, Theory, Trauma*. Ithaca: Cornell University Press, 1994.

Lancaster, Roger. "'That we should all turn queer?' Homosexual Stigma in the Making of Manhood and the Breaking of a Revolution in Nicaragua." *Culture, Society and Sexuality*. Ed. Richard Parker and Peter Aggleton. London: Routledge, 2002. 104–22.

Lauer, A. Robert. "El (homo)erotismo musical en la narrativa caribeña de Mayra Montero: *Púrpura profundo*." *Chasqui: Revista de Literatura Latinoamericana* 34.1 (2005): 42–50.

———. "La representación del deseo masculino en *La última noche que pasé contigo* de Mayra Montero." *Entorno* 43 (1997): 45–48.

Lefere, Robin. "*La fiesta del Chivo*, ¿mentira verdadera?" *Actas del XIV Congreso de la Asociación Internacional de Hispanistas.* Ed. Isaías Lerner, Robert Nival, Alejandro Alonso. Vol. 4. Newark, Delaware: Juan de la Cuesta, 2004. 331–38.

Legler, Gretchen. "Ecofeminist Literary Criticism." *Ecofeminism: Women, Culture, Nature.* Ed. Karen J. Warren. Bloomington: Indiana University Press, 1997. 227–38.

Lemebel, Pedro. "Censo y conquista." *Pedro Lemebel: Blog sobre el autor chileno.* 2005. Web. 1 May 2015.

———. Interview. *FILBA.* 2008. Web. 11 Sep. 2010.

———. "La esquina es mi corazón." *Pedro Lemebel: Blog sobre el autor chileno.* 2005. Web. 1 May 2015.

———. "Manifiesto." *Pedro Lemebel: Blog sobre el autor chileno.* 2005. Web. 1 May 2015.

———. *Tengo miedo torero.* Santiago: Planeta, 2001.

Lévi-Strauss, Claude. *The Savage Mind.* Chicago: Chicago University Press, 1966.

López, Irma M. "*La última noche que pasé contigo*: El crucero del placer y los excesos dionisíacos." *Latin American Literary Review* 33.66 (2005): 133–44.

López Morales, Berta. "Tengo miedo torero, de Pedro Lemebel: Ruptura y testimonio." *Estudios Filológicos* 40 (2005): 121–29.

Macías Rodríguez, Claudia, and Jung-Euy Hong. "Desde México para Corea: Entrevista a Cristina Rivera Garza." *Espacio Latino.* June 2006. Web. 14 March 2010.

Marsé, Juan. *El amante bilingüe.* Barcelona: Planeta, 1990.

Martín Sevillano, Ana Belén. "Violencia de género en la narrativa cubana contemporánea: Deseo femenino y masculinidad hegemónica." *Hispanic Review* 82.2 (2014): 175–97.

Martínez Sánchez, Carlos. "*Managua, Salsa City* ¡Devórame otra vez!" *El Nuevo Diario* 17 Jan. 2001. Web. 11 Sep. 2010.

McFarlane, Brian. "Novel to Film." *Film Theory and Criticism: Introductory Readings.* Ed. Leo Braudy and Marshall Cohen. New York: Oxford University Press, 2009. 381–89.

Meler, Irene. "La construcción personal de la masculinidad: Su relación con la precariedad de la inserción laboral." *Precariedad laboral y crisis de la masculinidad: Impacto sobre relaciones de género.* Ed. Mabel Burin, María Lucero Jiménez Guzmán, and Irene Meler. Buenos Aires: Universidad de Ciencias Empresariales y Sociales, 2007. 121–47.

Melgar Bao, Ricardo. "Entre lo sucio y lo bajo: Identidades subalternas y resistencia cultural en América Latina." *Tradición y emancipación cultural en América Latina.* Ed. Jorge Turner Morales and Rossana Cassigoli Salamón. México, D.F.: Siglo XXI, 2005. 30–56.

Menton, Seymour. *Latin America's New Historical Novel.* Austin: University of Texas Press, 1993.

Metz, Christian. *Film Language: A Semiotics of the Cinema.* New York: Oxford University Press, 1974.

Miller, Marilyn G., ed. *Tango Lessons: Movement, Sound, Image, and Text in Contemporary Practice.* Durham: Duke University Press, 2014.

Misael Hernández, Oscar. "Estudios sobre masculinidades: Aportes desde América Latina." *Revista de Antropología Experimental* 8 (2008): 67–73.

Montecino, Sonia. *Madres y huachos: Alegorías del mestizaje chileno*. Santiago: Ediciones CEDEM-Cuarto Propio, 1991.

Montero, Mayra. *La última noche que pasé contigo*. Barcelona: Tusquets, 2001.

Montoya Juárez, Jesús, and Ángel Esteban, eds. *Entre lo local y lo global: La narrativa latinoamericana en el cambio de siglo, 1990–2006*. Madrid: Iberoamericana; Frankfurt am Main: Vervuert, 2008.

Mosse, George L. *The Image of Man: The Creation of Modern Masculinity*. New York: Oxford University Press, 1996.

Novoa, Loreto. "Lemebel se ríe del Sida: Es la defensa de los homosexuales." Interview with Pedro Lemebel. *La Época* 25 (1996). Web.

Núñez Noriega, Guillermo. *Just Between Us: An Ethnography of Male Identity and Intimacy in Rural Communities of Northern Mexico*. Tucson: University of Arizona Press, 2014.

Ochoa Santos, Miguel Gabriel. "Cuerpo, dominio y escritura: *La fiesta del Chivo*." *Mario Vargas Llosa: Perspectivas críticas, ensayos inéditos*. Ed. Pol Popovic Karic and Fidel Chávez Pérez. México, D.F.: Miguel Ángel Porrúa, 2010. 211–46.

O'Flynn, John. "National Identity and Music in Transition: Issues of Authenticity in a Global Setting." *Music, National Identity and the Politics of Location: Between the Global and the Local*. Ed. Ian Biddle and Vanessa Knights. Burlington: Ashgate, 2007. 19–38.

Olavarría, José. "Hombres e identidad de género: Algunos elementos sobre los recursos de poder y violencia masculina." *Debates sobre masculinidades: Poder, desarrollo, políticas públicas y ciudadanía*. Ed. G. Careaga and S. Cruz Sierra. México, D.F.: Universidad Nacional Autónoma, 2007. 115–30.

———. "La investigación sobre masculinidades en América Latina." *Lo masculino en evidencia: Investigaciones sobre la masculinidad*. Ed. J. Toro-Alfonso. Puerto Rico: Publicaciones Puertorriqueñas, 2009. 315–44.

Ortega, Julio. "Bryce Echenique y los tiempos de la escritura." *Revista de Estudios Hispánicos* (U.P.R.) 30.1 (2003): 231–45.

Pacheco, Carlos. *Narrativa de la dictadura y crítica literaria*. Caracas: Centro de Estudios Rómulo Gallegos, 1987.

Pacini Hernandez, Deborah, Héctor Fernández L'Hoeste, and Eric Zolov. "Mapping Rock Music Cultures across the Americas." *Rockin' las Américas: The Global Politics of Rock in Latin/o America*. Ed. Deborah Pacini Hernandez, Héctor Fernández L'Hoeste, and Eric Zolov. Pittsburgh: University of Pittsburgh Press, 2004. 1–21.

Palaversich, Diana. "The Wounded Body of Proletarian Homosexuality in Pedro Lemebel's *Loco afán*." *Latin American Perspectives* 29.2 (2002): 99–118.

Payne, Judith. *Ambiguity and Gender in the New Novel of Brazil and Spanish America: A Comparative Assessment*. Iowa City: University of Iowa Press, 1993.

Paz, Octavio. *El laberinto de la soledad*. Madrid: Cátedra, 2007.

Pedreira, Antonio S. *Insularismo*. 1934. San Juan: Edil, 1992.

Piedra, José. "Nationalizing Sissies." *¿Entiendes?: Queer Readings, Hispanic Writings*. Ed. Emilie Bergmann and Paul Julian Smith. Durham: Duke University Press, 1995. 370–409.

Plata Ramírez, Enrique. "El Caribe cuenta y canta: Transversalidades del discurso narrativo y el discurso musical." *Voz y Escritura. Revista de Estudios Literarios* 16 (2008): 53–65.

Polit Dueñas, Gabriela. *Cosas de hombres: Escritores y caudillos en la literatura latinoamericana del siglo XX.* Argentina: Beatriz Viterbo, 2008.

Pons, María Cristina. *Memorias del olvido: la novela histórica de fines del siglo XX.* Madrid: Siglo XXI, 1996.

Pratt, Mary Louise. "Globalización, desmodernización y el retorno de los monstruos." *Globalización y diversidad cultural: Una mirada desde América Latina.* Ed. Ramón Pajuelo and Pablo Sandoval. Lima: Instituto de Estudios Peruanos, 2004. 399–415.

Puig, Manuel. *El beso de la mujer araña.* Barcelona: Seix Barral, 1976.

Quiroga, José. "Fleshing out Virgilio Piñera from the Cuban Closet." *¿Entiendes?: Queer Readings, Hispanic Writings.* Ed. Emilie Bergmann and Paul Julian Smith. Durham: Duke University Press, 1995. 168–80.

———. *Tropics of Desire: Interventions from Queer Latino America.* New York: NYU Press, 2000.

Quirós, Daniel. "Driving the City: Contesting Neoliberal Space in Franz Galich's *Managua, Salsa City.*" *Romance Notes* 54.1 (2014): 9–14.

Ramírez, Sergio. *Adiós muchachos: Una memoria de la revolución Sandinista.* México, D.F.: Aguilar, 1999.

———. *Margarita, está linda la mar.* Madrid: Alfaguara, 1998.

Rey Rosa, Rodrigo. *El cojo bueno.* Madrid: Alfaguara, 1996.

Rivera Garza, Cristina. *La cresta de Ilión.* México, D.F.: Tusquets, 2002.

———. *The Masters of the Streets: Bodies, Power and Modernity in Mexico, 1867–1930.* Diss. University of Houston, 1995. Ann Arbor: UMI, 1997.

———. *Nadie me verá llorar.* México, D.F.: Tusquets, 1999.

Rodó, José Enrique. *Ariel.* 1900. Madrid: Espasa-Calpe, 1971.

Rodríguez Juliá, Edgardo. *El entierro de Cortijo.* San Juan: Ediciones Huracán, 1983.

———. *Una noche con Iris Chacón.* San Juan: Antillana, 1986.

Rodríguez Matte, Hernán. *Barrio Alto.* Santiago: Alfaguara, 2004.

Rojas-Trempe, Lady. "Violencia político-sexual del Estado, trauma y la historia de una víctima en *La fiesta del Chivo.*" *Mario Vargas Llosa: Escritor, ensayista, ciudadano y político.* Ed. Roland Forgues. Lima: Editorial Minerva, 2001. 537–52.

Roncagliolo, Santiago. *Tan cerca de la vida.* Madrid: Alfaguara, 2010.

Rosario-Vélez, Jorge. "Somos un sueño imposible: ¿Clandestinidad sexual del bolero en La última noche que pasé contigo de Mayra Montero?" *Revista Iberoamericana* 68 (2002): 67–77.

Rubin, Gayle. "The Traffic in Women: Notes on the 'Political Economy' of Sex." *Toward an Anthropology of Women.* Ed. Rayna R. Reiter. New York: Monthly Review, 1975. 157–210.

Ruffinelli, Jorge. "Ni a tontas ni a locas: La narrativa de Cristina Rivera Garza." *Nuevo Texto Crítico* 21.41–42 (2008): 33–41.

Sánchez, Luis Rafael. *La guaracha del macho Camacho.* Buenos Aires: Ediciones de la Flor, 1976.

———. *La importancia de llamarse Daniel Santos.* Hanover: Ediciones del Norte, 1988.

Santos-Febres, Mayra. *Nuestra señora de la noche*. Madrid: Espasa, 2006.

———. *Sirena Selena vestida de pena*. Barcelona: Mondadori, 2000.

Sedgwick, Eve Kosofsky. *Between Men: English Literature and Male Homosocial Desire*. New York: Columbia University Press, 1985.

Serna, Enrique. *El miedo a los animales*. México, D.F.: Joaquín Mortiz, 1995.

———. *Fruta verde*. México, D.F.: Planeta, 2006.

———. *Giros negros*. México D.F.: Cal y Arena, 2008.

———. *La sangre erguida*. México D.F.: Planeta, 2010.

———. *Las caricaturas me hacen llorar*. México, D.F.: Joaquín Mortiz, 1996.

Sifuentes-Jáuregui, Ben. *The Avowal of Difference: Queer Latino American Narratives*. Albany: SUNY Press, 2014.

———. *Transvestism, Masculinity, and Latin American Literature: Genders Share Flesh*. New York: Palgrave, 2002.

Sommer, Doris. *Foundational Fictions: The National Romances of Latin America*. Berkeley: University of California Press, 1991.

Taylor, Claire, and Thea Pitman, eds. *Latin American Cyberculture and Cyberliterature*. Liverpool: Liverpool University Press, 2008.

Terán, Enrique. *El cojo Navarrete*. Quito: Americana, 1940.

Toro-Alfonso, José. "La investigación sobre masculinidades." *Lo masculino en evidencia: Investigaciones sobre la masculinidad*. Ed. J. Toro-Alfonso. Puerto Rico: Publicaciones Puertorriqueñas, 2009. 13–33.

———. *Masculinidades subordinadas: Investigaciones hacia la transformación del género*. Hato Rey: Publicaciones Puertorriqueñas, Universidad de Puerto Rico, 2008.

Torres, Vicente Francisco. *La novela bolero latinoamericana*. México: Coordinación de Difusión Cultural, Dirección de Literatura UNAM, 1998.

Ugarte, Elizabeth. "El lenguaje y la realidad social de *Managua, Salsa City*." *Istmo: Revista Virtual de Estudios Literarios y Culturales Centroamericanos* 3 (2001). Web. 11 Sep. 2010.

Vargas, José Ángel. *La novela contemporánea centroamericana: La obra de Sergio Ramírez Mercado*. San José: Perro Azul, 2006.

Vargas Llosa, Mario. *Cartas a un joven novelista*. México, D.F.: Ariel/Planeta, 1997.

———. *La fiesta del Chivo*. Madrid: Alfaguara, 2000.

———. *Travesuras de la niña mala*. Lima: Alfaguara, 2006.

Vasconcelos, José. *La raza cósmica*. 1925. México, D.F.: Espasa-Calpe, 1966.

Velasco, Xavier. *Diablo guardián*. México, D.F.: Alfaguara, 2003.

Venkatesh, Vinodh. "Androgyny, Football, and Pedophilia: Rearticulating Mexican Masculinities in the Works of Enrique Serna." *Revista de Literatura Mexicana Contemporánea* 49 (2011): 25–36.

———. "Growing up in Sanhattan: Cartographies of the Barrio Alto in Alberto Fuguet and Hernán Rodríguez Matte." *Hispanic Review* 80.2 (2012): 313–28.

———. "*La hermana perdida de Angélica María*: Enrique Serna Writes the Lost Decade." *Revista de Estudios Hispánicos* 47.1 (2013): 103–25.

———. "Outing Javier Fuentes-León's *Contracorriente* and the Case for a New Queer Cinema in Latin America." *Journal of Popular Romance Studies* 4.1 (2014). Web.

———. "Towards a Poetics of the Automobile in Contemporary Central American Fiction." *Letras Hispanas* 8.2 (2012): 66–80.

Viveros Vigoya, Mara. "Quebradores y cumplidores: Biografías diversas de la mascu-linidad." *Masculinidades y equidad de género en América Latina*. Ed. Teresa Valdés and José Olavarría. Santiago, Chile: FLACSO-Chile, 1998. 36–55.

Waxer, Lise, ed. *Situating Salsa: Global Markets and Local Meanings in Latin Popular Music*. New York: Routledge, 2002.

Williams, Gareth. *The Other Side of the Popular: Neoliberalism and Subalternity in Latin America*. Durham: Duke University Press, 2002.

Winterson, Jeanette. "The Erotics of Risk." *Following Djuna: Women Lovers and the Erotics of Loss*. Ed. Carolyn Allen. Bloomington: Indiana University Press, 1996.

Zapata, Luis. *Las aventuras, desaventuras y sueños de Adonis García, el vampiro de la Colonia Roma*. México: Grijalbo, 1979.

Zavala, Iris. "Con la música por dentro: La transculturación, la tropología y el enigma." *Intersecciones* 20.74–75 (2008): 11–32.

———. *El libro de Apolonia, o, de las islas*. San Juan: Instituto de Cultura Puertorriqueña, 1993.

Index

About the Author

Vinodh Venkatesh (Ph.D., University of North Carolina at Chapel Hill) is an associate professor of Spanish in the Department of Foreign Languages and Literatures at Virginia Tech. He has published over twenty articles and book chapters on such issues as gender, subjectivity, and the urban space in contemporary Spanish and Latin American cinema and narrative. His current research focuses on the circulations of affect and the framing of the body in recent Latin American films.